Princeton Theological Monograph Series

Dikran Y. Hadidian

General Editor

17

CRITICAL REALISM AND THE NEW TESTAMENT

CRITICAL REALISM
AND
THE NEW TESTAMENT

By

BEN F. MEYER

PICKWICK PUBLICATIONS
ALLISON PARK, PENNSYLVANIA

The author is grateful to the following publishers for permission to reprint:

"Conversion and the Hermeneutics of Consent,'" *Ex Auditu* 1 (1985) 36-46.
"Good Will Comes First, but Suspicion Has its Uses," published under the title
"The Primacy of Consent and the Uses of Suspicion," *Ex Auditu* 2
(1986) 7-18.
"Did Paul's View of the Resurrection of the Dead Undergo Development? *Theo-
logical Studies* 47 (1986) 363-87.
"Objectivity and Subjectivity in Historical Criticism of the Gospels," commis-
sioned by the International Institute for the Renewal of Gospel Studies
for the Jerusalem *Symposium on the Interrelation of the Gospels*, April,
1984.
"The 'Inside' of the Jesus Event," in **Creativity and Method: Essays in
Honor of Bernard Lonergan, S.J.**, ed. M. L. Lamb (Milwaukee:
Marquette University Press, 1981) 197-210.
"The World Mission and the Emergent Realization of Christian Identity," in **Jesus, the Gospels, and the Church: Essays in Honor of
William R. Farmer**, ed. E. P. Sanders (Macon: Mercer University Press, 1987) 243-63.
"Critical Realism and Biblical Theology," *Religious Studies and Theology* 6
(1986) 39-51.
"The Primacy of the Intended Sense of Texts" commissioned by the Conference
on the Development and Application of Lonerganian Hermeneutics, to
be published in **Lonergan's Hermeneutics**, ed. Sean E. McEvenue
and B. F. Meyer (Washington: Catholic University Press).

Library of Congress Cataloging-in-Publication Data

Meyer, Ben F., 1927-
  Critical Realism and the New Testament.
  (Princeton theological monograph series ; 17)
  Bibliography: p.
  1. Bible. N.T.--Criticism, interpretation, etc.--
History--20th century. 2. Lonergan, Bernard J. F.
I. Title. II. Series.
BS2350.M49 1989   225.6'01   88-31722
ISBN 0-915138-97-2

BS
2350
.M49
1989

For Mag, Dor, Ginny, Snook, Nan
and Imp

CONTENTS

Preface   ix

PART ONE

INTRODUCTION TO THE HERMENEUTICS OF CRITICAL REALISM

1. Locating Lonerganian Hermeneutics   1

2. The Primacy of the Intended Sense of Texts   17

3. Conversion and the Hermeneutics of Consent   57

4. Good Will Comes First, but Suspicion Has Its Uses   77

PART TWO

APPLICATION TO EXEGESIS, HISTORY AND THEOLOGY

5. Did Paul's View of the Resurrection of the Dead Undergo Development?   99

6. Objectivity and Subjectivity in Historical Criticism of the Gospels   129

7. Lonergan's "Breakthrough" and **The Aims of Jesus**   147

8. The "Inside" of the Jesus Event   157

9. The World Mission and the Emergent Realization of
    Christian Identity   173

10. Critical Realism and Biblical Theology   195

Index of Biblical Passages   213

Index of Names   221

PREFACE

The impulse to write these essays had two sources. The first was the biblical tradition. The more it revealed its breaks, tangents, oddly angled continuities, and the more I thought of the stunning shape taken by the fulfillment of its hopes, the more striking became the constant biblical affirmation of precedent and the triumphant achievement of ties with the past. The sustained effort of biblical authors to trace and affirm these ties was a hallmark of the tradition. The result in the New Testament was to project horizons allowing the elements of a rich, long history to be brought into deep coherence--a condition of the possibility of a truly "biblical" theology.

The second source was Bernard Lonergan's philosophic achievement--more concretely, the transformative impact of his phenomenology of knowledge and theory of objectivity on my efforts to make sense of the ways we make sense of things. I had grown up in the era of the new criticism: an affirmation of the "organic" nature of art and literature and an effort to get beyond impressionistic interpretation by text-centered attention to detail. The point was to respond "adequately" to works of mature sensibility (Valéry, Rilke, Yeats, Pound . . .). The forces that reformed my sense of "mature sensibility" were biblical literature and criticism (von Rad and Jeremias); Aquinas and Dante; Kierkegaard, Newman, and Lonergan; and remorseless moral realists from Waugh to Solzhenitsyn.

Philosophically, I had been raised on Thomism, a conceptualist tradition which I was unable to distinguish from the work of Aquinas himself. But the more I entered into biblical criticism, the less helpful the conceptualist account of knowledge became. Within my range I eventually experienced something of the tension Collingwood felt between Oxford realism and the practice of archaeology and intellectual history. Collingwood broke with realism under the influence of Croce. I learned from Lonergan that besides the doctrinaire realism of average scholasticism there was a realism that made room with the idealists for every ambition of intelligence but that, correcting the concessions and oversights in idealist critique, went decisively beyond idealism as well.

Many students of biblical literature and some of the very best have been content to do their own thing without having to make philosophic sense of it. But we do not choose our obsessions. If one is addicted to the effort to make philosophic sense of one's literary and historical work, so be it. My efforts in this direction have not been a straightforward success story. But in whatever measure they have succeeded I have been helped both to respect the distinctive exigences of this work and to shake free of alien encumbrances, especially prohibitions, foisted on it by contemporary hermeneutics. Lonergan's critical realism seemed to me to meet and remedy every one of these hermeneutical defects. The salient traits of this realism emerge in the course of the essays that follow, but it might be well to bring these traits together here and give a brief account of them.

A first feature of critical realism, then, is its focus on the concrete structures of human operations. The "existence" of the human subject consists in his "standing out" (*ex-sistere*) from the closed circle of natural routines; he moves from the real to the possible, from the familar past to a new future, from the seen to the unseen and from the finite to the infinite. At the root of this capacity for transcendence lies an inner dimension--the world of interiority or subjectivity--in which he finds himself. This world, indeed, is constituted by the presence of the subject to himself in the act of being a subject. Here he lives out the experiences of wonder and questioning, of bafflement and discovery, of self-orientation now headed for fulfillment, now for self-destruction. This experience is often disconcerting or mysterious, but it is not chaotic. On the contrary, it is spontaneously self-structuring; and the first trait of critical realism is the high premium put on the structures of conscious intentionality. The human subject in his conscious (but not yet objectified) functioning--his attentiveness, intelligence, reasonableness, and responsibility--is the living norm against which all theories on him are measured. Critical realism, in short, is intensely empirical. It acknowledges the primacy of performance as a particular instance of the authority of fact. The facts of human performance are accordingly the first object of inquiry and last court of appeal. It is a technique typical of this realism to reduce conflicting views respecting (for example) objectivity and subjectivity to coherence or incoherence with cognitional fact. Hence, to refute a position by

x

revealing it to be performatively self-reversing is a favorite critical-realist ploy.

Second, there is the defining correlativity of "true" and "real." Critical realism locates the issue of real/unreal at the level of sense only insofar as sense knowledge provides data for higher-level operations that terminate in judgment. It is perfectly true that what is sensed is, but this is ascertained not by the senses alone but by understanding and judgment taking account of sense data. Contrary to Samuel Johnson, the criterion of the real is not its kickability but its susceptibility to becoming known through true propositions. As the scholastic adage has it, *ens per verum innotescit*: reality becomes known through the (act of finding out what is) true.

Third, critical-realist hermeneutics accords a primacy to the grasp of individual meaning over generalization and the universal, for what interpretation envisages is not scientific analysis but insight into textual meaning that, however representative or allusive, is contextually unique. To get Euclid's meaning takes effort, but this is mathematical, not interpretative, effort.[1] Texts that call for interpretative effort do not deal with things clear in themselves, like mathematical ideas, but with human meaning and, typically, with a highly individual treatment of great issues, which are perennially divisive. The greater the text, the more pronounced its individuality; hence, the relative irrelevance of generalization to the construal and appreciation of literary texts. "There is only one **Divina commedia**, only one **Hamlet** by Shakespeare, only one two-part **Faust** by Goethe."[2] One understands the individual through attention not only to "codes," but beyond all codes, to unsystematically related particulars. The high degree of individuality

> found in artists, thinkers, writers, though beyond the reach of general rules or universal principles, is within easy reach of understanding. For what in the first instance is understood is what is given to sense or consciousness, or again, what is represented in images, words, symbols, signs. What is so given or represented is individual. What is grasped by understanding is the intelligibility of the individual.[3]

Fourth, the text has a *prima facie* claim on the reader, namely, to be construed in accord with its intended sense. The intended sense is what grounds the difference between language in general (*langue*) and particular utterance (*parole*), for it makes the latter to be what it is. Likewise, the intended sense differentiates "discourse," making it determinate. Numerous contemporary theorists, impelled by a variety of purposes and motives, have recently been testing the contrary view: language generates meaning autonomously, and texts are all intrinsically indeterminate. Views of this kind, however, may be entertained only on condition that the theorist abstract entirely from the qualitative difference between a sonnet of Keats or Hopkins and a sonnet produced by a minimally programmed computer. This is an arbitrary and ruthlessly reductionist abstraction. It signals the dead end of a long development in Western philosophy toward the disappearance of consciousness, selfhood, the responsible subject, the immortal soul.[4] "Relax," advises Denis Donoghue, "it's only a theory."[5] But Donoghue's view of theory as irrelevant to human living represents a return to the last days of the age of innocence. (It is derived from Ralph Barton Perry, writing in 1912.) The theory in question here exists primarily in the cultural superstructure, but is not confined to it. Simplified and popularized, transposed from technical statement to metaphor and image, catchphrase and slogan, it penetrates the culture, subverting good sense and confidence in good sense.[6]

Fifth, critical realism distinguishes between understanding and judgment and makes judgment integral to the task of interpreting. The content of understanding is intrinsically hypothetical; the step into "knowledge" (usually no more than probable knowledge) is effected by the grasp of evidence as "sufficient" and the consequently reasonable act of judgment. Critical realism is thus a break with the hermeneutics of innocence. It does not suppose that the meaning of the text is "already out there now," to be somehow read off the page. But if the interpreter conjures up the meaning of the text out of his own resources, he does not simply leave it at that, but goes on to the kind of critical reflection--Is this the meaning that the text is aiming at? What textual warrants make this meaning probable? With what measure of assurance?--that contributes to reasonable, probable, judgment.

Sixth, critical realism acknowledges the triangular structure of reader, text, and referent. The referent (*die Sache*) is what the text is about. Things (the referent) and words (the text) are reciprocally illuminating elements of a hermeneutic circle. (An example: Lonergan's hold on world process as revealed by modern science gave him a palpable edge over other interpreters of Aquinas's texts on world process.[7] By contrast, a negative example is given below: the modern recoil from apocalypticism has led modern interpreters to misunderstand Pauline apocalyptic texts.[8])

Finally, critical realism takes sober account of the interpreter's need to measure up to the text and to be attuned to it. When the literature to be interpreted is great, it may well call for an understanding of the world and a self-understanding on the part of the interpreter that at the moment are simply beyond him. Again, great literature generates a tradition of interpretation. The tradition may be authentic, representing remarkable reach and a steady accumulation of insightful adjustments and reinterpretations. On the other hand, it may be inauthentic, representing a falling-off, a watering down, a tailoring of the text to the mediocrity of its readers. The task of interpretation is essentially modest, but the demands it imposes remain unsparingly in force. Literary critics often seem to bring invulnerable confidence to their treatment of poets and philosophers; and, though biblical exegetes must somehow come to terms with astonishing texts, from the powerful currents of Isaian faith to the agony of Job, from the symbolic acts of Jesus to the audacious theology of Paul, they rarely confess feeling unprovisioned in the face of the task, or daunted by it. But the major texts, as Lonergan has argued, "not only are beyond the initial horizon of their interpreters but may also demand an intellectual, moral, religious conversion" before the interpreter can measure up to his task.[9]

These seven traits--the authority of fact, the correlativity of "true" and "real," the primacy of insight into the text as individual, the "intended sense" as constitutive of discourse, the indispensability of judgment, the circle of things and words, and the requisite that the interpreter measure up to the text--set critical-realist hermeneutics apart as sane, rigorous, and productive. This is a far cry from current theory: first, from the game but misguided effort to make linguistics the interpreter's main resource and, second, from a biblical hermeneutics still tied up in knots over "the senses of scripture." Both have left subject and subjectivity entirely out of account. Superficial hermeneutics takes the interpreter's intellectual, moral, and religious authenticity for granted and concentrates on objective resources and procedures. Deep hermeneutics takes nothing for granted and ultimately concentrates on the above threefold authenticity, for this is the key both to gross differences, e.g., between the views of Jesus proposed respectively by Joachim Jeremias and by the editor of *Der Spiegel*, and to the subtler differences between, for example, Barth's fideist view, Bultmann's existentialist view, and Stuhlmacher's theologically more open and critically better calibrated view, of Pauline theology.

Of the ten essays presented here, six have appeared elsewhere, one is about to appear elsewhere, and three are printed only here. Most of them were invited papers, and one of the invitations deserves special mention. Under the leadership of Prof. David Dungan (University of Tennessee) an ecumenical study group in Madison, Wisconsin, having spent months studying my book, **The Aims of Jesus** (London: SCM, 1979), asked me to answer their questions in a paper for a conference on historical-Jesus research (held in Madison, Oct. 14-16, 1983). This was the background to "Lonergan's 'Breakthrough' and **The Aims of Jesus**." All the essays have been chosen for their explicit concern with interpretation or historical method. All date from the 1980s, several from my sabbatical year which the administrative officers of McMaster University allowed me to divide between 1983 and 1984, and which the Social Sciences and Humanities Research Council of Canada generously funded. All were written in the village of Les Verrières, near Neuchâtel, Switzerland. Peter Stuhlmacher's calling attention to my hermeneutical work (in the second edition of his **Vom Verstehen des Neuen Testaments**, 1986)[10] was among the encouragements to bring this book out. It is dedicated, with love, to my sisters.

Burlington, Ontario
June, 1988

NOTES

1. Bernard Lonergan, **Method in Theology** (London: Darton, Longman and Todd, 1972) 153-54.
2. Ibid., 209.
3. Ibid.

4. See William Barrett, **Death of the Soul** (Oxford: Oxford University Press, 1986).

5. Denis Donoghue, "Relax, It's Only a Theory," *New York Times Book Review*, March 1, 1987.

6. Bernard Lonergan, "The Absence of God in Modern Culture," in **A Second Collection**, ed. W. F. J. Ryan and B. J. Tyrrel (London: Darton, Longman and Todd) 101-116, at 112.

7. See Bernard Lonergan, **Grace and Freedom**, ed. J. P. Burns (London: Darton, Longman and Todd, 1971) 72-76.

8. See the conclusion of the essay, "Did Paul's View of the Resurrection of the Dead Undergo Development?"

9. Lonergan, **Method in Theology**, 161.

10. Peter Stuhlmacher, **Vom Verstehen des Neuen Testaments** (Göttingen: Vandenhoeck & Ruprecht, ²1986).

PART ONE

INTRODUCTION TO THE
HERMENEUTICS
OF
CRITICAL REALISM

I

LOCATING

LONERGANIAN HERMENEUTICS

In 1958 the situation of philosophy in England came under the severe scrutiny of an Oxford Hegelian in G. R. G. Mure's **Retreat from Truth**.[1] Mure's somber analysis focused on the horizons and field of vision inherited from British empiricism and shared, though quite diversely, by the philosophies cultivated in England then as now: Marxism, logical atomism, and, above all, language analysis. Whether or not they were direct descendants of classical empiricism, they shared an empiricist assumption about the world: there was no world but the world envisaged by the practical man as the condition of his activity. Against this scheme of things--void of value, having no *raison d'être* of its own--Mure affirmed truth (as genuineness in self-transcendence) and a universe of value. The book ended, however, not on a note of serene, much less joyous, affirmation, but in deep depression at the spectacle of philosophy in its last throes.

Twenty years later, in **Idealist Epilogue**,[2] Mure matched the clarity and incisiveness of **Retreat from Truth**, again affirming a value-charged universe, yet deepening, if possible, the mood of philosophic despair. What ally did truth have in a world wracked with violence and yet riveted to its empiricist premises? For Mure--steady, sober opponent of myth--the ally of truth was. . .the *Weltgeist*! But the *Weltgeist* was never in a hurry. There was hope, no doubt, in the long run, a distant hope, too distant to appear as more than a speck on an old man's horizon.

Mure was a slightly older contemporary of Bernard Lonergan, and the example of Mure's thought might serve as a point of orientation allowing us to locate Lonergan on the scene of philosophy. He appeared on that scene in 1957--out of nowhere, so to speak--with **Insight**,[3] a packed account of the understanding of understanding: a phenomenology of cognitional acts (which included an account of world process), a critical-realist epistemology, a non-necessitarian metaphysics, a briefly sketched but dense hermeneutics, an ethics of freedom, a positive account of general transcendent knowledge (the rational affirmation of God) and of special transcendent knowledge (the anticipation of religion that emerges from the antithesis of God and evil).

Like Mure, Lonergan was acutely aware of the contemporary debacle of philosophy. Like Mure, he grasped how ruinous the legacy of empiricism had been. He profoundly sympathized with the idealist critique of empiricism, the idealist aspiration to self-transcendence, and the idealist affirmation of value. Yet Lonergan's realism differed fundamentally and consistently from all the modes of idealism, including that of Hegel and his heirs, for "every statement made by a realist denotes an object in a realist's world; every statement made by an idealist denotes an object in an idealist's world; the two sets of statements are disparate. . ."[4]

Difference of horizon implied not only a different set of objects but a deeply different subject. Here even the difference of mood between Mure and Lonergan--deep depression versus serene affirmation--was an index irreducible to temperament. The critical realist found decisive allies of truth in the radically disinterested human drive to know, in the radical recoil from the existential vacuum of meaninglessness, in the ineradicable human longing for fulfillment. The affirmation of God exorcised the *Weltgeist*. It reaffirmed divinity as Act and a divine governance of the world that elicited a positive expectation of salvation, the divine solution of long-term and otherwise irreversible decline. Given this rationally affirmed divine governance of the world, it followed that the drive to know, the recoil from meaninglessness, the longing for fulfillment were effective allies of truth.

The key to this movement of reflection was not "the intuition of being" posited by the Neo-Scholastic form of realism, nor the empiricist's resolute removal from the real world of everything not given in immediate experience, nor the idealist's addition of understanding, reason, and value to the world of appearances. It was "the upset of crisis and conversion"[5] involved in breaking cleanly with the realism of sense-perception and in affirming access to the real in a sequence of cognitive acts that reached its term only with true judgment.

The first group of philosophers to whom Lonergan commended the strategy making the phenomenology of knowledge the first moment of the philosophic task were classical Thomists, deeply committed to the primacy of metaphysics. Against the traditionalism of the Thomists Lonergan argued for the order: first, cognitional operations and epistemology, then metaphysics. Against the modernity of continental hermeneutists and their allies, he argued, in **Insight** and subsequent works, for the order: first cognitional operations and epistemology, then hermeneutics.

On the first front Longeran's argument highlighted a basic structure in the thought of Aristotle and Aquinas: the distinction between priority *quoad se* (ontological causes) and priority *quoad nos* (cognitional reasons). He pointed out that one could not assign ontological causes without having cognitional reasons. To this he added the observation that "development" in the sense of progress in human thought "must come from the cognitional reasons."[6] Cogent illustration touched developments specifically associated with Aristotle and Aquinas. "What began with Aristotle was, not form, but knowledge of form," and "what began with Aquinas was, not existence, but knowledge of existence."[7] The strategic order "knowledge before metaphysics turned out in the last analysis to belong precisely to the legacies of Aristotle and Aquinas, for, though it did not mime the order most prominent in their written works, it took its point of departure from their principles and the historic example of their achievements.

Lonergan's argument on the second front took account of modes of understanding particularized by the diversity of objects, but it relocated these modes within a comprehensive inquiry into the understanding of understanding. As success in the understanding of understanding led to success in particular cases such as understanding the understanding of texts, so failure in the one led to failure in the other.[8] Again, a deeply and solidly based epistemological critique was not to be derived from inquiry into this or that particular mode of understanding. But without epistemological critique hermeneutics could well lead, as in fact it had led, to Troeltschean historicism.[9] Finally, the rise of the historical consciousness and of the human sciences, in which "meaning" was a basic category, had complicated hermeneutics to the point of requiring just that methodical clarity on cognitional structures that was offered in **Insight**.

For example, the confusions attendant on a hundred years of debate about *erklären* and *verstehen* were resolved, not by attention to discrete modes of understanding, but by attention to the understanding of understanding. The result was to find "somewhat artificial" the distinction between *erklären* and *verstehen*.[10] Both scientists and historians understood *(verstehen)*; both communicated the intelligibility that they had grasped *(erklären)*. The difference lay, not on the side of the subject grasping, but on the side of the intelligibility being grasped. Scientific intelligibility was of a sort that was headed toward a coherent structure valid in any of a set of specified instances.[11] Historical intelligibility was a sophisticated extension of commonsense understanding, headed toward a reconstruction of the past.[12] "Insight" or "understanding" was both more precise in meaning and had a broader range of reference than *verstehen*.[13] Insight occurred in response to inquiry and with respect to sensible presentations (=sense data) or representations (=spontaneously assembled or deliberately devised images). It consisted in a grasp of intelligible unity or relation in sense-data or in the natural image or in the symbol, linguistic or otherwise.

If insight was the pivotal moment, judgment was the decisive moment in human cognition. True judgment was an affirmation following upon a grasp of sufficient evidence for a proposition, or, in Lonergan's technical formulation, following upon a grasp of "the virtually unconditioned," i.e., a condition whose conditions were known and known to be fulfilled.[14] If a judgment was true, its content was unconditioned. Though ontologically at home only in the judging subject, it was intentionally independent of that subject. True judgment was accordingly an instance of self-transcendence.

This self-transcendence was lost, however, just as soon as its one and only home, namely, the mind of the judging subject, was forgotten and "language" was allowed to usurp its place. For, truth is not a matter of language; it is a product of reflective understanding.[15] If this product is expressed in words, still the words are merely "adequate" or "inadequate" with reference to what exists exclusively in the judging mind.

A powerful counterposition in contemporary hermeneutics turns on maintaining that truth and falsity reside, not in judgment, but in expression[16] and that, accordingly,

> the public or common field through which men can
> communicate is not an absolute, independent of all
> subjects because reached through the virtually uncon-
> ditioned, but simply the atmosphere which, as we
> breathe it in common, so also we set vibrating in the
> various manners that carry our words from one to an-
> other.[17]

When this happens, and it has happened with disastrous cultural and political effect in our world, community is deprived of its foundations. Community exists on the basis of common experience and
common and complementary understanding. Moreover, it cannot do
without common judgments grounded on evidence accessible in common, and common values that presuppose those judgments. Once
"atmosphere," be it in the literal sense or in the figurative sense of a
common field created by language, is allowed to replace the common
field reached through the virtually unconditioned, community is undermined at every level and begins to sag and collapse. Its foundation is
not merely linguistic. The foundation of community lies in the fact that
"we hold these truths. . ."

Insight was a creative act of retrieval. It retrieved the conditions of the possibility of real meaning and real value. The retrieval
promised to benefit the individual person, but it promised, above all, to
benefit human communities. Its ultimate intention had been to clear the
way for the service of the ecclesial community, without forgetting for a
moment the subordination of the Christian cause to "the cause of mankind."[18] More specifically, **Insight** had been meant to clear the way
for a critical renewal of method in theology. Lonergan's later treatise,
Method in Theology,[19] gave final expression to this central task of
his life. Between **Insight** and **Method**, the most notable development
in Lonergan's thought bore upon the breakdown of hermeneutics into a
sequence of four functional specialities: interpretation, history, dialectic, and foundations.[20]

It is difficult to say whether in the first instance it was as philosopher or theologian that Lonergan accented the fundamental and crucial distinction between consciousness and intentionality. The definition
of consciousness is basic to cognitional theory; it is no less crucial to
christology (the part of theology that deals with Christ and includes the
question of his psychological make-up). In any case, Lonergan reasoned

as follows: acts of sensing, imagining, and remembering; of wondering, questioning, and question-answering; of weighing the answers and pronouncing on them; of deliberating, evaluating, and deciding, are all transitive not only in the grammatical sense that they are denoted by transitive verbs but in the psychological sense that by each operation one is aware of an object. In each case, that is, the presence of the object to the subject is a psychological event. "Intentionality" and "consciousness" denote distinct but inseparable aspects of the event. "Just as operations by their intentionality make objects present to the subject, so also by consciousness they make the operating subject present to himself."[21]

Here the central insight lay in the recognition that, whereas conscious acts have an object-oriented dimension (intentionality), they exhibit still another dimension, namely, the presence of the subject to himself (consciousness). This living, familiar, and variable, but tacit and unarticulated presence is, indeed, what makes the subject to be subject.

Consciousness is variable, for it varies with distinct levels of intentionality. Lonergan differentiated four such levels. First, there is the empirical level of presentations: awareness of the data of sense (colors, shapes, sounds, odors, etc.) and of the data of consciousness (conscious acts of sensing, attending, wondering, questioning, construing, pondering, judging, etc., in short, the gradated experience of the conscious subject). On this empirical level we sense, perceive, imagine, feel, speak, move. Second, there is the level of intelligence: wondering, questioning, hypothesizing, understanding, conceiving. On this intellectual level we inquire, come to understand, express what we have understood, and work out its significance. Third, there is the level of reason: marshalling evidence, weighing, reflecting, judging. On this rational level we differentiate between true and false and between certain and probable. Fourth, there is the level of decision: deliberating, evaluating, choosing, deciding. On this responsible level we are concerned with ourselves, our ends and means, our loves and hates, the courses of action open to us and their likely results; on this level, too, we carry out our decisions or fail to do so.

This differentiation is a retrieval of human intentionality, and a retrieval relatively immune to revision. For any revision would have to appeal to data; so any revision would have to presuppose an empirical level of operations. Again, revision would have to offer a better explanation of the data; so any revision must presuppose an intellectual level of operations. Again, revision supposes the claim that the better explanation is more probable; so revision would presuppose a rational level of operations. Finally, no one undertakes the labor of revision unless he takes it to be worthwhile; so revision would suppose a responsible level of operations.[22]

What exactly is it that this scheme is schematizing? Lonergan called it "the rock." It is the conscious, intentional operations proper to the human being, and it is these operations as given in consciousness. In other words, "the rock" is the subject himself "in his conscious unobjectified attentiveness, intelligence, reasonableness, responsibility."[23] Lonergan's most fundamental achievement lay in bringing this "rock" to light.

The task included locating the "operator" that effected the promotion of human intending from the empirical, through the intellectual, to the rational level. This operator was "the notion of being." In developmental terms it was a drive to the intelligible (intellectual level) and the true (rational level); but since, as the scholastic adage has it, "reality becomes known through one's knowing what is true" *(ens per verum innotescit)*, this same drive is to being/the real. Sense intends the sensible and intelligence the intelligible, but because cognitive desire does not come to rest in insight alone, we conclude on the basis of this empirical observation that our real goal is reality and that all human beings are naturally and spontaneously realists. It takes no little theorizing to cut conscious intentionality off at the empirical level, or, conceding to the empiricist his truncated conception of "the real," to suppose that the domain of operations transcending sense is merely "ideal."

In **Insight** "hermeneutics" was Lonergan's comprehensive theory of meaning. Its forefront was dominated by a certain paradigm: an interpretation of philosophers by no means limited to grasping their meaning in their own terms. He conceded that there were advantages in interpreting Plato by Plato, Aquinas by Aquinas, Kant by Kant.[24] But interpretation of this kind was non-explanatory, and it is clear that Lonergan's real goal as hermeneutist was an explanatory account of why Plato was Plato and no more; Aquinas, Aquinas and no more; Kant, Kant and no more--yet why Plato, Aquinas, and Kant were utterly indispensable to the dialectical process by which philosophy properly and profitably kept driving beyond them all toward a goal that would sublate them all.[25]

Apropos of this dialectic, it might be appropriate to reconsider our locating of Lonergan, now not only by reference to the latter twentieth century and by comparison and contrast with a contemporary idealist such as G. R. G. Mure, but in a far larger context. The last time that original systematic thought found expression in comprehensive syntheses was with Kant and Hegel. Scholasticism, to be sure, had retained something of the vast sweep of Aquinas. But, whether measured against its original expression in the thirteenth century or against such contemporary movements as German idealism, scholasticism in the Enlightenment and post-Enlightenment eras cut in some respects a poor figure. It lacked the *élan vital* of the medieval synthesis and it lacked the critical spirit of Kantian and post-Kantian thought.

Lonergan, first a deft historian of certain of Aquinas's philosophic and theological achievements,[26] effected a stunning transposition of the scholastic heritage to the domain of modern thought. The key to this transposition was the phenomenology of knowledge. He met the epistemological issue by differentiating between the intending that defined elementary knowing (e.g., seeing and hearing) and the intending that defined fully human knowing (grasping intelligently and affirming reasonably). The kind of metaphysics that emerged on the basis of this phenomenology and epistemology seemed tame and confined by comparison with the metaphysics that structured the theology of Aquinas, for it was not coterminous with being. Lonergan did affirm that the intending that was wondering and questioning related the wonderer/questioner immediately to being. But Lonerganian metaphysics was limited to the proper object of human knowing, i.e., to "being proportionate to human knowing." On the other hand, this metaphysics gained "critical" status from the isomorphism of the structures of human knowing with the structures of being proportionate to it. Nor did the limits of this critical metaphysics undercut the possibility of transcendent knowledge, i.e., the rational affirmation of God and the anticipation of religion that emerged from the antithesis of good and evil.

Thus there appeared, surprisingly, in the mid-twentieth century a philosophy that was critical, systematic, and comprehensive. It was characterised by a critique that matched, corrected, and sublated that of Kant and a system the heuristic categories of which made it more open

as well as more fully rounded and comprehensive than that of Hegel.
If the hermeneutics of **Insight** was deeply concerned with the
dialectic of philosophy, it is noteworthy that after **Insight** Lonergan
found that there was something to be gained by acknowledging a limited, integral, interpretative task: the act of clarifying, without changing,
the intended sense of texts. This certainly did not mean abandonment of
the explanatory ideal. In fact, Lonergan had become clearer than ever on
its usefulness. Principally, it belonged to the functional specialty
"dialectic,"[27] but it had another use, of potentially great value to ordinary interpretation. By moving from the description of the common
sense of a past age to an explanatory grasp precisely pinpointing that
age's insights and oversights, values and biases, the interpreter would
no longer find himself surprised by his own findings, for he would have
entered, more consciously and securely than he might have thought possible, into the writer's world of meaning.

Interpreters usually recognize that those for whom they are
working out an interpretation have no difficulty in grasping X (a particular part or aspect of the meaning of the text) but great difficulty in
grasping Y. The interpretation, then, concentrates on Y. The case will
be different for a different audience, having different resources. Explanatory interpretation, on the other hand, does not deal with parts or aspects of the meaning of the text in their relation to a particular audience; it deals with them in their relation to (a) each other, and (b) the
totality of meanings. This kind of interpretation supposes an audience
than can understand and profit from it. What do the explanatory interpreter and his audience have in common?

Lonergan's answer is: a comprehensive or universal viewpoint. This is a heuristic structure. It draws on (a) generalized empirical
method, i.e., the objectification of conscious intentionality, its levels
and chief "operator," the notion of being or drive to reality. (This
"generalized empirical method" is also called "transcendental method,"
for, as the normative pattern of intelligent operations, it grounds and
pervades all particular methods, while transcending their limits.) (b) It
draws on diverse ways of retrieving the rock and diverse appreciations of
objectivity: naive realism and empiricism, naive and critical idealism,
and finally critical realism. (c) It draws on the understanding of the subject to whom common sense relates everything. Basic to this subject
are the patterns of experience: biological, aesthetic, intellectual, dramatic (subject to bias, blind-spots, repression, and inhibition, drawn to

authenticity and hindered by a many-rooted history of disorder).[28] Further, it draws on the understanding of common sense itself, together with the biases to which common sense is inevitably subject.[29] (d) It draws on the basic differentiations of consciousness. These differentiations respond to exigences.[30] Science responds to the exigence of explanation. Philosophy responds to the "critical" exigence. Established in the sphere of interiority or subjectivity, it is able, on the basis of generalized empirical method, to grasp the procedures of common sense, or mathematicized science, of religion, of philosophy and of theology.

The heuristic structure so assembled is a hold on the elements of meaning, their possible combinations and differentiations. It includes a hold on objectivity and on how differences respecting objectivity are reducible to diverse accounts of cognitional fact. All possible viewpoints and all possible relations among them are potentially included in this hold on the elements of meaning and all of them are subject to critique.

To the present writer it appears that virtually all Lonerganians have been bitten by the bug of the explanatory idea. But it is easier to grasp the ideal in principle than to realize it is practice. It is not so surprising, then, that we do not yet have the explanatory account of philosophy that Lonergan sketched[31] but left unrealized in **Insight**. We do not yet have the account--lightly sketched in the epilogue to **Insight**--of how, historically, theology has worked.[32] We do not yet have an explanatory account of the common sense of any age, although the procedure of developing one is sufficiently indicated in **Method in Theology**.[33] The sole example of the explanatory ideal realized in a historical account has been provided by Lonergan himself. It is his tracing of the dialectical development of Trinitarian thought in **The Way to Nicea**.[34]

Meantime, instead of further Lonerganian developments of the solid and original schemes produced by Ernst Cassirer and Bruno Snell,[35] we are being offered today simplistic and inevitably misleading schemes of cultural development like that borrowed in part from Roman Jakobson and sponsored by Northrop Frye in **The Great Code**.[36] Clearly, there is room here for efforts to meet contemporary needs in many fields by developing Lonergan's suggestions, leads, and example in explanatory hermeneutics.

This introductory effort to locate Lonergan in the field of hermeneutics might conclude by specifying some of the functions of Lonergan's hermeneutics at the present time.

First, it could supply solid phenomenological and epistemological foundations for "the hermeneutics of consent."[37] This hermeneutics eloquently attests the currently widespread hunger for theological exegesis of biblical works that, by contradistinction to the flawed exegetical programs proposed by liberal theologians and kerygma theologians over the past hundred years or so, aspires to measure up without *arrière-pensée* to the affirmations and celebrations, the commitments and hopes of the biblical text.[38]

Second, Lonerganian hermeneutics could advance a much needed clarification. Arnold Toynbee thought that in his many-volumed masterwork he had produced a massive work of empirical history. Lonergan's clarification consisted in redefining Toynbee's achievement as a source-book of grand-scale ideal-types useful for many enterprises, including that of empirical history.[39] There are interpreters from Kierkegaard through Freud to Frye, whose works on the Bible call to be reclassified under rubrics other than biblical interpretation.

Third, a needed critical function today is to separate the wheat from the horrendous mass of chaff in contemporary literary theory. This will inevitably include the debunking of all those modes of pretentious sophistication ballyhooed as insight: *langue* without *parole* and *Sprache* without *Sache*,[40] sign without signified,[41] text without author,[42] and scholarship in recoil from "coherence" and "validity."[43]

Fourth, it belongs to Lonerganian hermeneutics (among other schools of sober thought) to differentiate between confused and undiscriminating attacks on "the historical-critical method" itself and the real limitations and perversions that have shown up in the practice of the method. It is not the fault of the method if its practitioners find themselves without engaging questions to ask. When the questions are worthwhile--as in such works as F. M. Cross's **Canaanite Myth and Hebrew Epic** (1973), E. P. Sanders's **Paul and Palestinian Judaism** (1977), Raymond E. Brown's **The Birth of the Messiah** (1977), Rudolf Pesch's **Das Abendmahl und Jesu Todesverständnis** (1978), Joseph Fitzmyer's **Gospel According to Luke** (1981-85), Peter Stuhlmacher's **Reconciliation, Law and Righteousness** (1981, ET 1986), Richard A. Horsley and J. S. Hanson's **Bandits, Prophets, and Messiahs** (1985), to mention only a few among many excellent works--the historical-critical method functions lucidly and incisively.

Fifth and finally, Lonerganian hermeneutics seems to be particularly well provisioned for the task of finding the truth in the heresy, for in exemplary fashion Lonergan himself repeatedly found, not (or not only) what was wrong, but above all what was right, in Barth and Bultmann, Freud and Frye, Gadamer and Habermas, Parsons and Piaget, Ranke and Ricoeur, Scheler and Simmel, Teilhard de Chardin and Eric Voegelin.

NOTES

1. G. R. G. Mure, **Retreat from Truth** (Oxford: Blackwell, 1958).

2. G. R. G. Mure, **Idealist Epilogue** (Oxford: Clarendon, 1978).

3. Bernard Lonergan, **Insight, A Study of Human Understanding** (New York: Longmans, 1957).

4. Bernard Lonergan, **Collection**, ed. F. E. Crowe (New York: Herder & Herder, 1967) 214.

5. **A Second Collection**, ed. W. F. J. Ryan and B. J. Tyrell (London: Darton, Longman & Todd, 1974) 30.

6. **Collection**, 154.

7. **Collection**, 154.

8. Bernard Lonergan, **Method in Theology** (London: Darton, Longman & Todd, 1972) 154 on the third factor heightening the problem of interpretation in modernity.

9. **Second Collection**, 207.

10. **Method**, 229.

11. **Method**, 229.

12. **Method**, 230.

13. **Method**, 212.

14. **Insight**, 208-9 and 343-45; **Method**, 102.

15. **Insight**, 271-78.

16. **Insight**, 557.

17. **Insight**, 557.

18. **Second Collection**, 158.

19. See above, note 8.

20. Second Collection, 275.

21. Method, 8.

22. Method, 19.

23. Method, 19.

24. Insight, 583-84.

25. Insight, 389.

26. Bernard Lonergan, Verbum: Word and Idea in Aquinas, ed. David Burrell (Notre Dame: Notre Dame University Press, 1967), and Grace and Freedom: Operative Grace in the Thought of St. Thomas Aquinas (New York: Herder & Herder, 1971).

27. Method, 235-66.

28. Insight, 173-81.

29. Insight, 207-44.

30. Method, 83-85.

31. Insight, 389.

32. Insight, 739-42.

33. Method, 90-99, 172-73.

34. Bernard Lonergan, The Way to Nicea (Philadelphia: Westminster, 1976).

35. Ernst Cassirer, The Philosophy of Symbolic Forms (New Haven: Yale University Press, 1953-57); Bruno Snell, The Discovery of the Mind (Cambridge, MA: Harvard University Press, 1953; repr. New York: Harper & Row [Harper Torchbook] 1960).

36. Northrop Frye, The Great Code (New York: Harcourt Brace Jovanovich, 1982).

37. See Peter Stuhlmacher, Historical Criticism and Theological Interpretation of Scripture. Toward a Hermeneutics of Consent (Philadelphia: Fortress, 1977).

38. See my essay below: "Conversion and the Hermeneutics of Consent."

39. Method, 228; Bernard Lonergan, A Third Collection, ed. F. E. Crowe (New York-Mahwah: Paulist, 1985) 103-6, 214.

40. Offering cogent resistance to these theoretical tendencies: Paul Ricoeur, on "discourse," in Interpretation Theory. Discourse and the Surplus of Meaning (Forth Worth: Texas Christian University Press, 1976) 1-23; and Emerich Coreth on the dialectic of Sache and Sprache, in Grundfragen der Hermeneutik (Freiburg: Herder, 1969) 64-65, 116-17, 123-24.

41. On this fallacy, see Valentine Cunningham, "Renoving That Bible: The Absolute Text of (Post) Modernism" in The Theory of Reading, ed. Frank Gloversmith (Sussex: Harvester, 1984) 1-51, esp. 1-13.

42. Cunningham, "Renoving That Bible," 13-17, on Roland Barthes,

Hillis Miller, Jacques Derrida. See also David Lodge, **Language of Fiction** (London: Routledge & Kegan Paul, 1966, 21984), especially the 1984 "Afterword."

43. Derrida (in 1967, at least) would relativize coherence in the name of "play." Again, validity is among the targets of his assault on "logocentrism." See Cunningham, 6, 16.

II

THE PRIMACY OF THE
INTENDED SENSE OF TEXTS

**Part One: Ninety-Five Theses on General and Biblical
Hermeneutics**

The purpose of the following theses is to outline a full rationale for the following hermeneutical proposition: the text has a primary claim on the reader, namely, to be construed in accord with its intended sense.

The effort to state the full rationale of this proposition seems to me especially worthwhile at a time when interpretation--the construal of the intended sense--is widely rejected in theory, e.g., with the counter-thesis that an "intended" sense is neither the primary nor even a possible goal of interpretation, and abandoned in practice by literary critics, classical scholars, and biblical exegetes in favor of analytic studies either alternative to interpretation (e.g., structuralist analysis) or logically presupposing interpretation (social-scientific, psychological, or historical analysis). But the outline, in thesis form for the sake of succinctness, is also meant to serve as the basis for a follow-up study, part two of the present essay, offering further detail on "intention," "the historical consciousness," and contemporary possibilities of the theological interpretation of scripture.

1. Communications

1.1 To deprive an adult of all or nearly all communication is to subject him to a severe ordeal, and to deprive a child in this way would fundamentally damage him. The capacity and appetite for communication is rooted in man's rational and social nature. He is a meaning being with a natural drive for the mediation of meaning to and from his fellow human beings.

1.2 Of man's resources for the mediation of meaning, language is primary and peerless. By analogy, other resources are so many languages (the alphabet of symbols, body language, the languages of art and architecture, etc.).

1.2.1 Language is an encoding resource shared by a speech community. From this resource we choose words and phrases that by the conventions of ordinary usage are more or less apt to encode the meanings that we wish to express.

1.2.2 Language is thus conventional and instrumental: conventional inasmuch as its ordinary meaningfulness is established by common usage, and doubly instrumental inasmuch as it is used to express meaning and the expression of meaning itself serves ulterior human purposes.

1.2.3 Both the classical view of language (namely, that it is the vehicle of thought) and the Leibnizian view of language (namely, that it is the determining medium of thought) are true as affirmations and false insofar as either is made to negate the other. They are reconciled in a higher viewpoint, which permits the distinction between ordinary linguistic meaning and original linguistic meaning. "All men enjoy flashes of insight beyond meaning already stabilized in etymology and grammar" (Whitehead).[1]

1.3 The drive to communicate is as complex as the entire social dimension of the life of man. But there is a common note that runs through its many performative modes (to request, to inform, to persuade, to command, to entertain, etc.) and other modalities (spontaneous/ deliberate, private/public, oral/written, etc.): the will to transmit intended meaning.

1.3.1 Transmission envisages reception and normally envisages some response from the receiver. Response effects a reversal of roles: the receiver becomes a transmitter and the original transmitter now receives.

1.3.2 By his response the receiver indicates how he has construed (=decoded) the original transmission. To the extent that this does not correspond to what the transmitter intended, grounds appear for distinguishing between "intended transmission" and "effective transmission."

1.3.3 There are two possible sources for the gap between the two: the original transmission failed to express adequately the sense that the transmitter intended; the receiver failed to construe the transmission accurately. By repeated efforts of exchange defects in either source or in both are eliminated or at least reduced.

2. Writing and Reading

2.1 Writing calls for a more deliberate use of language than is usual in ordinary speaking. This deliberateness reflects a recognition that by writing one may transmit without being personally present and so able to enter into an exchange with the receiver, making good any failures of communication. The deliberateness of writing, then, is first of all the writer's special efforts to insure that the transmission adequately incorporate his intended meaning and that it meet in advance the foreseeable receivers' foreseeable problems in construing it.

2.1.1 In writing, the transmission is a "text," i.e., a written word-sequence encoding the message of the writer. The "message" is whatever the writer intends to encode and succeeds in encoding. The writer, then, expresses a message in a text and the reader construes a text with a view to receiving its message. ("Message" so defined is a technical term to be differentiated from the "lesson" or "moral" of a story, or from the noble sentiments that many Victorians looked for in poetry.)

2.1.2 "Intention" or "intended meaning" is thus not only in the writer; it is also intrinsic to the text insofar as the text objectifies or incorporates or encodes or expresses the writer's message.

2.1.3 It follows that the dismissal of the *mens auctoris* as irrelevant to
interpretation (Gadamer)[2] and the rejection of the so-called "intentional
fallacy" (Wimsatt and Beardsley)[3] are themselves products of an oversight: intended meaning is not merely in the writer and extrinsic to the
text; it is precisely the text's main intrinsic determinant.

2.1.4 The prime object of interpretation is that sense which is the for-
mal cause *(causa essendi)* of the singular configuration of the text, and
to which this singular configuration is, in turn, the index *(causa cog-
noscendi)*. Inasmuch as this is none other than the sense that the writer
has managed to encode or objectify in the text, hermeneutics is "author-
based."[4]

2.1.5 It does not follow from this that the intended sense is *a priori*
deeper or truer or humanly more interesting or important than senses
that accrue to the text in the course of its journey through time. What
does follow is the need to distinguish these diverse senses so as to do
justice respectively to the text, to the history of its impact *(Wirkungsgeschichte:* Gadamer),[5] and to the ties--be they fragile and fortuitous,
or firm, intrinsic, and intricate--between the two.

2.1.6 We should distinguish with Ferdinand de Saussure between
"language" (the linguistic resources shared by a speech community) and
"utterances" (instances of actual linguistic expression);[6] with E. D.
Hirsch between "sense" (i.e., originally intended sense) and
"significance" (new, superadded senses);[7] and with Gottlob Frege between "meaning" (the intelligible content of an expression) and
"reference" (the object[s] to which the expression refers or applies).[8]

2.1.7 From the vantage point of the interpreter, the study of
"language" is ordered to the study of "utterances"; the prime concern is
with "sense," though "significance" is a resource for the quest of the
sense as well as a distinct concern in its own right; finally, both concerns break down into the effort to grasp "meaning" and "reference."

2.2 To read signifies, first, to construe a text with a view to grasping
its message or intended sense.

2.2.1 One construes a text progressively and cumulatively, by spiraling into its sense, i.e., attending to the reciprocally mediating opposites that define the hermeneutic circles, e.g., "whole and parts," "things and words," "reader and text."

2.2.2 The circle of whole and parts: "I understand the whole only in function of understanding the parts; I understand the parts only in function or understanding the whole." Logically, the circle is vicious; actually, it is broken open by acts of insight that, alternating between whole and parts, mediate an ever firmer grasp of the work in both aspects.

2.2.3 The circle of things and words: "I understand words by understanding the things they refer to; I understand things by understanding the words that refer to them." The first limb states a fundamental insight: "Whoever does not understand the things cannot draw the sense from the words" (Luther).[9] The second limb states how one moves through a grasp of words to a firmer grasp of things: the reader understands things, with the writer, by means of his words.

2.2.4 If it is a fact that readers regularly understand things through the mediation of the writer's words, the so-called "myth of transparency" (Kermode)[10] is itself mythical, i.e., mistaken and misleading. On the contrary, readers are and always have been spontaneously and keenly intent on the realities evoked by the text and as evoked by the text.

2.2.5 The circle of reader and text: "I understand myself in virtue of understanding the text; I understand the text in virtue of understanding myself." This is a straightforward specification of the circle of things and words, focusing on one of its fundamental aspects: the limitations on understanding imposed by the limits of one's self-understanding. It also suggests the possibility of modifying one's self-understanding under the stimulus of even fragmentary insight into another's meaning.

2.3 As geometric figures are functional to geometric ideas, so in some kinds of writing language is severely functional to abstract meaning. Thus, the sound of the words is irrelevant; other words with other sounds might do as well. But in poetry the medium is part and parcel of the message, i.e., the material text is included in the intended sense. The words as sounded (and, often enough, as seen printed on the page) belong as well to what the writer intends to communicate as to how he intends to communicate it. As the meaning of a statue is inseparable from its embodiment in the statue itself, so the meaning of a poem is imperfectly separable from its unique material text.

2.3.1 Interpretation takes account of aspects inadequately distinct from the message, namely, the text's illocutionary intentions (such performative modalities as to attest, to argue, to promise, to threaten, etc.) and its perlocutionary intentions (i.e., the intending of effects, e.g., to move to shame, to instill pride, to elicit wonder, provoke reflection, incite enthusiasm).[11]

2.3.2 The intrinsically appropriate stance of the interpreter is not doubt nor scepticism nor suspicion, but goodwill, empathy. the readiness to find truth, common understanding, agreement (Newman, Gadamer, G. Ebeling, Peter Stuhlmacher).[12]

2.3.3 To grasp another's meaning I must not only have a pre-understanding *(Vorverständnis)* of and, indeed, vital relationship *(Lebensverhältnis)* [13] to the things that he refers to; I must furthermore project horizons approximating those of his message and find in myself a range of resources akin to those actualized in and called for by his message. This is hardly possible apart from an antecedent stance of openness, receptiveness, empathy vis-à-vis his word.

2.3.4 This initial stance does not foreclose critique. It supposes a distinction between understanding and critique, between their respective objects and requisites, and so between the stances appropriate to each. Finally, this view acknowledges accurate understanding as a *sine qua non* condition of valid critique.

2.3.5 The dynamism of interpretation is toward "encounter," i.e., vital contact with another's intended sense. "All real living is meeting" (Buber);[14] so is all real interpreting.

2.3.6 The circles of things and words and of reader and text underscore the ordering of interpretation to encounter. The labor of construing an eminent text yields to vital contact with the new world thus brought to light. In one's understanding of Hosea or Heracleitus, of Dante or Rilke, there may occur modifications both of horizon and of self-understanding on the part of the interpreter. (On the other hand, some changes of this sort may, in accord with the limits of the prospective interpreter, be prerequisite to his understanding of Hosea or Heracleitus, of Dante or Rilke.)

2.3.7 Encounter is the nexus between interpretation and critique, and critique is above all a report on encounter.

2.3.8 Among specific objects of critique: the text as work of art, as representation of reality, as claimant to truth, as qualitatively comparable to other works. Here critical distance and "the hermeneutic of suspicion" in the sense of attention to bias, to ideology, to rationalizing explanations, screening devices, etc., not only in the text but in the critic himself, are indispensable to critique (Lonergan).[15]

2.4 Immediately and variously related to interpretation (though, unlike interpretation, not limited to the harmonics of authorial intention) is the placement of the text in the history of tradition before and after it.

2.4.1 The text generates a tradition of interpretation and critique, which thereafter conditions access to it. Ideally, the consciousness of the interpreter is informed not only by the tradition that the text to be interpreted has generated *(wirkungsgeschichtliches Bewusstsein:* Gadamer)[16] but by the critically illuminated history of the tradition, as well. Tradition constitutes a contextual unit of literary intelligibility, an intelligibility heightened by critical history.

2.5 Reading primarily regards the intended sense. Nevertheless, readers may read with other, special, purposes. Such is the police detective's reading of a ransom note, or a social historian's reading of an ancient encomium. Such special purposes, however, suppose rather than detract from the primacy of reading for the intended sense. If the detective did not recognize the note as a demand for ransom, he would not bother with further analysis of it. If the social historian did not recognize the encomium as an encomium, it would not serve the purposes of his further, specialized, inquiry.

2.5.1 Reserving "interpretation" for reading in the primary sense, we shall use "analysis" for all the secondary, specialized kinds of reading (structural analysis, psychological analysis, socio-economic analysis, etc.). Some modes of analysis (text-critical, form-critical, etc.) prepare the way for interpretation; others, however, make interpretation a point of departure for some ulterior goal.

2.5.2 If the dynamism of interpretation is toward "encounter," the dynamism of analysis is toward problem-solving. A satisfactory definition of the phenomenon of myth, for example, is an analytic solution of a problem. Though relevant to the interpretation of mythical texts, it is not itself interpretation. Analysis directly centered on texts may degenerate all too easily into pure application or illustration of what the analyst already knew before he analyzed the text (e.g., that all consciousness is socially determined; that human motivation operates as Freud described it, etc.).

2.5.3 Insofar as the analyst is looking through or past patent meaning is search of latent meaning, his appropriate stance is one of critical distance, scepticism, "suspicion" (Ricoeur).[17]

2.5.4 Just as psychoanalysis is a kind of analysis, not a kind of literary critique, so there are modes of analysis, equally distinct from literary critique, appropriate to texts consciously or unconsciously distorted by psychic bias, individual bias, group bias, general bias.[18] As concerned with latent and even unintended meaning, such modes of analysis instantiate a hermeneutic of suspicion, as psychoanalysis does.

3. The Historical Consciousness

3.1 A historical consciousness--a tendency to view all things human in an overarching context of historical change--has increasingly pervaded the West over the past two hundred years and the world at large in the course of the present century.

3.1.1 This historical consciousness was gradually established by complementary insights into the potent but limited impact of human acts of meaning. First, by his acts of meaning man is equally the maker of himself and of the world he lives and moves in. Second, every act of meaning is embedded in a context, and these contexts inexorably change.

3.1.2 Man makes himself what he is in accord with a process whereby, acknowledged or not, all his acts of meaning enter into the forging of his selfhood. Though man has always been a self-maker and a maker of his own worlds of meaning, only historically conscious man is aware of this. He has discovered autonomy: the possibility of deliberately setting out to reshape himself and his world.

3.1.3 If every act of meaning is embedded in a context subject to inexorable change, man in time is never wholly one and the same. He is not what he was; he will not be what he is.

3.2 This new consciousness and the insights that have generated it are transforming, but neither foundational nor complete. Transforming: among a vast public the historical consciousness has massively demystified tradition, culture, society, wealth, power. Not foundational: the historical consciousness has differentiated the consciousness of rationalists, idealists, empiricists, materialists, existentialists, etc., while inducing neither a revision of their principles nor a reconciliation of their differences in a higher synthesis. Nor complete: theories of knowledge and reality, of man and history, give concrete shape to the historical consciousness as it actually exists in groups and individuals.

3.2.1 Thus, the autonomy implied in self-making is open to interpretation and realization as absolute or as "under God." The grasp of relativity to context may be accompanied by the affirmation or by the denial of transcontextual constants and the transposability of meaning from context to context.

3.2.2 A leading theory, which has successively taken Enlightenment, nineteenth-century and twentieth-century shapes, proposes freedom as the goal of man. If the chief expression thereof has been an emancipation from the normative past and an ever more thoroughgoing secularization, one of the twentieth-century variations on the theme has celebrated man's coming of age as "son" (Gal 4:5) and as "heir of the world" (Rom 4:13) (Gogarten),[19] so demonstrating that the historical consciousness and even secularization itself are open to potentially decisive redefinition.

3.2.3 Antedating the rise of the historical consciousness and in time widely merging with it was the Cartesian recoil from any but indubitable affirmations. The first of Descartes' four rules was

> to avoid precipitation and prejudice in judgments, and to accept in them nothing more than was presented to my mind so clearly and distinctly that I could have no occasion to doubt it (*Discours de la méthode*).[20]

3.2.4 The mind-set betrayed by this principle became the Enlightenment's "prejudice against prejudice" (Gadamer);[21] it debunked belief and tradition; it defined "critical" intelligence as methodically sceptical. A potentially anti-historical element thus entered into the historical consciousness.

3.2.5 For Descartes the immediate data of consciousness were a rock of certitude in a sea of doubt. For Marx and Freud, "masters of suspicion" (Ricoeur),[22] the immediate data of consciousness were sources of illusion.

3.2.6 In its commonsense mode the contemporary historical consciousness of the West is Cartesian and Marxian, Vichian and Nietzschean, Hegelian and Freudian--in short, rife with latent contradiction.

3.2.7 If modern Western culture is consciously experimental and developing, and pervaded by a historical consciousness charged with competing and incompatible tendencies, it nevertheless derives some unity from a central ideal, controlling in theory and at least significant in practice, which northern Europeans and North Americans established in the late Enlightenment: the dignity of man, conceived in terms of political self-determination and individual human rights.

3.3 The thesis of the more or less radical unknowability of the past (hard-line historical relativism) is doubly grounded: first, in the practical difficulty of reconstituting the common sense of another time and place; second, a more fundamentally, in one or another mistaken theory of knowledge (e.g., to know anything, one must know everything; the human subject, since he exhibits no transcontextual constants, is flatly discontinuous with both forbears and progeny, etc.).

3.3.1 While the historical consciousness has intensified the recognition of difficulties (i.e., historically conditioned diversity of common sense) in interpreting texts from outside the horizons and perspectives habitual to the interpreter, it has also set at his disposal a hitherto unimagined array of interpretative resources designed to meet and resolve these difficulties.

3.3.2 The root possibility of understanding texts, including even texts from another time-zone and language-zone, another culture and civilization, is grounded in invariant structures of human intentionality (e.g., experience-understanding-judgment).[23]

3.3.3 True judgment bearing on the past is grounded, like every instance of true judgment, in a grasp of the virtually unconditioned (i.e., of a conditioned whose conditions are known and known to be fulfilled).[24] Inasmuch as these conditions and their fulfillment are finite and knowable in principle, valid interpretations of texts from the past and true judgments bearing on past reality are possible and in fact occur.

3.4 History studies historical reality, i.e., man as he was, or man as he made himself and his world to be what they were. The inquiry alternates between efforts to know (a) who wanted what, and (b) what possibilities actually found fulfillment, and why.

3.4.1 "Historical criticism" globally signifies the resources, techniques, and proximate norms of historical inquiry. Such criticism presupposes not only the historical consciousness but some view of what, in principle, is knowable, of what is proper and what alien to historical inquiry, of what is worth knowing and what most worth knowing, etc.

3.5 The rise of the historical consciousness, its determination by diverse and partly conflicting theories of knowledge, of man, of history, the widespread cultivation of historical curiosity and knowledge and the sophistication of historical criticism have had an irresistible impact on contemporary thinking, writing, reading.

3.5.1 Among the more conscious results: the reader today no longer assumes that he is on a seamless historical continuum with writers of other times and places. Moreover, it is widely recognized that the reading of an eminent text requires an account of its historical context as well as an introduction to its conceptual and linguistic idiom.

3.5.2 Among the less conscious results: without the slightest effort in the direction of theory, contemporary commonsense readers have taken in bits and pieces of conflicting theories and ideals--Cartesian, Vichian, Kantian, Hegelian, Marxian, Freudian, etc. Cultural clarity is thus muddied by cultural confusion, adding to the alloy of common sense by common nonsense.

3.5.3 In the modern age the ideal of working out an understanding of the intended sense of a text, judging how accurate this understanding is, and expressing what one judges to be an accurate understanding of the intended sense of the text[25] has often been realized by professional interpreters more fully and effectively than ever before, owing to the exploitation of more exact and elaborate resources (textual criticism, lexicography, linguistics, social, cultural, and literary history) than have ever previously been available to interpreters.

3.5.4 Professional interpreters appear to differ markedly from commonsense readers and, on technical aspects of interpretation (use of linguistic, philological, historical resources), they do. In other respects, however, e.g., encounter with the text, report on encounter, critique of truth and value, the superiority of the professionals is random and unreliable.

3.6 Eminent texts are eminent in virtue of their bringing "things counter, original, spare, strange" into deep coherence. Since the full secret of their sweep and unity defies definition, "a classic is a writing that is never fully understood" (Friedrich Schlegel).[26]

3.6.1 The difficulty of interpretation does not, however, explain the contemporary flight from interpretation (i.e., from construal of and encounter with intended meaning): the limiting of interpretation to elucidation of detail; the drift into trackless historical conjecture;[27] the preferring of analysis (sociological, structuralist, Marxian, Freudian, etc.) to interpretation, together with an accompanying domestication of intended meaning, either by translating it systematically into more congenial terms or at any rate by judging it on the basis of some conventional standard or some closed system.

3.6.2 Eminent texts and the effort to interpret them bring to light the cultural confusions of the interpreter. Recoil from cognitive dissonance is accordingly a key factor in the contemporary flight from interpretation.

3.6.3 Inasmuch as encounter with eminent texts enlightens, corrects, and refines, perseverance in interpretation is the primary schooling of the interpreter.

3.6.4 A more radical and thoroughgoing solution supposes the discovery of an adequate account of human intentionality[28] and its personal appropriation. It proceeds to a dialectic of competing theories of knowledge, man, and history. It consists in the act of discriminating among them between true and false, real and illusory.

4. Theology and the Bible

4.1 Biblical literature has a twofold claim to eminence: literary and religious. Though distinct, these are inseparable aspects of one phenomenon. The literary excellence of the Bible is interwoven with the quality of the response to God of God's people. This is a communitarian and public response, calling for linguistic and, eventually, literary expression.

4.2 By the resurrection of Christ Christianity was bound to the scriptures of Israel, for the resurrection vindicated Jesus' election-historical mission, which supposed and climaxed the election history of biblical Israel.

4.2.1 The first Christians understood salvation in Christ as fulfillment: the coming to realization of what had been foreshadowed (1 Cor 10:6; Rom 8:32), promised (Gal 3:8; 4:28f.; Rom 4:13-25; 15:8; Acts 2:16-21,33), and prophesied (Luke 24:26f.,46f.; Acts 2:23,34f.; 3:18,22); the coming to perfection of what had been provisional (Matt 5:17); the coming to completion, i.e., to foreordained eschatological measure, of time (Mark 1:15), sin (Matt 23:32; 1 Thess 2:16; Rom 1:29) suffering (Col 1:24), and the whole drama of history (Eph 1:9f.; cf. 2 Cor 1:20). Hence, the scriptures of Israel were both the word of God and an indispensable source of the understanding of salvation in Christ.

4.2.2 Jesus himself initiated the interpretation of his career as the fulfillment of biblical type (e.g., the motifs of "Son of man," Matt 10:23; Luke 17:24-30; Servant, Mark 9:31; 10:45 par.; 14:24 par.; covenant, Mark 14:24 par.), promise (e.g., Matt 5:3f.; cf. Isa 61:1f.), and prophecy (e.g., Matt 11:5 par.; cf. Isa 35:5-7; 29:18f.; 61:1f.), the perfecting of the provisional (Matt 5:17), and the filling up of eschatological measure (Matt 5:21f.,33f.,38f.,43f.; cf. Luke 14:22-24.

4.2.3 If for early Christianity the scriptures of Israel were the word of God, so was the proclamation of their fulfillment (1 Thess 2:13; 2 Cor 2:17; 5:19f.; cf. 1 Cor 9:16f.).

4.2.4 Marcionite repudiation of the Old Testament and gnostic interpretation of biblical and liturgical texts elicited orthodox responses reaffirming the Old Testament as the word of the one and only God and appealing to "the rule of faith" (cf. Gal 6:16; Rom 12:6) as the norm of scriptural interpretation.

4.2.5 The formation of an authoritative canon of New Testament scriptures attests early Christian commitment to the unity of faith; the concrete content of the canon (cf. especially the maintenance of distinct gospels) attests commitment to the particularity, variety, and fulness of normative faith-witness.

4.3 The practice of Christian interpreters in the early centuries likewise attests their commitment both to the particularity of particular texts and, in accord with the analogy or rule of faith, to their coherence with the faith heritage attested by the scriptures as a whole.

4.3.1 Their treatment of the literal sense of biblical texts exhibited both aspects; their treatment of the "spiritual" sense, by which, for example, the Old Testament scriptures pointed to Christ and to the sacraments of baptism and the eucharist, highlighted the second aspect.

4.3.2 Rooted in New Testament practice and developed by expositors from the second to the fourth century, the Fathers' favorite method of exposing the spiritual sense of scripture was allegorical interpretation. The positive function of this interpretation was to witness repeatedly and creatively to the faith as a comprehensive unity.

4.3.3 Conceptual tools borrowed (partly through Arabic mediation) from Greek philosophy transformed the interpretative resources of theologians in the high Middle Ages. Among the results were an analytically penetrating style of interpretation and an elegant systematization of "the senses of scripture."[29]

4.3.4 From the late fifteenth century to the present the most significant changes in theological interpretation, as in interpretation generally, related to the rise of the historical consciousness. Renaissance humanists introduced a rudimentary use of philological methods. The Reformers' appeal to "scripture" against "Church" gave impetus to the break with allegory.

4.3.5 Catholic hermeneutics from Irenaeus to the present appeals to the faith heritage of the apostolic Church as theological criterion (the "analogy" or "rule" of faith). Protestant hermeneutics from the Reformers to the present has restructured the role of tradition in interpretation, maximizing concentration on the literal sense and appealing to the *claritas interna* and *externa* of the scriptural text as well as to the Spirit's unmediated illumination thereof.[30]

4.3.6 To determine what the precise theological differences are that currently control these two hermeneutic stances is a task unfinished until the differences are not only located but refined and resolved.

4.3.7 Immeasurably more significant than the historic theological differences between Protestants and Catholics was the sheer fact of the shattering of Church unity. "Nothing could have made Christian faith more unbelievable at the dawn of the modern age than the splitting apart of the Church" (H. U. von Balthasar).[31]

4.3.8 However deep, however true, however relevant the message of the scriptures to "a world split apart" (Solzhenitsyn),[32] a Church split apart witnesses not only for but also against the credibility of that message.

4.4 Once biblical scholarship in the historical-critical mode had made its appearance under unlikely auspices (Benedict Spinoza and Richard Simon, followed by the English deists), it was taken over by European Protestants, who sponsored its most striking advances.

4.4.1 Historical-critical methods have been historically associated with many intellectual movements (rationalism, idealism, positivism, historical relativism, existentialism, etc.), so repeatedly giving the impression that the methods were not of themselves ideologically neutral, but were locked into this or that theory of knowledge, of man, of history, etc. But since these methods have been laboriously separated from one ideology after another, it now appears that of themselves they are, in fact, ideologically neutral, functional to whatever controlling theories are adopted by the interpreter. Theological problems are accordingly traceable, not to the methods, but to the theories with which they have been fused in particular cases.

4.5 Apart from confessional disputes, the theological problems in question derive from all the sources of cultural dissonance in the modern West, e.g., the Cartesian conception of critical intelligence; rationalist repudiation of transcendence and tradition; Kantian subversion of the assurance of knowing the real; undifferentiated historical relativism, as in Ernst Troeltsch; hermeneutic systems that eliminate "false scandals" by eliminating whatever exceeds the limits of reason (demythologizing, etc.).

4.5.1 Three theological roots of allegorical interpretation from the primitive to the medieval Church point up, by contrast, what is often lacking in modern New Testament interpretation: a sense of the text's theological depth-dimension, a grasp of its total religious context, and responsiveness to the note of definitive fulfillment.

4.5.2 If "Antioch" be taken to signify the primacy of the literal (i.e., intended) sense of the text, and "Alexandria," the affirmation (e.g., by allegory) of the full scope and unity of divine revelation, the ascendancy of Alexandria in the eras before the rise of the historical consciousness was a theological necessity. The lack of a sense of history, of historic change, development, and reversal, of the unpredictable and far-reaching diversity that human development entails, and the corresponding lack of historically oriented interpretative resources made it impossible simultaneously to affirm the unity and coherence of divine revelation and to maintain in practice the primacy of the literal sense of scripture.

4.5.3 When Antioch and Alexandria are not brought together in synthesis, Antioch signifies a hermeneutics closed to transcendence or, as Newman put it apropos of the historic school of Antioch, bound to the principle that "there is no mystery in theology."[33] Under this constraint, devotion to the literal sense is wholly unequal to encounter with the New Testament.

4.5.4 The most pressing exigence in biblical hermeneutics today is for a critical synthesis of Antioch and Alexandria, i.e., for the projecting of horizons at once fully differentiated by a historical consciousness and fully open to the transcendent mystery of salvation.

4.5.5 Inasmuch as scripture carries its own powerful if mysterious warrants, the satisfaction of such theological exigences comes first of all from a persevering quest of the intended sense of the scriptures.

4.5.6 Openness to the transcendent mystery of salvation, though realized in significant measure by vital contact with the scriptures, is antecedent to the scriptures as a question is antecedent to an answer, for the ground of this openness is the radical question that man not only has, but is, whereas the scriptures present themselves as the answer to this question.[34]

4.5.7 Communion in faith with the Church of apostolic times is hardly more than an illusion if it fails to include credal commitments to the same revelation. Thus, the maintenance of authentic Christian identity is the ultimate theological rationale of insistence on the intended sense of scriptural texts. Communion in faith with the Church of all times imposes a like commitment to the intended sense of credal, liturgical, and doctrinal texts.

4.5.8   A particular theological problem at the present time is the widespread incapacity among biblical and especially New Testament interpreters to differentiate between texts that are genuinely contradictory and
texts that are conceptually diverse and unharmonizable, but whose
meanings are neither contradictory nor incompatible.

4.5.9   The radical and thoroughgoing solution of the theological problems besetting biblical interpreters lies in the practice of three functional specialities: dialectic, foundations, and doctrines (Lonergan).[35]

Summary of Part One

The hermeneutical primacy of the intended sense of texts is
gounded in the social character of communications (1.1; 1.3-1.3.3), particularly in the use of language (1.2-1.2.2), and still more particularly
in the correlative acts of writing and reading (2.1-2.3.3). The rise of the
historical consciouness (3.1-3.1.3) has differentiated hermeneutics, facil-
itating a more effective grasp of the intended sense (3.5.3), but also un-
derscoring and in some sense increasing its difficulty (3.3f., 3.6). Theology adds its own reasons (4.5.3-4.5.8) for insisting on the primacy of
the intended sense of biblical, credal, liturgical, and doctrinal texts.

The contemporary flight from interpretation on the part of literary critics (3.6.1), their preference for analysis (cf. 2.5-2.5.3), and the
increasingly ideological character of critique (cf. 2.3.9 and 3.6.1) are indices to cultural crisis and confusion (3.2.3-3.2.7; 3.5.2, 3.5.4,
3.6.1f.).

Partly similar results in the field of biblical scholarship are the
product of a hermeneutics closed to transcendence (4.5.3). The challenge
today is accordingly to articulate a critically grounded hermeneutics
open and committed on the one hand to history and the intended sense
of the text, and on the other to the transcendent intelligibility and unity
of the mystery of salvation (4.5.2-4.5.6).

As "self-correcting," interpretation holds out an element of
hope for interpretative progress (3.6.3, 4.5.5). But it would be excessively optimistic to suppose that attention to the intended sense of the
scriptures would be sufficient of itself to meet the complex cultural situation reflected in the shortcomings of current biblical interpretation

(3.6.4, 4.5.9). This calls, rather, for a vital realization of the functional specialities of dialectic, foundations, and doctrines (4.5.9).

Part Two: Intention, History, and Theology

The first part of this paper has several purposes and uses, but for the present I am happy to weight them in favor of two aims. The first is to restore the intelligibility of the intended sense of the text as the object of interpretation. The second is to integrate this view of the object of interpretation into a program of biblical interpretation open to divine revelation as the transcendent and coherent *mysterium Christi*. If the aims are two, the headings below will be three: a contemporary debate on the intended sense; the impact of the historical consciousness on the issue; application to biblical interpretation.

The thesis form adopted above had the advantage of being concise, and concision allowed a large context to be outlined in a few pages. But among the disadvantages of the form is to leave unarticulated much of what pertains to persuasion: leisurely clarification and the consideration of objections. I would like to offer just these clarifications and considerations in this second part of this essay.

Finally, I am especially concerned with interpretation as indispensable to Christian life and, within that broad sphere, with interpretation as indispensable to the enterprise of contemporary Christian theology. As indispensable to Christian life in general, interpretation belongs under the functional specialty "communications";[36] but as indispensable to the collaborative enterprise that is theology, interpretation is a functional specialty in itself.[37] "Communications" calls for as many modes and styles of interpretation as there are audiences with a right to the Christian heritage. My own primary interest here, however, is in the functional specialty "interpretation." Interpretation in this sense is weighted, above all, in favor of precision, and excellence among interpreters and their work shows a tendency toward convergence.

An Unsatisfactory but Instructive Debate

In 1967 E. D. Hirsch tried to make the case for the intended sense of the text as the object of interpretation.[38] His position, however, as well as the arguments that supported it, were defective at several points. First, he failed to differentiate consistently between the intention of the author as in the author and extrinsic to the text and the intention of the author as intrinsic to, or encoded in, or expressed by the text. So Hirsch, from the first chapter of his book, could envisage the marginal case in which the author himself decided: "by these words [i.e., his text] I meant so and so, but I insist that from now on they shall mean something different." An event of this kind, Hirsch says, is "unlikely," but it "*could* occur." In that case the single text, according to Hirsch, has not changed in meaning; it now had two meanings, and it is up to the interpreter "to decide which of the author's two meanings he is going to concern himself with."[39]

Here Hirsch has indeed fallen victim to an intentional fallacy. He has converted the text into an index to the history of the author, which has thus become the real object of interpretation. At one time the author meant such and such by the text; later, he meant something else.

We should pause over this example. Hirsch does not work it out in any detail, perhaps because it is exceedingly unpromising for his thesis. He does not, for example, say whether the author's second meaning is as well supported by the text as his first. Why not? Here as elsewhere Hirsch has so one-sidedly insisted on meaning as an act of "authorial will" as to pass over without notice the series of practical insights--bearing, for example, on the choice and arrangement of words--by which the author realizes or implements the authorial will to communicate something to some audience.

We can make up for Hirsch's lack of detail by supposing, first of all, that the author's second act of authorial will offers as plausible a sense of the text as his first. But, second, we must insist that the object of interpretation be, not the history of the author, but the sense of the text itself. It then follows that we are not dealing with actually known, successive meanings of a text that is clear, but with possible meanings of a text that is ambiguous. The interpreter would be wise not to begin by taking the author's word on the successive meanings of the text, nor to settle simply on one of its purported meanings, nor even to take up both in isolation from one another. His task is to construe the text as it stands, determining whether more than one possible meaning is textually actualized, and, if so, how the meanings are related--by reference not to the testimony of the author but to the particulars of the text. Otherwise, the to-be-interpreted ceases to be the text itself. (For the quite legitimate but, in our context, irrelevant task of investigating the author, the testimony of the author on his change of mind about the meaning of the text is, of course, a useful and interesting datum.)

Another of Hirsch's examples: a poet intends in a four-line poem to convey a sense of desolation. It turns out, however, that even the most competent readers fail to catch this. "Obviously," says Hirsch, the poet's "intention to convey desolation is not identical with his stylistic effectiveness in doing so." Does the poet's lack of effectiveness make any difference? Not to Hirsch. The only universally valid meaning of the poem is the sense of desolation.[40] How awkward. The only valid interpretation of the poem is one that, owing to the poet's incompetence, readers cannot find their way to, other than by interrogating the poet or his diaries. Besides being awkward, the conclusion is fallacious. The sense of desolation that the poet lacked the effectiveness to express is *eo ipso* extrinsic to the text, a merely unrealized intention that belongs to the personal history of the poet. In the absence of successful expression, authorial will is futile.

So, from the opening pages of his 1967 book, Hirsch had subverted in advance the long, hard, and in many respects admirable and effective following effort to establish the intended sense as the object of interpretation. On the other hand, his critics outdid him in obscuring the issues, easily matching Hirsch's confusions with their own flimsy and sophistical critiques.

Monroe C. Beardsley mounted an attack on Hirsch's "identity thesis" (the meaning of the text is the meaning of the author) soon after Hirsch's book appeared.[41] The identity thesis, claimed Beardsley, could be "conclusively disproved" by three arguments.[42]

The first argument: some texts, formed without authorial meaning, nevertheless have a meaning and can be interpreted. The first example is provided by the *New Yorker*, citing the *Portland Oregonian*:

> It showed that there is at least one officer on the Portland police force who had not seen Officer Olsen drunk," Apley quietly observed.

> In contrast to Apley, Jensen argued like a man filled
> with righteous indigestion.

Beardsley's one-sentence analysis: "Here there is no 'authorial will,' since the final phrase is inadvertent."[43] But this analysis fails. It is true that the authorial will of the reporter did not find apt expression (whether by his own fault or that of the printer). Still, we are on safe ground in reconstructing from the text the reporter's authorial will to evoke Jensen's "righteous indignation." Moreover, the comic effect of the text as it stands depends on the final phrase, to which Beardsley denies an authorial will; but final phrase and comic effect alike are fully intended by the **New Yorker**. Conclusion: Beardsley's first example has failed to illustrate "meaning" but without "authorial meaning."

Beardsley's second example:

> When Hart Crane wrote "Thy Nazarene and tender
> eyes," a printer's error transformed it into "Thy Naza-
> rene and tinder eyes"; but Crane let the accident ver-
> sion stand as better. [44]

No analysis is provided. The example is presumed to illustrate, self-evidently, meaning without authorial meaning. But does it? Hardly. The only reason why the second reading is not a mere misprint is that Crane "let the accident version stand as better." It thus entered into the intended sense of Crane's text.

Beardsley's third example is computer poetry:

> While life reached evilly through empty faces
>   While space flowed slowly o'er idle bone
> And stars flowed evilly on vast men
>   No passion smiled.

Here Beardsley anticipates the objection that "there is something like a hovering 'authorial will,' expressed in the instructions of the programmer." Quite right. Is the objection answered by noticing that, whereas the instructions were general, the poem "is a particular new composition of words," and that "it has meaning, but nothing was meant by anyone"?[45] Hardly. That there is "meaning" in this piffling twaddle is unmysterious: the programmer used words, especially "poetic" words, saw to it that they were used in accord with intelligible syntax, and even provided line divisions. But, in accord with the generality of the instructions, the meaning is suspended somewhere in the no-man's-land between *langue* and *parole*. Measured as *parole*, it is failed meaning. Confused and flat, the computer product fails to meet the specification of real meaning without real authorship.

What Beardsley really needs is an exception to the principle of causality. The computer can hardly be credited with providing one. If one were to add another ten or twelve lines of computer poetry to these four, the text would be still less meaningful. The theoretical issue, on the other hand, would be that much clearer: the text improves only in the measure in which the programmer's instructions are controlling. Beardsley has done no more than prove the undisputed point that words and syntax are elements of meaning, and that the ratio of more or less "happy" combinations of words will rise in accord with reduced randomness and fall in accord with increased randomness. So much for the examples meant to make Beardsley's first argument persuasive.

His second argument is that the meaning of a text can change after its author has died. The probative instance is from Mark Akenside's mid-eighteenth-century poem, "The Pleasures of Imagination," II, 311-313, referring to "the Sovereign Spirit of the world":

> Yet by immense benignity inclin'd
> To spread about him that primeval joy
> Which filled himself, he rais'd his plastic arm. . .

"Plastic arm," says Beardsley, has acquired a new meaning in the twentieth century. This "forces" us to distinguish between what these lines meant and what they mean today.[46]

I would say, rather, that this forces us to look up "plastic" in the Oxford English Dictionary, inasmuch as the dominant twentieth-century sense is evidently inappropriate here, yielding only interference, a jarring, irrelevant comic effect. Beardsley's "proof" is thus counterproductive.

His third and last argument is that a text can have a meaning that its author is not aware of. Hirsch had offered an example of this: a critic points out to an author that he had emphasized an intended similarity by a parallel construction. "How clever of me!" says the author, welcoming the observation, but admitting that he had not previously adverted to the rhetorical device.[47] But Hirsch, as Beardsley pointed out, did not know how to incorporate the example into his theory, and so dealt with it in terms of distinctions tangentially relevant at best (meaning vs. subject matter, consciousness vs. self-consciousness).[48] This, it seems to me, is of a piece with Hirsch's overlooking or undervaluing the fundamental distinction between intention and the textual realization of intention. Just as a hapless poet may well fail to realize his intention textually, so a competent poet may in some particular realize it better than he knew. This tells us a truth, if a minor truth: the textual realization of intention sometimes involves effects not specifically intended, and not all of them are bad. Beardsley and many others think that it tells us a great and hermeneutically seminal truth: the text is simply autonomous vis-à-vis its author. But such a judgment is far from exigent. It would take much more than Hirsch's example to prove Beardsley's thesis, through Beardsley and the many who agree with him seem to be invincibly unaware of this.[49]

What emerges from this brief review of an unsatisfactory debate is, first, Hirsch's failure to make the intended sense explicitly intrinsic to the text. Hirsch might have successfully fielded all objections if he had defined the object of interpretation as the sense that the author both intended and managed to encode or express in the text.

Second, Beardsley, the inventor (with William K. Wimsatt, Jr.) of "the intentional fallacy," offers a not atypical critique of Hirsch. He understands his refutations of Hirsch to be "conclusive." On examination, however, they turn out to be jerry-built and easily dismantled.

Finally, out of the enormous influx of French and German theory into North American literary criticism since the time of the debate on Hirsch's **Validity in Interpretation**, we can offer no more than a comment, and that on a tendency of many movements, but expecially of the movement called reader-reception theory. The quite unjustified break with the notion of "the intended sense of the text" prepared the way for abandoning the age-old idea epitomized in Max Weber's correlative terms, *Sinnsetzung* (expression of meaning) and *Sinndeutung* (interpretation of meaning) in favor of *Sinndeutung* alone. The rise of reader-reception theory was accordingly no surprise. If it is qualified, under alien influence, by an exaggerated view of "intertextuality" and the denial of "reference" to extratextual reality, it becomes manifestly indefensible. Normally, however, it takes the familiar form of trying to convert the text's unknown meanings and references into knowns. In particular cases, then, actual interpretation may turn out to differ only marginally from application of the theory defended here.[50]

There is a sense in which the active correlative, *Sinnsetzung*, is a constituent element of interpretation theory, for it is necessarily implied by the object of interpretation, i.e., the *intended* sense of the text. Nevertheless, there is an observation made by the ancients and sporadically repeated across the centuries: unlike living speech, texts are helpless. They "question" the reader only metaphorically; they cannot literally "enter into dialogue" with him, calling attention, for example, to the earlier but now forgotten passage, the significant but overlooked detail. Regardless of how careful the writer, he is finally at the mercy of the reader. The readership's reading determines what actual impact a book is to have, what in fact it will mean to the world.

Shall we conclude that the reader is king? Not exactly, for he is still obliged to measure up to the text. So, there are two sides to the matter. On the one hand, "a book is a mirror," as G. C. Lichtenberg observed: "If an ass peers into it, you can't expect an apostle to look out."[51] On the other hand, interpretation is a matter of finding a reader who can meet the challenge of the text, a matter of sending a thief to catch a thief--and if the history of modern exegesis tells us anything, it tells us over and over again that asses do not catch apostles.

Aspects of the Impact of the Historical Consciousness on Interpretation

Interpretation is an effort to meet questions that have arisen about a text. The questions that interpretation (as distinct from analysis and from critique) seeks to answer are specifications of the general query, "what does the text mean?" Still, one era's, and even one generation's, questions about the text differ from another's. With few exceptions, nineteenth-century biblical commentaries are painfully dated and unreadable today. The problem is not so much that the resources--say, the philological resources--of the interpreters are obsolete. Not infrequently they are richer than in average exegesis today. The difficulty is rather that a shift in the focus of interest has taken place. We are just not interested, for example, in what were once the burning questions of liberal theology.

Over the past two hundred years there has hardly been a shift in focus to compare with the rise of the historical consciousness. Philology and history generated extraordinary new possibilities for biblical interpretation. Their reduction to act has been a continuing triumph of "historical-critical" interpretation especially of the Old Testament but also quite markedly on the New. Deuteronomy has become, for the first time in two millennia of Christian interpretation, the biblical book of *agape, par excellence.* Owing to the analysis of new linguistic finds, texts from the Psalms, from Job, from Qoheleth and other works, that had been misunderstood for well over two millennia of guesswork sanctified by tradition, now yielded a clear and solidly grounded original sense. Lengthy, thematically unified passages such as Rom 9-11, which through almost the whole Christian era had been thoroughly and disastrously misunderstood, were now recovered in their pristine passion and lucidity. *Dikaiosyne theou* in Paul was no longer allowed to be misconceived on the model of the *justitia* of Roman law. I pass over in Ciceronian silence the revolution in textual emendation, lexicography, morphology and syntax, analysis of genres and forms, chronology and geography.

We might pause, however, over the new possibility of a critical history of traditions opened up by historical interpretation. Such interpretation insists on the original sense of the text not only for its own sake but as a condition and starting point of such history. Some have supposed that this insistence on an original sense entails maximizing it as the only sense that counts or at any rate as the truest or most significant sense. If that were the case, the new possibility of the critical history of traditions would have lost much of its point before getting underway. The exclusivist supposition, however, is mere bias and is happily separable from historical interpretation itself (cf. thesis 2.1.5). So far from stifling the pursuit of the text's history of impact *(Wirkungsgeschichte),* historical interpretation makes possible an ever fuller, more exact and instructive, history of tradition. One need think only of the studies of Isa 53 by Dalman, Billerbeck, Zimmerli, and Jeremias and his students,[52] who collectively have traced the journey of this text through time, its formative influence on key texts in Zechariah, Daniel, and Wisdom, on Synagogue traditions both Greek and Aramaic, on Christianity at its birth and on Judaism and Christianity respectively through the ages. This hermeneutically rational inquiry has taken over a good part of the functions of "multiple sense" theories from patristic and medieval times.

The idea of the intended sense is age-old, but, as the possibility of retrieving it underwent fundamental transformation under the impact of a historical consciousness in Europe, new resources and tools of inquiry came into being that allowed the intended sense to be retrieved far more fully and precisely than had ever previously been thought possible. While twentieth-century theoreticians were making the "intended sense" an object of deep suspicion--often misunderstanding it in the light of poor theory and worse practice on the part of those who made biographical research the interpretative key to texts--twentieth-century practitioners have repeatedly succeeded in recovering the intended sense of even quite short, self-contained texts. Here, to be sure, the experts are not all of one mind. But I would propose as representative examples of extraordinarily adroit recovery, over the past fifty years or so, of short but charged New Testament texts the pre-Pauline faith formulas in the Epistle to the Romans (e.g., 1:3f.; 3:25f.; 4:25; 8:34; 10:9f.) and the work of Karl Georg Kuhn,[53] Joachim Jeremias,[54] and others[55] on the Our Father as word of Jesus and as diversely shaped liturgical text.

The exploits of historical-critical method have not, of course, preserved biblical interpretation from perversity and triviality, as Western society and culture abandoned its religious and philosophic legacies. Biblical interpreters were not exempt from these currents and biblical interpretation from Spinoza to the present has often betrayed a crippling estrangement from the biblical text. The methodical limits of historical interpretation allowed it to be pressed into the service, first, of a religiously neutral, then of an alienated and hostile, vantage point. As Screwtape explained to Wormwood, "The Historical Point of View, put briefly, means that when a learned man is presented with any statement in an ancient author, the one question he never asks is whether it is true."[56] Historical relativism, taken in by the modern with his mother's milk, tended to make implicitly moot the whole array of truth claims from the ancient world. Undiscriminating religious critics thought that historical method was itself to blame for this. More discerning spirits differentiated historical method from the philosophic assumptions that were often gratuitously fused with it. Despite appearances, Enlightenment ideology has always been gratuitous, though leading lights from Strauss through Troeltsch to Bultmann could not free themselves from identifying selected aspects of this ideology with the techniques that constituted historical method itself. The question today is, why anyone should willingly prolong this ever more evidently bankrupt philosophic tradition.

For, there are alternatives. Collingwood has long been read and admired, but it has been too little noticed what a work of demolition and liberation his **Idea of History** was.[57] On a still broader front, Lonergan has performed a like task, tracing the collapse of the cult of necessity from the Renaissance critique of Aristotle down to our own time. Mistaken philosophies can blend with science, but, like the theories of early sociologists of religion such as Tylor and Spencer, fanciful and wrong-headed opinions are finally exposed

> and, once exposed, forgotten. Forgotten like the Euclidean structure of space exorcised by Einstein and Minkowski, like the necessity that ruled physical process up to quantum theory, like the iron laws of economics trumpeted on political platforms up to the depression of the early thirties.[58]

Gradually cleansed of ideological parasites, the procedures of historical interpretation are today more than ever a peerless (though by no means the exclusive) tool at the disposal of biblical scholarship. But they are just a tool. A tool is not to be blamed for its use in the pursuit of perverse or trivial objects. Tools can as well be made to function in the service of the drive to truth as in that of overt or covert ideology or of the spell of trivia *(fascinatio nugacitatis)*.

In his treatment of interpretation as a functional specialty in theology, Lonergan has outlined the conditions of the possibility of interpretation and has left the matter at that. "Anyone can. . .interpret," he says, and "conversion is not a requisite."[59] But, of course, not anyone can interpret well. To interpret well and especially to interpret biblical literature well, calls precisely for the authenticity that hinges on a manifold conversion.[60] Once we pass beyond considering the conditions of the possibility of interpretation to consider the conditions of the possibility of excellence in interpretation, the main focus of hermeneutics shifts to the authenticity of the interpreter. Given this authenticity, the clean beauty of the technical resources of historical-critical interpretation has, in fact, often appeared and still appears and will, no doubt, continue to appear.

This, as I remarked above, is not the exclusive tool of biblical scholarship. It is suitably supplemented by other tools, such as structuralist interpretation.[61] With the passage of time it will itself develop, and will be diversely supplemented, in ways that we cannot foresee. But we are concerned with the present. My intention is to say how the main resources of the present might be made to serve the religious and theological needs of the present. The precise context is the functional specialty "interpretation." (I do not intend to treat the question of how this relates to the functional specialty "communications.")

A Synthesis of Antioch and Alexandria

Some years ago, taking a cue from Newman's remarks on the ancient schools of Antioch and Alexandria (Antioch, he said, was "the fountain of primitive rationalism"[62] and "the very metropolis of heresy,"[63] in accord with the principle that "there is no mystery in theology"[64]), I argued that the issue on which Christian theologians fundamentally defined themselves was whether salvation was a transcendent mystery, i.e., the kind of mystery that came to be defined, following Philip the Chancellor in the thirteenth century, as "supernatural". Those who said yes I called Alexandrines and those who said no, Antiochenes. Among contemporary Antiochenes I took Bultmann, then still living, to be *facile princeps.* [65]

To Alexandrines the gospel is an invitation and initiation into the secret *(to mystērion)* that is Christ (see 1 Cor 2:1,7; Col 1:24-29; Eph 1:3-10; 3:1-13; cf. Rom 16:25f.). This description would satisfy most Antiochenes, as well, with the proviso that it be understood in concrete human terms and, accordingly, that all objectifications--incarnation and expiation, redeemer and redemption, the scheme of the future: parousia (1 Cor 15:23), the transformation of the living and the resurrection of the dead (1 Cor 15:50f.), the final delivery of "the reign" to God the Father (1 Cor 15:24)[66] --be so resubjectified as at one stroke to dispose of Christianity's mythical remnants and lay bare its existential thrust. In this proviso it was authenticity that was at stake: authentic proclamation, authentic response, the authentic existence (radical obedience symbolized by the cross) into which the respondent stepped.

Authenticity, in fact, is the heart of the matter in both Antiochene and Alexandrine worlds of discourse. Though both are intent on the twofold authenticity of human subjectivity and of the Christian heritage, it would be fair to say that whereas the contemporary Antiochene puts a premium on what is authentically human, his Alexandrine counterpart puts it on what is authentically Christian. In the millennium and a half prior to the rise of the historical consciousness these two ways of settling priorities could find no resolution in a higher synthesis (thesis 4.5.2). Today, however, these pivotal choices invite the question of whether we can find a third point of vantage and field of vision in which one is no longer constrained to favor one set of demands over the other. Such an ideal solution would impinge in conspicuous fashion on the practice of interpretation. In patristic Christianity the concern for coherence stood behind the ancient Alexandrine's recourse to allegorical interpretation; recoil from the arbitrary governed the ancient Antiochene's insistence on the letter of the text. This kind of tension has persisted into modern times. Ronald Clements, for example, has recently traced the laborious retreat, under pressure of commitment to the intended sense of the text, from classic schemes of messianic prophecy and fulfillment to the fall-back position of a generalized history of messianic hope.[67]

So there will be a least three elements in a theologically responsible biblical hermeneutics: first, the claims of the biblical text, i.e., the primacy of its intended sense; second, the claims of human authenticity, i.e., Antiochene rejection of premature and artificial interpretative solutions; third, the claims of Christian authenticity, i.e., Alexandrine insistence on the intelligibility and cohesiveness of salvation and of the scriptures that attest it in hope and in celebration.

Antioch and Alexandria signal opposed hermeneutic faults. Thus, "Antiochene" means not only the interpreter's commitment to the literal sense but also the rationalist's recoil from mystery. The historic Antiochene[68] seized on the Alexandrine weak point, the recourse to exegetical artifice in affirming the mystery of salvation. So far, so good; but in the face of New Testament texts the Antiochene style in any age is slated for failure. The text is an initiation into mystery. Rationalism is a recoil from mystery. The fatal flaw in Antiochene exegesis has been a resultant flight from unwanted meaning.

This is what made hermeneutics so important in Bultmannianism. Its task was to justify the flight from the intended sense whenever the text called for belief in what "we cannot sincerely consider true."[69] To Bultmann mystery was contradiction. The New Testament did indeed intend a mystery to the will, i.e., the contradiction of appetite. At the deepest level of its intending, however, it did not intend a mystery to the mind, i.e., the contradiction of intelligibility. "The deepest level of intending" posited a duality in intending: the surface level of the text attested an ostensible intending; its deep level, an authentic intending. For example, in 1 Cor 15 Paul did and did not intend "a history of final things."[70] The result was a rupture between the act of meaning and its consciously produced internal term, namely, what is meant.

At one level the Bultmannian interpreter was aware that in 1 Cor 15:21-28 "a history of final things" was precisely what was meant. But besides being unacceptable in itself, this failed to correspond to the interpreter's hard-won understanding of what was most genuinely Pauline. How could Paul have been so un-Pauline and anti-Pauline? This kind of question has tortured dogma-free exegesis in Germany for over a hundred years.[71] The only real breakthrough answer has been that of Bultmann, who had recourse here to cognitional theory. Experience engendered expressive symbols; meaning was this act of expressing; and interpretation recovered the act of meaning. The crucial point was that the recovery took place, not by fixing attention on the objectified symbols generated by the act of cognition, but rather by finding in one's own life the experience that generated them. The interpretative question, then, was not, what did Paul's symbols symbolize? What did it mean that all died by solidarity with Adam and would be brought to life again by solidarity with Christ, that Christ must reign until all enemies will have been put "under his feet," but that once this had happened, he would turn over the reign to his Father? The controlling question, rather, was: what was the vital drive and experience that engendered this set of extravagant symbols? Thus, the authentic, undogmatic, existential Paul comes into view--but at the price of the exegete's having deconstructed the correspondence between meaning and meant.[72]

Alexandrine exegetes and theologians, by definition committed to the *mysterium salutis,* interpret the Christian heritage in transcendent terms. But there is also a hermeneutic fault that is specifically Alexandrine. It, too, is a selective flight from the intended sense of the text, but for reasons diametrically opposed to those of the Antiochene. For the Alexandrine is tender-minded. In the name of theological postulates, e.g., the internal unity of divine revelation, he is self-blinded to concrete problems and tempted to affirm premature, unverifiable, hermeneutic harmonies. There is no need to rehearse grossly uncritical instances of the Alexandrine syndrome. A refined example, one of many, is the stout refusal of many a New Testament scholar to acknowledge that the scheme of the future supposed by Jesus corresponds to none of the eschatological schemes proposed in early Christianity.[73] The kind of rounded unity and coherence that the Alexandrine formerly affirmed in the guise of interpretation must now be reconceived as an object of anticipation likely at best to find laborious, discontinuous, piecemeal verification. This sober sense of limits clips the wings of Alexandrine "interpretation." Such is the indispensable contemporary transposition from triumphant exegesis to the explicit recognition that the exegetical task is perennially unfinished and that there are exegetical problems either permanently or at least currently irresolvable. Where once the Alexandrine had recourse to interpretative artifice and skilled evasion, his contemporary successor will incorporate into his results the products of *docta ignorantia*: embarrassingly numerous instances of acknowledged uncertainty and impasse.

It seems to me important that the task envisaged here be differentiated, on the one hand, from interpretation in the context of the secular university, where biblical literature is treated under the heading of the history of religions, and, on the other hand, from interpretation as a "communications" task in the Church. As a functional specialty in theology, interpretation cannot simply abstract from such questions and projects as biblical theology and the correlation of the Old and New Testaments. To that extent, the characteristic foci of interest in modern secular history of religions do not quite measure up to the challenge of interpretation as a functional specialty in theology. That is, by comparison with the quite distinct interests, ethos, and practice in contemporary history of religions, interpretation as functional specialty is a kind of *kirchliche Schriftauslegung* (ecclesial interpretation of scripture), but it is very different indeed from the *kirchliche Schriftauslegung* recently proposed by Heinz Schürmann.[74]

Schürmann, who does not distinguish between interpretation as a functional specialty in theology and interpretation as an immediate resource for preacher and catechist, urges a *kirchliche Schriftauslegung* in what I would call the Alexandrine mode. The categories of Old Testament prophecy and New Testament fulfillment are boldly rehabilitated in the light of "faith." As elements of "scripture," all individual affirmations are "dehistoricized" and transposed to the "time of the Church," "relativized" by being connected at once to the "center" of scripture and to its total ambit, and "actualized" to apply to the present. The New Testament is conceived on the model of an ellipse with two poles: the kerygma of the resurrection of Jesus and Jesus' proclamation of the advent of the reign of his Father. Each makes the other intelligible, and the result is avoidance both of a pure kerygma theology and a pure Jesus theology.

My purpose in evoking the tenor of Schürmann's proposals is not to contest particular points in the context of "communications" (though I find much here that calls for further discussion). It is simply to clarify, by contrast with "communications," the traits of interpretation as a functional specialty in theology. Here, ideally, the interpreter sublates and synthesizes Antioch (as precise a retrieval as possible of the intended sense of texts) and Alexandria (as deft a retrieval as possible of the text's depth-dimension and salvation-historical context; see thesis 4.5.1). Interpretation conceived in these terms does not do everything. It does not trace or evaluate the canonization of the scriptures; it does not offer a theory of inspiration; it does not present a ready-made resource for preacher and catechist. It does not try to do all theology, but limits itself to the single question: what is the intended sense of the text?

NOTES

1. A. N. Whitehead, **Adventures of Ideas** [1933] (Harmondsworth: Penguin, 1942) 263.

2. Hans-Georg Gadamer, **Wahrheit und Methode** (Tübingen: Mohr, 31972) xix, 276f: ET, **Truth and Method** (New York: Seabury, 1975) xix, 259f.

3. W. K. Wimsatt and Monroe D. Beardsley, "The Intentional Fallacy" [1954], **The Verbal Icon** (New York: Noonday, 1958) 3-18.

4. E. D. Hirsch coined the phrase and made the point in "Carnal Knowledge. Review of Frank Kermode **The Genesis of Secrecy**," *New York Review of Books* 26 (June 14, 1979) 18.

5. Gadamer, **Wahrheit und Methode**, 285 and *passim* thereafter; ET, **Truth and Method**, 267 and *passim* thereafter.

6. Ferdinand de Saussure, **Course in General Linguistics** (New York: Philosophical Library, 1959) 17-20.

7. E. D. Hirsch, **Validity in Interpretation** (New Haven: Yale University Press, 1967) 210f., attributes this distinction to August Boeckh; but, since Boeckh does not clearly draw it, Hirsch should be credited with having invented it.

8. See Anthony Quinton, "Connotation and Denotation," in **The Fontana Dictionary of Modern Thought,** (eds.) Alan Bullock and Oliver Stallybrass (London: Fontana Books, 1977). This entry correlates Frege's distinction with those of John Stuart Mill (connotation and denotation) and of Adolf Carnap (intention and extension).

9. Cited by Gadamer, **Wahrheit und Methode,** 162; ET, **Truth and Method,** 151.

10. Frank Kermode, **The Genesis of Secrecy. On the Interpretation of Narrative** (Cambridge, MA: Harvard University Press, 1979) 118f.

11. On the terms "illocutionary" and "perlocutionary," see J. L. Austin, **How to Do Things With Words,** ed. J. O. Urmson (Oxford: Clarendon, 1962).

12. John Henry Newman, **Essay on the Development of Christian Doctrine** [1878], Ch. 3, Sect. 1, para. 1 and 2 (Garden City: Doubleday, 1960) 115-117; Gadamer, **Wahrheit und Methode,** 276-281; 529; ET, **Truth and Method,** 259-265; Gerhard Ebeling, "Dogmatik und Exegese," **Zeitschrift für Theologie und Kirche** 77 (1980), 269-285, esp. 274-276; Peter Stuhlmacher, **Historical Criticism and Theological Interpretation of Scripture** (Philadelphia: Fortress, 1977) 83-87.

13. On pre-understanding, see Rudolf Bultmann, "The Problem of Hermeneutics" [1950], in **Essays Philosophical and Theological** (London: SCM, 1955) 234-261, see 239; 252f.; "Is Exegesis Without Presuppositions Possible?" [1957], in **Existence and Faith. Shorter Writings of Rudolf Bultmann** (Cleveland: World [Meridian], 1960) 289-296; **Jesus Christ and Mythology** (New York: Scribner, 1958) 49f.; on "vital relationship," see "The Problem of Hermeneutics," 241-243, 252f.; 255f.; "Is Exegesis Without Presuppositions Possible?"; **Jesus Christ and Mythology,** 50-52.

14. Martin Buber, **I and Thou** [1923] (New York: Scribner, 21958) 11.

15. On "the hermeneutic of suspicion," see Paul Ricoeur, **Freud and Philosophy** (New Haven: Yale University Press, 1970) 32-36. On how to make the hermeneutic of suspicion function productively rather than subversively, see Bernard Lonergan, "The Ongoing Genesis of Methods,'" **Studies in Religion/Sciences Religieuses** 6 (1976-77) 341-355, pp. 349-353; reprinted in **A Third Collection** (New York: Paulist, 1985) 146-165, pp. 156-163.

16. Gadamer, **Wahrheit und Methode,** 285 and *passim* thereafter;

ET, **Truth and Method**, 267 and *passim* thereafter.

17. Paul Ricoeur, "Philosophical Hermeneutics and Theological Hermeneutics," **Studies in Religion/Sciences Religieuses** 5 (1975-76) 14-33, see 31f.

18. On individual, group and general bias, see Bernard Lonergan, **Insight. A Study of Human Understanding** (London: Longman, 1957; reprinted London: Darton, Longman & Todd, 1983) 218-242; on psychic bias, see Robert M. Doran, **Psychic Conversion and Theological Foundations** (Chico: Scholars Press, 1981) 149-154. One example of the modes of analysis referred to in this thesis is "ideology critique."

19. Larry Shiner, **The Secularization of History. An Introduction to the Theology of Friedrich Gogarten** (Nashville-New York: Abingdon, 1966) 25-35 offers an excellent summary of Gogarten's mature thought on this theme.

20. René Descartes, **Discourse on Method**, (ed.) L. J. Lafleur (New York: Liberal Arts, 1950) 12.

21. Gadamer, **Wahrheit und Methode**, 256-261, ET, **Truth and Method**, 241-245.

22. Ricoeur, **Freud and Philosophy**, 32-36.

23. Lonergan, **Insight**, 271-278; "Cognitional Structure," in **Collection. Papers by Bernard Lonergan** (New York: Herder & Herder, 1967) 221-239, esp. 222-227.

24. Lonergan, **Insight**, 280-287; "Insight Revisited," in **Second Collection** (London: Darton, Longman & Todd, 1974) 263-278, esp. 273-275.

25. Bernard Lonergan, **Method in Theology** (New York: Herder & Herder, 1972) 155-173.

26. Cited by Gadamer, **Wahrheit und Methode**, 273, note 2; ET, **Truth and Method** 524, note 194.

27. See Dennis J. McCarthy, "Exod 3:14: History, Philology and Theology," **Catholic Biblical Quarterly** 40 (1978) 311-322, esp. 319-322.

28. "An adequate account of human intentionality" refers to Lonergan's **Insight**, to his essay "Cognitional Structure" (see note 23 above), and to the chapters "Method," "The Human Good," and "Meaning" in **Method in Theology**, 3-99.

29. See Henri de Lubac, **Exégèse médiévale. Les quatre sens de l'Ecriture**, 4 vols. (Paris: Aubier, 1959-63) vol. 1, 11-39; 110-118.

30. Peter Stuhlmacher, **Vom Verstehen des Neuen Testaments. Eine Heremeneutic** (Göttingen: Vandenhoeck & Ruprecht, 1979) 92-95; see 93 on Luther's readiness to cite the Apostles' Creed and other Church symbols and dogmas as "valid signposts" to his theology.

31. Hans Urs von Balthasar, **Glaubhaft ist nur Liebe** (Einsiedeln: Johannes Verlag, 1963) 12.

32. Alexander Solzhenitsyn, "A World Split Apart," in **East and West** (New York: Harper & Row [Perennial], 1980) 39-71.

33. Newman, **An Essay on the Development of Christian Doctrine** [1878] ch. 5, sect. 2, para. 3 (Garden City: Doubleday, 1960) 186.

34. Karl Rahner, **Foundations of Christian Faith. An Introduction to the Idea of Christianity** (New York: Seabury, 1978) 17-43 and *passim* thereafter. Compare Augustine's sudden act of self-understanding, under the impact of a friend's death: "Factus eram ipse mihi magna quaestio."

35. On these functional specialties, see Lonergan, **Method in Theology**, 235-333.

36. See "Communications" in **Method in Theology**, 355-368.

37. See "Interpretation" in **Method in Theology**, 153-173.

38. E. D. Hirsch, **Validity in Interpretation** (New Haven: Yale University Press, 1967).

39. **Validity**, 9.

40. **Validity**, 12.

41. Monroe C. Beardsley, "Textual Meaning and Authorial Meaning," **Genre** 1 (1968) 169-181.

42. "Textual Meaning," 174.

43. "Textual Meaning," 174f.

44. "Textual Meaning," 175.

45. "Textual Meaning," 175.

46. "Textual Meaning," 175.

47. **Validity**, 21.

48. "Textual Meaning," 176f.

49. In the 1984 "Afterword" to his **Language of Fiction** (London: Routledge & Kegan Paul, 1966, 21984), David Lodge rightly rejects on the basis of "practice," i.e., his own practice as a novelist, the currently popular literary critical view of the text as "authorless." And he does this, it should be noted, while considering himself an anti-intentionalist "in the Wimsattian sense." (In fact, Lodge has attributed to Wimsatt and Beardsley his own better balanced and more discriminating grasp and formulation of the issue of intention.)

50. Still, there is a world of difference between the characteristic mentalities associated with the two theories. For Joachim Jeremias, an outstanding seeker after the intended sense of the text, "Exegese ist Sache des Gehorsams!" **Die Abendmahlsworte Jesu** (Göttingen: Vandenhoeck & Ruprecht, 31960) 6, whereas Stanley Fish, a proponent of reader-reception theory, announces: "No longer is the critic the humble servant of texts. . ." (cited in *Encounter* 65 [July-August, 1985] 21). Such lively proclamations of autonomy are commonplace in the literature of the movement.

51. Wystan Hugh Auden cited this text, without, unhappily, providing references.

52. Out of the large number of works (brought together in numerous bibliographies on Isa 53, e.g., that prepared by Joachim Jeremias for the article *"pais theou" in Theological Dictionary of the New Testament* V, 654-656) I would signal the following: S. R. Driver and A. Neugebauer, **The Fifty-Third Chapter of Isaiah According to the Jewish Interpreters** 1876-77, repr. New York: KTAV, 1969); Gustaf Dalman, "Der Leidende und der sterbende Messias der Synagoge im ersten nachchristlichen Jahrtausend," **Schriften des Institutum Judaicum Berlin** (1888); Paul Billerbeck, "Hat die alte Synagoge einen präexistenten Messias gekannt?" Nathaniel 21 (1905) 89-150; Walther Zimmerli and Joachim Jeremias, **The Servant of God** (London: SCM, 1957, 21965); Harold Hegermann, **Jesaja 53 in Hexapla, Targum und Peschitta** (Gütersloh: Bertelsmann, 1954).

53. Karl Georg Kuhn, **Achtzehngebet und Vaterunser und der Reim** (Tübingen: Mohr, 1950).

54. Joachim Jeremias, "The Lord's Prayer in the Light of Recent Research," in **The Prayers of Jesus** (London: SCM, 1974) 82-107 [German original, 1962].

55. R. E. Brown, "The Pater Noster as an Eschatological Prayer," in **New Testament Essays** (New York-Ramsay: Paulist, 1965) 217-253; Philip B. Harner, **Understanding the Lord's Prayer** (Philadelphia: Fortress, 1975).

56. C. S. Lewis, **The Screwtape Letters and Screwtape Proposes a Toast** (London: Bles, 241966) 121.

57. R. G. Collingwood, **The Idea of History** (Oxford: Oxford University Press, 1946). A striking anomaly: Collingwood's clear and coherent theory subverts in advance the thinking of roughly half the people who cite him favorably. An example: J. M. Robinson, **A New Quest of the Historical Jesus** (London: SCM, 1959).

58. Bernard Lonergan, "Method: Trend and Variations," in **A Third Collection. Papers by Bernard J. F. Lonergan**, ed. F. E. Crowe (Mahwah, N.J.: Paulist, 1985) 13-22, at p. 20.

59. **Method in Theology**, 268. In "An Interview with Fr. Bernard Lonergan," **Second Collection. Papers by Bernard J. F. Lonergan**, eds. W. F. J. Ryan and B. J. Tyrrell (London: Darton, Longman & Todd, 1974) 217, Lonergan makes it clear that the word "can" in the phrase "anyone can do research, interpretation, history" stands for "is welcome to." The functional specialties do not set up conditions of membership: everyone is welcome to try. But Lonergan does not expect that all will do these things well, for undifferentiated consciousness "finds any message from the worlds of theory, of interiority, of transcendence both alien and incomprehensible" (**Method**, 287). Diversi-

ty in self-definition (cf. B. F. Meyer, "On Self-Definition" in **The Early Christians: Their World Mission and Self-Discovery** [Wilmington: Glazier, 1986] 23-31) accounts for why one man understands and welcomes a message from the world of transcendence whereas another misconstrues or ignores or despises it. The manifold "conversion" thematized by Lonergan is calculated to effect such changes in self-definition as would open the subject to the boundless sweep of the intelligible, the true, the real, the good, the beautiful, the holy.

      60. See B. F. Meyer, "Conversion and the Hermeneutics of Consent," *Ex Auditu* 1 (1985) 36-46 (reprinted in this volume).

      61. See John J. Collins, "The Meaning of Sacrifice: A Contrast of Methods," **Biblical Research** 22 (1977) 19-34.

      62. **Essay on the Development of Christian Doctrine**, ch. 4, sect. 2, para. 10 (Garden City: Doubleday, 1960) 155.

      63. **Essay on Development**, ch. 7, sect. 4, para. 5 (Garden City: Doubleday, 1960) 327.

      64. See above, note 33.

      65. B. F. Meyer, **The Church in Three Tenses** (Garden City: Doubleday, 1971) 171f.; cf. 151-154.

      66. See J. M. Robinson, "Hermeneutic Since Barth," in **The New Hermeneutic**, eds. J. M. Robinson and John C. Cobb (New York: Harper & Row, 1964) 31-33.

      67. Ronald Clements, "Messianic Prophecy or Messianic History?" **Horizons in Biblical Theology** 1 (1979) 87-104.

      68. On historic Antioch, I am referring, first of all, to a period from the mid-fourth to the mid-fifth century (and specifically to Diodore, who became bishop of Tarsus in 378; to Theodore, who became bishop of Mopsuestia in 392; and to Nestorius, who became bishop of Constantinople in 428); secondly, to a tendency in interpretation (accent on the literal and historical, suspicion of allegory); thirdly, to a style of christological theorizing that was stronger on duality than on the unity allowing a *communicatio idiomatum* in christological predication. On historic Alexandria, I am referring to the tradition that ran from Clement and Origen through Athanasius to Cyril, a tradition quite at home with allegory, inclined to put a high premium on mystery, and especially to champion a high christology against the "inspired man" christology of Antioch.

      69. Bultmann, **Jesus Christ and Mythology** (New York: Scribner, 1958) 17.

      70. See note 66 above for reference to Bultmann's view.

      71. For a particular instance, see my "Did Paul's View of the Resurrection of the Dead Undergo Development?" in *Theological Studies* 41 (1986) 363-387 (also reprinted in this volume).

      72. Objectification is an aspect of intentionality, i.e., of acts of

meaning. We objectify the self by meaning the self and we objectify the world by meaning the world. Of its nature this meaning is related to a meant, and what is meant may or may not be so. The short-circuiting into which the pre-World War II theorizing of Hans Jonas and Rudolf Bultmann fell was the failure to acknowledge this intrinsic correspondence. Thus, what was meant by 1 Cor 15 was not, according to Bultmann, a *Schlussgeschichte* (history of final things)--all that was mere objectification. What was meant was the pinning of all hope on commitment to the Christ of faith. I have nothing against this thesis of hope, so far as it goes. But since meaning projects a meant, since to posit a severing of this tie is to posit the impossible, I would say that what was meant by 1 Cor 15:21-28 was precisely a *Schlussgeschichte*, a scenario of post-historical salvation, Christ's triumph over the last enemy, death, and the realization of the reign of God in its fullness; and I would connect Paul's passionate expression of hope with this same scenario.

73. On the altogether distinctive eschatological scenario of Jesus (recovered by brilliant detective work in C. H. Dodd's **Parables of the Kingdom** [London: Nisbet, 1935] and brought to the high polish of precise formulation in an essay of Joachim Jeremias [**Theologische Blätter** 20 (1941) col.216-222]), see B. F. Meyer, **The Aims of Jesus** (London: SCM, 1979) 202-209. Though the work of Dodd and Jeremias has not been refuted, neither has it been accepted. One cannot help suspecting that the explanation lies in a simple recoil of contemporary scholars from unwanted meaning.

74. Heinz Schürmann, "Thesen zur kirchlichen Schriftauslegung," **Theologie und Glaube** 72 (1982) 330f.

III

CONVERSION AND THE
HERMENEUTICS OF CONSENT

In 1977 Peter Stuhlmacher's essay on historical critique and theological exegesis appeared in English,[1] establishing at once that a significant new voice had entered the North American discussion of where New Testament studies were headed. Thus far the post-Bultmannian era had arrived at no more than a negative self-definition: not just post-Bultmannian but non-Bultmannian. Part of the community of New Testament scholarship in North America had already transposed its whole enterprise from a theological context to the larger, more secular context of the history of religions, this history to be enhanced by social description[2] and the application of sociological and anthropological theory.[3] Another part of the community of scholars had turned to literary study, shifting from "history" to "story" and drawing on linguistic and literary theory.[4] Though this work has been theologically more promising than contemporary history-of-religions research,[5] technical literary analysis has so far usually won out over theology, existentialist or otherwise.

Still, theology is not to be denied. As Stuhlmacher's essay rightly supposes, in one or another form theology is bound to assume a controlling role wherever New Testament scholarship remains intent on the intended sense and thrust of New Testament texts. While Bultmann (d. 1976) was still living, there was a long moment when it seemed that the new bearers of the torch would be precisely his disciples. Thus, Ernst Käsemann called for a revised return to the historical Jesus (1954),[6] Günther Bornkamm set it in motion, (1956),[7] James M. Robinson analyzed and publicized it in the English-speaking world (1959),[8] and the "new quest" soon became a category of research and a topic of non-stop discussion. Meantime, Ernst Fuchs[9] and Gerhard Ebeling[10] proposed a hermeneutical program grounded in a later-Heideggerian variation on neo-Kantian cognitional theory, designed to secure the retreat from "objectifying knowledge" (cf. the Cartesian "subject-object schema"), and presented under the catchword "the new hermeneutic," which the indefatigable Robinson introduced to North America with a thoroughly informed and up-to-the-minute essay on Protestant hermeneutics from Karl Barth's commentary on Romans (1918) to the publication (1964) of the essays on "the new hermeneutic" discussed at the Drew University consultation on hermeneutic.[11] Again, in 1961 Käsemann gave characteristically forceful new expression to the theme "the righteousness of God" (Rom 1:17; 3:21f.; 25f.; 10:3),[12] so launching a discussion that for several years quickened Pauline studies in Germany.[13]

In retrospect, Bultmann's own alertly exploratory theological career was the unhurried implementation of a far-reaching theological reform. Salient moments included the "Introduction" to his 1926 book on Jesus,[14] the 1941 essay on demythologizing the New Testament,[15] the climactic theology of the New Testament (1948-53),[16] and the full statement of its history-of-religions presuppositions (1940).[17] Measured against the liberal theology that it supplanted, Bultmann's kerygma theology was a long forward step. It insisted, like liberal theology, on illuminating for modern man the continuing religious relevance of the New Testament, but it displaced "the essence of Christianity"--the kingdom of God and its coming; God the Father and the infinite value of the human soul; the higher righteousness and the commandment of love[18]--in favor of the New Testament's own center of gravity: the gospel of Christ's death and resurrection.

Moreover, all the above-mentioned contributions by Bultmann's followers--a new quest, a new hermeneutic, a new perspective on Pauline theology--were positive achievements, despite Bultmann's distancing of himself from all of them. The new quest, while maintaining both the privileged status of the kerygma and the core of Bultmann's critique of the quest as practiced by liberal theology, went no little distance, particularly in the work of Ernst Fuchs,[19] toward relieving the danger of docetism inherent in kerygma theology. The new hermeneutic, profiting from a partial fusion of horizons with the thought of Hans-Georg Gadamer, brought to thematic status a stance only adumbrated by Bultmann: the critic consciously allowed and invited the text to call his self-understanding into question and to correct it.[20] Finally, Käsemann's appreciation of "the righteousness of God" redressed the balance of Bultmann's excessively anthropological and individualistic soteriology.

In view of all this, how is it that Bultmannianism, especially in America, its second home, all but died with Bultmann?

Before offering an answer of our own, we might recall a few observations that others have made. In part, then, the Bultmannian project simply ran out of steam. Heinz Schürmann remarked in 1973 on the painfully meager results of the "new quest,"[21] and eventually *New Testament Abstracts* ceased to reserve a special heading for it. Again, the intense German concern with "the righteousness of God" found little echo in American exegesis. In part, success was attended by a loss of original contour. Thus, impulses from Fuchs and Ebeling were received, absorbed, transformed, but the new hermeneutic in its continental form took, at best, tenuous root in North America.

But there were deeper reasons for the collapse of the Bultmannian program. Stuhlmacher's essay offered three. First, the ostensible biblical basis for Bultmann's existentialist interpretation (Pauline and proto-Johannine preaching) was overly narrow. Second, this interpretation, which accorded ontological priority to possibility (e.g., the individual's "openness to the future") over actuality, was finally played out; large, non-existentialist themes such as history as a total process, its teleology and meaning, "have imperiously reappeared." Finally, "Bultmann's rejection of all dogmatics" was "no longer viable, if the church is not to abandon every missionary, catechetical, and apologetic witness and explication of its faith."[22] In a word, Bultmann's program collapsed in virtue of just those traits that had lent it profile and cachet-- namely, its ruthless exclusions and denials.

Among these denials, what could have been more basic, and more fateful, than the denial of mystery? Bultmann, to be sure, acknowledged a "mystery of the will," i.e., the gospel's contradiction of man's self-regarding appetites; but he equated the acknowledgement of mystery to the mind with *sacrificium intellectus*, making this term qualify belief in what one cannot sincerely take to be true.[23]

If we distinguish between "Alexandrine" and "Antiochene" theologians--the first term referring to those who understand the object of faith and theology to be mystery (e.g., the school of Alexandria, Augustine, Aquinas), the second referring to those who hold that "there is no mystery in theology"[24] (e.g., the school of Antioch, Abelard, the dogma-free current in Protestantism)--there can hardly be any doubt that Bultmann was *facile princeps* among twentieth-century Antiochenes.[25] His straightforward reduction of mystery to contradiction and unintelligibility marked him as a rationalist, not in the sense specific to Cartesian and Enlightenment a-priorism, nor in the sense of that eighteenth- and early nineteenth-century school of biblical critics that David Friedrich Strauss targeted for destruction, but in the generic sense of thinkers who reduce intelligibility as such to the intelligibility proportionate to human intelligence. Such is the generic rationalism we would call Antiochene. Profoundly congenial to much of Western modernity, it is wholly out of tune with the world of New Testament meaning. In the sphere of exegesis, accordingly, the Antiochene must either offer interpretations that latently or patently subvert the intended sense of the text, or work out a hermeneutic that systematically requires the transposition of this sense into other terms. The Rationalists whom Strauss ridiculed took the first tack; from Strauss to Bultmann, their critics took the second.

Neither the Hegelian Strauss nor the existentialist Bultmann was tempted in the slightest to follow the Enlightenment Rationalists in folding, bending and spindling New Testament texts, contrary to their evidently intended sense. Strauss acknowledged an originally intended sense, which he refused to reshape to agree with his own views. This assuredly did not mean that he accepted it at face value. "The matters narrated in the biblical books," he said, "must be viewed in a light altogether different from that in which they were regarded by the authors themselves."[26] Texts, for example, that named Jesus "Messiah" or "Son of God" exhibited a mythological mode of thought that, however appropriate to antiquity, had to yield in the present new and climactic stage of historic spiritual development to a vastly superior, philosophic, mode of thought. The texts were not false--far from it. They simply called for another hermeneutical operation: transposition into the new categories that Strauss devised under the influence of Hegel.[27]

In Bultmann, though the material elements were all changed, the pattern remained the same. For example, according to the intended sense of "the Word was made flesh," a pre-existent heavenly being became man.[28] But this was a precipitate of mythical thinking (technically defined as the presentation of the otherworldly in this-worldly guise), blocking modern man's access to the text. The text was not false, but it called for another hermeneutical operation: transposition into existentialist terms. Gone was Strauss's metaphysical style of demythologizing and gone the pseudo-eschatology that identified Hegelian philosophy with the goal of world process. In place of Hegelian categories there were existentialist categories; in place of the Hegelian scheme of the transition from representation *(Vorstellung)* to idea *(Begriff)* there was an account of the origin of myth in the objectifying function or moment in cognitional process.[29] Bultmann and Strauss, then, had much in common; and though there were significant divergences among Enlightenment rationalism, Straussian idealism, and Bultmannian existentialism, this should not be allowed to conceal the common ground (i.e., the rejection of mystery as unintelligible) that accounted for their ultimately common flight from the intended sense of New Testament texts.

It would not be accurate to say that the contemporary community of New Testament scholars has suddenly been moved to concentrate on the dimension of mystery in the New Testament, or that Bultmannianism has been widely abandoned precisely because of its generic rationalism. What can, however, be said is, first, that New Testament scholarship has proved on the whole to be equivocal or frankly sceptical about the virtues of transposing intended meaning into supposedly superior categories, and in any case has refused to be systematic in this matter; second, that serious commitment to the intended sense of New Testament texts inevitably translates into the intending of events and states of affairs that transcend the intelligibility proportionate to human intelligence: the incarnation of the Word of God (John 1:14), his saving death and resurrection (Rom 3:25f.; 4:25), a Church that, though many, is one body "because we all share in the one loaf" that is Christ (1 Cor 10:17).

It is significant that the opening of the post- and non-Bultmannian era had been heralded by widespread reservations (e.g., Pannenberg, Stuhlmacher, Roloff, Hengel, Schürmann, Goppelt) on the historical relativism of Ernst Troeltsch.[30] The attack on Troeltsch, however, was grounded less in any fully worked out cognitional theory than in the pragmatic observation that Troeltschean critique, elaborated in explicit opposition to "dogma," was itself a merely dogmatic positivism. Its central postulate, "the similarity in principle of all historical events" *(die prinzipielle Gleichartigkeit alles historischen Geschehens),* put access even to the most baffling historical reality at the disposal of all,[31] thanks to the "all-leveling" power of analogy, a perfect expression of what Troeltsch took to be enlightened emancipation from dogmatic prejudice.

Stuhlmacher refers to Troeltsch's account of historical criticism as "thus far unexcelled."[32] But set beside Collingwood's **The Idea of History**,[33] it gives an impression of dated ideology, its abstractions yielding little hint of the distinctive autonomy of historical thought vis-à-vis all forms of science, including psychology and sociology. The cardinal role of the historian's own freely formulated questions is entirely overlooked, nor is there any Troeltschean counterpart to what for Collingwood is the goal of historical investigation, namely, penetration to "the inside of the event," the intentionality that promotes historical occurrence to the status of historical action and gives it its characteristic density. By contrast to Collingwood's literating account of historical knowledge, Troeltsch's views incorporated a cramped rationalism brought to bear on the history of religions as an inhibiting principle. The current dissatisfaction with Troeltschean ideology can therefore only be welcomed, though in the awareness that it has yet to take the form of a thorough dismantling of its philosophic postulates.

A final comment on the era in biblical studies that is being left behind bears, again, on hermeneutics. Like Troeltsch, Bultmann conceived of historical process in classic Enlightenment fashion as a closed cause-and-effect continuum; but, unlike Troeltsch, he dispensed with the concrete particulars that filled this continuum from the New Testament to the present. In his day Troeltsch was intensely concerned with the historical mediations of meaning that had both widened chasms and sought to bridge chasms between the New Testament and its interpreters. Bultmann appealed to Luther, though his was a distinctly post-Enlightenment retrieval of Lutheran themes. Otherwise Bultmann operated like the chess player who, having no need to know by what sequence of moves the present situation on the board has been reached, simply sizes it up as it stands and decides what move to make. Abstraction from history did not mean, however, that Bultmann lightened the interpeter's task. Just the opposite. Since history did nothing, the interpreter had to do everything. He became a solitary hero charged with translating the whole biblical heritage into the whole theology of the present.

Bultmannians have continued to commend this lonely hermeneutical feat, witness James M. Robinson's essay on the future of New
Testament theology.[34] In the Bultmannian manner Robinson conceives
of biblical theology as a self-contained operation. It neither supposes
nor requires any mediation outside itself, e.g., by the myriad strands
that already bind Christians to their scriptural legacy. "Hermeneutic" is
called on to supply all that is needed. Hence, Robinson takes no more
account than Bultmann did of the afterlife of New Testament texts in
the life of the Church *(Wirkungsgeschichte)*.

Why should he? The meaning that counts is not the biblical
writer's consciously intended meaning in any case. It is rather the meaning that is "latent behind the text," i.e., an understanding of existence
inherent in New Testament language, whether or not it is made thematic in New Testament texts--indeed, whether or not it is contradicted by
New Testament texts.[35] Here it should be noticed that intended meaning
is measured by "the understanding of existence latent behind the text,"
and not vice-versa. Even the best of the New Testament writers, Paul
and John, repeatedly, inevitably, entered into opposition to themselves,
speaking--against their own deepest intentions, which remained "latent
behind the text"--of incarnation (John 1:14), or of the attesting of the risen Jesus by witnesses (1 Cor 15:3-8) or of a coming "history of final
things" that will include the parousia and the reign of God, the transformation of the living and the resurrection of the dead (1 Cor 15:22-28,
50-57). Thanks to his grasp of the understanding of existence latent behind the text, the Bultmannian interpreter knows that all such texts require content-criticism *(Sachkritik)*, that dogmatic and mythological
meaning is to be not just decoded but, as Robinson frankly puts it,
"eliminated" in the interests of stating "more adequately" the authentic
thrust of the text.[36] The interpreter understands Paul and John far better
than they understood themselves, for he understands, as they could not,
when their language is appropriate to its subject matter and when it is
not, and roughly how appropriate to the subject matter it is in any giv-
en case.

Robinson outlines several possible ways of expanding this
"front opened up by Bultmann."[37] Presumably, they are ways that have
the greatest hermeneutical significance for the Church; the Church,
however, has no hermeneutical significance for them. There appears to
be no real need of any but biblical theologians, and to the work of these
biblical theologians the drama and heritage of two millennia of Chris-

tian experience--the simultaneous and the successive translations of Christianity into a world-wide variety of cultures, the precipitate in Christian dogma of the great battles for the maintenance of Christian identity, the thesaurus of Christian spirituality and reflection, the legacy of division between East and West and in the West between Catholic and Protestant--call for no acknowledgement or comment and so are reduced to irrelevance to the matter at hand.

The presuppositions and procedures urged by Stuhlmacher are at several points directly antithetical to all this. First, Stuhlmacher defines his own vantage point (on "the boundaries between kerygmatic theology, Pietism, and biblically-oriented Lutheranism")[38] and purpose ("to clarify the possibilities and limits of historical-critical exegesis within the framework of Protestant theology today").[39] Second, he sets his hermeneutical reflections in the context of the history of biblical interpretation from the ancient Church to the present. Third, he puts a high premium on an exegetical consciousness informed by the tradition that the texts to be interpreted have generated *(wirkungsgechichtliches Bewusstsein).*[40] Fourth, he attributes to dogmatics--a dogmatics, that is, that does not exhaust itself in theological-historical analyses, but moves on to its own affirmations--an indispensable role, namely, "to correct and guide" Protestant exegesis.[41]

Evident here is a sober realism about the limits of the individual scholar and of biblical scholarship as a whole. This scholarship is not an absolutely autonomous project. Neither ahistorical nor unecclesial, it cannot do without the Christian past. It promotes no particular philosophic orthodoxy, and it is far removed from the Antiochene mindset.

Stuhlmacher's review of the "extravagant experimental results" of radical New Testament criticism[42] amounts, no doubt, to an indictment of current practice, but, at a deeper level, to a recognition of "the vacuum and exegetical uncertainty in which we find ourselves."[43] He reviews several theological responses to this situation, responses that · commend the abandonment of exegesis in favor of a political theology expected to generate its own new truths, or the abandonment of historical-critical exegesis in favor of "self-evident Bible exposition within the circle of the reborn."[44] Finally, he makes his own proposal, under the heading "the hermeneutics of consent." This is "a new openness to the world," which breaks down into "a willingness to open ourselves anew to the claim of tradition, of the present, and of transcendence."[45]

Openness, consent, and what Stuhlmacher names "the principle of hearing" all recall Gadamer's observation that readers are and always have been primarily intent on the realities evoked and envisaged by the text, and that the reader's attention shifts to the intentions and limits of the writer only when there occurs some loss of focus on *die Sache,* the reality that the text intends. The initial and primary stance of openness, hearing, consent subverts that "prejudice against all prejudices" which the West adopted in the Enlightenment. It prepares the way for a recovery of tradition in principle and in fact. It does not, on the other hand, rule out critical dialogue with tradition. Stuhlmacher introduces a critical principle by his insistence that exegesis attempt to take the measure not only of the *die Sache* but of the text in its particularity, as well, and that exegetical operations be thoroughly "reasoned out in respect of method."[46] What openness and hearing and consent rule out is an "absolutist stance toward emancipation," the "insolent attitude" that regards all claims on the individual as alienating.[47]

The hermeneutics of consent, then, is the recovery of an attitude making it possible once again that men and women should be hearers of the word and of the word in its full integrity.

II

Among the responses to Stuhlmacher's proposal special importance attaches to the annual, entitled *Ex Auditu,* published by Pickwick Publications, incorporating articles, representing various disciplines and denominations, on a single theme based on theological interpretation of Scripture. Meantime, responses offered to Stuhlmacher's initial proposal from a variety of hermeneutical vantage points can only promote reflection on the issues and so help the cause, which is soon to find institutional but open and dialogical embodiment. The pages to follow make up one such response.

Stuhlmacher's essay was designed to be of immediate service to the cause of German Protestantism; hence, its perspectives and resources, as James Barr observed in the "Introduction" to the edition of the essay published in Great Britain, were exclusively German and Protestant. But the substance of the proposal--a specification of the conditions that would enable "historical criticism" to become "theological interpretation of scripture"--transcends national and confessional boundaries. Likewise, the reflections to follow are not, I trust, hermetically sealed off and confined to a Catholic or North American context. They do not bear on what differentiates hermeneutical postures as "Catholic" and "Protestant," and they have no hidden agenda. They are animated by sympathy with Stuhlmacher's critical assessments and positive proposals. They are concerned with how to bring to fulfillment the conditions that he has specified for a theologically more satisfactory interpretation of scripture.

Let us begin with an ending: the final image in Matthew Arnold's "Dover Beach."

> And we are here as on a darkling plain
> Swept with confused alarms of struggle and flight,
> Where ignorant armies clash by night.

This image, Nicholas Lash assures us,[48] was inspired by a passage from one of John Henry Newman's *University Sermons:*

> Half the controversies in the world are verbal ones;
> and could they be brought to a plain issue, they would
> be brought to a prompt termination. Parties engaged
> in them would then perceive, either that in substance
> they agreed together, or that their difference was one
> of first principles. This is the great object to be aimed
> at in the present age, though confessedly a very ardu-
> ous one. . . . Controversy, at least in this age, does
> not lie between the hosts of heaven, Michael and his
> angels on the one side, and powers of evil on the oth-
> er; but it is a sort of night battle, where each fights
> for himself, and friend and foe stand together. When
> men understand each other's meaning, they see, for the
> most part, that controversy is either superfluous or
> hopeless.[49]

In our age, too, "the great object to be aimed at" is to find out which controversies are not verbal but substantial, not trivial but basic, not reconcilable in a higher viewpoint but simply irreducible. The achievement of this "great" but "very arduous" object would produce a stunning clarification. Its result would be new alignments, as the parties to the now clarified controversies discovered who in reality were adversaries and who, allies.

What we need to know in the field of biblical scholarship and hermeneutical reflection is first of all "each other's meaning." But from that point of departure we need even more to know what the finally significant issues are, and what we can do to make our way to the truth on these issues. Disagreement must become a daylight affair. Since our time and energy are limited, an end to "superfluous" controversies would be a boon. It would be an equally welcome boon to find some light on controversies that are "hopeless."

The matter might be put more concretely and the discussion carried a step further by reconsidering the present situation in New Testament studies. By common consent there is much from the era of existentialism that ought to be inherited and not allowed to be lost. But in the realm of the human spirit inheriting is not a passive occurrence; it is a work of discernment and appropriation. How are we to discern and appropriate the authentic legacy of the existentialist era?

Consider the demythologizing program. Its proponents did not set themselves the straightforward task of disengaging and highlighting the existential thrust of New Testament texts. Rather, they were intent on translation, the translating of mythical meaning into existentialist terms. Too often, the observer complained, the intended meaning (e.g., the incarnation of the Word) was lost in the translation. The existentialist would respond: deliberately lost, for unbeknownst to the biblical writer, an objectification such as the incarnation of the Word obscured and subverted the authentic intention at work in the very production of the objectification. In the existentialist's view, the appropriate task was to re-subjectify the objectification, and it was this hermeneutical effort that revealed to him the existential thrust of the text.

Now, Stuhlmacher's essay favors maintaining the gains of existentialism without incurring its losses. But I do not find in the essay suggestions as to how this might be done. However fully justified in its immediate context, the dismissal of Bultmann's program as exhausted and no longer viable does not meet the challenge of discerning and appropriating his genuine legacy. Debate with the existentialist becomes most significant when test cases such as the interpretation of the Johannine prologue are satisfactorily resolved. But this leads us into issues that Stuhlmacher's essay seems hardly to envisage, e.g., issues of cognitional theory.

Exegesis moved in a circle of things and words, in accord with the lapidary principle that Gadamer adopted from Luther: "Whoever does not understand the things cannot draw the sense from the words" *(Qui non intelligit res non potest ex verbis sensum elicere)*.[50] But what are "the things"? This question divides the existentialist demythologizer from his fellow exegetes. For, though he acknowledges that it is through the words that we determine what the things are, he would add two clarifications. First, by "words" he primarily means "language" *(Sprache/langue)*, and only secondarily "utterances" *(Worte/paroles)*, and by "things" he means subject matter *(Sache)*. Second, in the case of the Johannine prologue, John's objectifying language has deformed the subject matter, contrary to John's own deepest intentions. Now, whoever would differentiate true from false in the kind of interpretation that complies with these principles must deal, among other things, with "objectification." This is the hinge issue, not a historical nor a literary nor a philological issue alone, but an issue in cognitional theory. My point is, first, that a hermeneutics of consent that truly measures up to its vocation must meet this issue and, indeed, all such issues; second, that a hermeneutics of consent *can* meet such issues, on condition that it learn to exploit resources that are already at hand. For there are resources at hand for a clarification of root issues, prominently including those of cognitional theory, for a constructive grasp of basic and irreducible conflicts, and for an end to superfluous controversies and even for light on and a possible way out of controversies that are otherwise hopeless.

Ultimately, the resources in question can only be the collective exercise of our wonder, questioning, imagination, insight, reflection, judgment, decision. But these resources find their full potential when their normative and essentially spontaneous structures are brought to thematic consciousness. This is the meaning and the attraction of "transcendental method." The claims made above respecting a clarification of root issues and a grasp on irreducible conflicts suppose that transcendental method, which includes this clarification and grasp among its functions,[51] is a success, i.e., that it has already found signally successful thematization. This supposition is grounded in an extraordinary philosophic performance.[52] Transcendental method, to be sure, is of itself merely human and not yet theological. But it can supply theology with its crucial anthropological component. It is accordingly full of promise for the renewal of theology, including "the theological interpretation of scripture."

Nothing characterizes transcendental method so much as its irreducibility to "method" as Gadamer uses the term, namely, to signify technical efforts devised to secure a closed circuit of control. Transcendental method refers primarily to the spontaneously self-assembling structure of human intentionality; secondarily, to the detailed objectification[53] of this structure. In the primary sense, then, this "method," so far from being in tension with "truth," is a condition of the possibility of truth. At the same time, it is well called "method," for it is not only itself methodical in the sense of producing progressive and cumulative results, it is also the core of all successful particular methods. Even those who might bridle at the term "transcendental method" practice it whenever their work proceeds intelligently and effectively. To that extent, it is clear that transcendental method introduces nothing new, i.e., no new, hitherto inoperative kind of act. It is, rather, a heightening of consciousness, a new attentiveness to and understanding of acts that have always been in operation. But the effects of this heightening of consciousness are not to be overlooked. They include new sureness and new precision in dealing, for example, with hermeneutical issues. The challenge, then, is to appropriate in fully conscious fashion the sequence of wonder, inquiry, insight, judgment, decision already concretely at work in ourselves.

It is a challenge not easily met, for two reasons: its intrinsic difficulty (David Hume wryly observed that whenever the operations of the mind become the object of scrutiny they seem involved in obscurity) and its liability to alien intrusions (fears and aversions and short-circuitings founded on cultural routine, settled preferences, personal commitments). Realism respecting the difficulties that attend both a satisfactory descriptive retrieval of human intentionality and its introduction as a critical component into theological reflection has led Bernard Lonergan to bring "horizon" and "conversion" to the center of the discussion.[54]

Horizon, literally, is the limit of what can be seen from any given vantage point. Metaphorically, it is the limit of what one knows and cares about. Conversion is a revolutionary transition from one horizon to another. Intellectual conversion is a transition from the horizon of cognitional myth (knowing is something like seeing) to that of transcendental method made fully thematic and affirmed. Moral conversion is a transition from the horizon of satisfactions to the existential primacy of values. Religious conversion is a transition from the horizon of this-worldly commitments to the primacy in one's life of the love of God.

Internally related as modalities of the single drive to self-transcendence, these conversions can be conceived, when all three occur within a single subject, in terms of sublation, i.e., of a transcending that includes, preserves, and deepens what has been transcended. Intellectual conversion carries the subject confronted by baffling issues past imagination and myth, supposition and conjecture, wishful thinking and peer group thinking, to the act of affirming what is so. Moral conversion establishes him on a level of consciousness that goes beyond the value, truth, to values generally, but this only solidifies the attachment to truth. Religious conversion goes beyond the sphere of values to the ground of values, wherein the subject is "grasped, possessed, owned through a total and an otherworldly love."[55]

Such sublations, however, do not establish the genetic order: first intellectual, then moral, finally religious conversion. Commonly the order is the exact opposite. First, there is God's gift of his love. The eye of this love reveals the world of values. These include the value of believing the truths taught by the religious tradition, and in such belief and tradition lie the seeds of intellectual conversion.[56]

To the student of the scripures the gift-character of religious and moral conversion, and the emergence of moral from religious commitment, are not novel ideas but themes of Deuteronomistic and prophetic tradition and of Pauline and Johannine theology. Nor is it any new idea that the theologian lacking in religious and moral conversion cannot function. These conversions are to religious thought what praxis is to social thought. What may be new to biblical scholars is the pointed relevance of intellectual conversion as defined above to the theory and practice of interpretation.

For, intellectual conversion as defined above supposes the discovery of an adequate account of human intentionality; it consists in the immanently generated affirmation of this account as true, and in its appropriation as a heuristic and critical resource. The foundational moment of this resource is a description of cognitional fact, i.e., a certain description of certain data of consciousness, all of which are open to introspection. Discrimination among conflicting descriptions of cognitional fact (the acceptance of positions and the rejection of counterpositions) grounds the discrimination between true and false, real and ilusory, precisely with reference to such issues as Stuhlmacher has raised, e.g., that of historical criticism's inevitable dependence on some controlling view of history and reality, and the diversity and incompatibility among the available views (rationalist, idealist, existentialist, materialist, etc.).[57] The biblical scholar who supposes that his own seemingly untheoretical view of history is straightforward and sufficient may well be unaware of ideological components in it derived from an unacknowledged, uncriticized, and unsatisfactory philosophy. Common sense "is commonly unaware of the mixture of common nonsense in its more cherished convictions and slogans."[58] In any case, the functional dependence of historical criticism on some view of reality, including historical reality, pointedly illustrates the relevance of intellectual conversion to biblical scholarship.

Lonergan acknowledged the evidence of religious and moral conversion in the work of Barth and Bultmann, but he urged that their work, though in different manners, revealed the need of intellectual conversion as well, and for its thematization in method:

> Only intellectual conversion can remedy Barth's fideism. Only intellectual conversion can remove the secularist notion of scientific exegesis represented by Bultmann. Still, intellectual conversion alone is not enough. It has to be made explicit in a philosophic and theological method, and such an explicit method has to include a critique both of the method of science and of the method of scholarship.[59]

It already takes the exegete too many years to assemble the tools of his trade. If he nevertheless wishes to go to the heart of the matter, which is where the hermeneutics of consent directs him, he is willy-nilly enlisted in time-consuming ventures that go still further. They are called into being by the drive to human authenticity, which is simply the dynamism of self-transcendence. Though longer on labor and shorter on glamour, this is not unlike a sport in which the athlete's life is on the line.

"Dialectic" in the Lonerganian sense is concerned with contradictory views, and aims at discovering which of them are rooted in irreducibly opposed horizons. Of itself this is an exercise of clarification, but its ulterior purpose is truth. For, dialectic inevitably solicits the further question of human authenticity (intellectual, moral, religious conversion) and the question of its presence or absence in oneself as well as in others. These two questions generate the light, referred to above, that can be thrown on hopeless controversies. And conversion itself is the "possible way out of controversies that are otherwise hopeless." Such conversion is rare, but it occurs (as we have seen, for example, even in that public paradigm of hopeless controversy, the abortion debate). The dialectician's method, then, is calculated to make the question of authenticity acute. "It is not an infallible method, for men easily are unauthentic, but it is a powerful method, for man's deepest need and most prized achievement is authenticity."[60]

My proposal, in short, is that the hermeneutics of consent take its stand here. I would invite those who have already felt the justice of Stuhlmacher's critique and the attractiveness of his suggestions, to consider whether any basis will better serve the cause he has outlined than this one: the appropriation of transcendental method and its implementation in a hermeneutics commanded by human authenticity itself, conceived as a threefold conversion.

NOTES

1. Peter Stuhlmacher, **Historical Criticism and Theological Interpretation of Scripture. Toward a Hermeneutics of Consent,** ed. Roy A. Harrisville (Philadelphia: Fortress, 1977; with an introduction by James Barr, London: SPCK, 1979).

2. See Jonathan Z. Smith, "Social Description of Early Christianity," *Religious Studies Review* 1 (1975) 19-25; Robert M. Grant, **Early Christianity and Society** (San Francisco: Harper & Row, 1977); Abraham J. Malherbe, **Social Aspects of Early Christianity** (Baton Rouge: Louisiana State University Press, 1977).

3. Gerd Theissen, **The Sociology of Early Palestinian Christianity,** (Philadelphia: Fortress, 1978); Howard Clark Kee, **Christian Origins in Sociological Perspective** (Philadelphia: Westminster, 1980); see also the review article of J. G. Gager in *Religious Studies Review* 5 (1979) 174-180; Robin Scroggs, "The Sociological Interpretation of the New Testament: The Present State of Research," *New Testament Studies* 26 (1980) 164-

179; Daniel J. Harrington, "Sociological Concepts and the Early Church: A Decade of Research," *Theological Studies* 41 (1980) 180-190. Bruce J. Malina, **The New Testament World. Insights from Cultural Anthropology** (Atlanta: Knox, 1981).

    4. See J. J. Collins, "The Rediscovery of Biblical Narrative," *Chicago Studies* 21 (1982) 45-58.

    5. See John Navone and Thomas Cooper, **Tellers of the Word** (New York: Le Jacq, 1981).

    6. Ernst Käsemann, "The Problem of the Historical Jesus," in **Essays on New Testament Themes** (London: SCM, 1964) 15-47 (German original, 1954).

    7. Günther Bornkamm, **Jesus of Nazareth**, tr. I. and F. McLuskey with J. M. Robinson (New York: Harper & Row, 1960; German original, 1956).

    8. James M. Robinson, **A New Quest of the Historical Jesus** (London: SCM, 1959).

    9. Ernest Fuchs, **Hermeneutik** (Bad Canstatt: Müllerschön, 1954 21958); **Zum hermeneutischen Problem in der Theologie. Die existentiale Interpretation** (Tübingen: Mohr, 1959).

    10. Gerhard Ebeling, **The Nature of Faith** London: Collins, 1961); **Theologie und Verkündigung** (Tübingen: Mohr, 1962); **Word and Faith** (Philadelphia: Fortress, 1963).

    11. James M. Robinson, "Hermeneutic Since Barth," in **The New Hermeneutic**, eds. James M. Robinson and John B. Cobb, Jr. (New York: Harper & Row, 1964) 1-77.

    12. Ernest Käsemann, "The Righteousness of God in Paul, " in **New Testament Questions of Today** (London: SCM, 1969) 168-182 (German original, 1961).

    13. See Christian Müller, **Gottes Gerechtigkeit und Gottes Volk** (Göttingen: Vandenhoeck & Ruprecht, 1964); Rudolf Bultmann, "DIKAIOSYNE THEOU," *Journal of Biblical Literature* 83 (1964) 12-16; Peter Stuhlmacher, **Gerechtigkeit Gottes bei Paulus** (Göttingen: Vandenhoeck & Ruprecht, 1965); Karl Kertelge, **"Rechtfertigung" bei Paulus** (Münster: Aschendorff, 21967); Hans Heinrich Schmid, **Gerechtigkeit als Weltordnung** (Tübingen: Mohr, 1968); Hans Conzelmann, "Die Rechtfertigunglehre des Paulus: Theologie oder Anthropologie?" (1968) in **Theologie als Schriftauslegung** (Munich: Kaiser, 1974) 191-206.

    14. Rudolf Bultmann, "Introduction," in **Jesus and the Word**, (New York: Scribner's 1934, 21958) (German original, 1926).

    15. Rudolf Bultmann, "New Testament and Mythology," in **Kerygma and Myth**, ed. H. W. Bartsch (London: SPCK, 21964) 1-44 (German original, 1941).

16. Rudolf Bultmann, **Theology of the New Testament**, 2 Vols., (New York: Scribner's, 1951-55; German original 1948-52).

17. Rudolf Bultmann, **Primitive Christianity in its Contemporary Setting** (New York: World, Meridian, 1956; German original, 1949).

18. See Adolf von Harnack, **What is Christianity?** (London: Williams & Norgate, 1901) 51.

19. See, for example, Ernst Fuchs, **Jesus, Wort und Tat** (Tübingen: Mohr, 1971).

20. Ernst Fuchs, **Hermeneutik,** 2 1958 (see note 9 above), **Engänzungsheft.**

21. Heinz Schürmann, "Zur aktuellen Situation der Leben-Jesu-Forschung," *Geist und Leben* 46 (1973) 300-310, esp. 304f.

22. Stuhlmacher, **Historical Criticism** 61f.

23. Rudolf Bultmann, **Jesus Christ and Mythology** (New York: Scribner's 1958) 17.

24. John Henry Newman, **An Essay on the Development of Christian Doctrine,** 2d rev. ed., 1878 (Garden City: Doubleday, 1960) 186.

25. Ben F. Meyer, **The Church in Three Tenses** (Garden City: Doubleday, 1971) 151-155.

26. David Friedrich Strauss, **The Life of Jesus Critically Examined** (Philadelphia: Fortress, 1972) 40.

27. Strauss, **Life of Jesus,** 757-784.

28. Bultmann, **Jesus Christ and Mythology,** 17.

29. James M. Robinson cites the relevant passages from Hans Jonas and indicates their significance for Bultmann's theory of demythologizing in two essays: "Hermeneutic Since Barth" (see note 11 above), 37, and "The Prehistory of Demythologization," *Interpretation* 20 (1966), 65-77.

30. Ernst Troeltsch, "Über historische und dogmatische Methode in der Theologie," in **Gesalmmelte Schriften. II. Zur religiosen Lage, Religionsphilosophie und Ethik** (Tübingen: Mohr, 1922) 729-753, esp. 730-733. Wolfhart Pannenberg, **Jesus--God and Man** (Philadelphia: Westminster, 1968) 109; Peter Stuhlmacher, "Neues Testament und Hermeneutic--Versuch einer Bestandsaufnahme," in **Schriftauslegung auf dem Wege zur biblischen Theologie** (Göttingen: Vandenhoeck & Ruprecht, 1975) 9-49; Jürgen Roloff, "Auf der Suche nach einem neuen Jesusbild," *Theologische Literaturzeitung* 98 (1973) 561-572, esp. col. 565-570; Martin Hengel, "Historical Methods and the Theological Interpretation of the New Testament," in **Acts and the History of Earliest Christianity** (London: SCM, 1979) 129-136; Heinz Schürmann, "Zur aktuellen Situation," esp. 307; Leonhard Goppelt, **Theology of the New Testament. I. The Ministry of Jesus in its Theological Significance,** ed. Jürgen Roloff (Grand Rapids: Eerdmans, 1981), Appendix.

31. Hengel, "Historical Methods," 129 (proposition 1.2.4).

32. Stuhlmacher, **Historical Criticism**, 44f.

33. R. G. Collingwood, **The Idea of History** (Oxford: Oxford University Press, 1946).

34. James M. Robinson, "The Future of New Testament Theology," *Religious Studies Review* 2 (1976) 17-22.

35. Robinson, "The Future of New Testament Theology," 20.

36. Robinson, "Hermeneutic Since Barth," 34.

37. Robinson, "The Future of New Testament Theology," 20-22.

38. Stuhlmacher, **Historical Criticism**, 21.

39. Stuhlmacher, **Historical Criticism**, 21.

40. Stuhlmacher, **Historical Criticism**, 83, 87.

41. Stuhlmacher, **Historical Criticism**, 76f.

42. Stuhlmacher, **Historical Criticism**, 71-74.

43. Stuhlmacher, **Historical Criticism**, 75.

44. Stuhlmacher, **Historical Criticism**, 70.

45. Stuhlmacher, **Historical Criticism**, 84f.

46. Stuhlmacher, **Historical Criticism**, 86.

47. Stuhlmacher, **Historical Criticism**, 84.

48. Nicholas Lash, **Theology on Dover Beach** (London: Darton, Longman and Todd, 1979) 5, note 7.

49. J. H. Newman, **Newman's University Sermons** (London: SPCK, 1970) 200-201.

50. Hans-Georg Gadamer, **Truth and Method**, (New York: Seabury, 1975) 151.

51. See Bernard Lonergan, **Method in Theology** (New York: Seabury, 21979, 20f.

52. See Bernard Lonergan, **Insight: A Study of Human Understanding** (New York: Longmans, 1958).

53. See **Insight**, 250-254 and **Method**, 262-265, 341-343, on the diverse senses assumed by "object" and its derivatives according as the words relate respectively to "the world of immediacy" (made present by acts of sensing) and "the world mediated by meaning" (made present by acts of appropriating the words and phrases, customs, convictions, and values, etc., of others)--an empirically grounded distinction crucial to Lonergan's "critical realism."

54. Lonergan, **Method**, 235-244.

55. Lonergan, **Method**, 242.

56. Lonergan, **Method**, 243.

57. Stuhlmacher, **Historical Criticism**, 62.

58. Lonergan, **Method**, 53.

59. Lonergan, **Method**, 318.

60. Lonergan, **Method**, 254.

IV

GOOD WILL COMES FIRST
BUT SUSPICION HAS ITS USES

This essay proposes a set of propositions on subject and subjectivity in interpretation: on the hermeneutical centrality of subjectivity, on the conditions of authentic subjectivity, and on authentic subjectivity as the condition of or key to objective interpretation.

We begin (part one) with the passing of the age of innocence, when issues of subjectivity were overlooked or underrated or suppressed or merely presupposed. There follows (part two) an account of the kind of subjectivity that is calculated to measure up fully to the task of interpretation. Here the accent falls on the role of critical realism in establishing a deeply and solidly based hermeneutics. Finally (part three), we discuss biblical interpretation, distinguishing conditions of possibility and conditions of excellence. Orientation to consent is the appropriate stance for interpretation in the strict sense, but "suspicion" is allotted a twofold role: first, in "analysis", whether antecedent to or consequent on interpretation; second, in critique, brought to bear not only on the text but on the interpreter himself.

I

...the more human studies turn away
from abstract universals and attend to concrete human beings, the more evident it

> becomes that the scientific age of innocence has
> come to an end; human authenticity can no longer
> be taken for granted.
>
> Bernard Lonergan [1]

The age of innocence was objectivist, a time when problems and solutions were discussed exclusively in terms of "objective data" or, at best, of "objective data and objective arguments." A late-blooming work markedly emblematic of this objectivism was Oswald Spengler's **Decline of the West,** according to which the life and death of Western, as of every, civilization is as pre-determined as the evolution and life-span of a butterfly.[2] In this view, nothing that we, the bearers of Western civilization, think or decide or do makes any difference.

The passing of the age of innocence has been signaled by the emergent theme of the subject, whose thinking, deciding, and doing make all the difference. The subject, celebrated in a cloud of unknowing by the Romantic movement, was diversely thematized in the works of Schopenhauer and Nietzsche, of Kierkegaard and Newman, and the theme moved toward maturity in our century with Heidegger, Jaspers, Marcel, and Maritain. Perhaps the most fundamental forward step on the philosophic and hermeneutical front has been the grasp of objectivity, not as the absence of subjectivity, but as the fruit of authentic subjectivity.[3]

Though the age of innocence has passed, there is hardly a day in which we do not hear the voice of yesterday. Not long ago the philosopher, Sidney Hook, responded in a mellow mood to a question about his atheism:

> I may, when I die, wake up in the presence of the Almighty, and if He were to ask me why I did not profess my belief in Him, I would reply, "Lord, You did not give me enough evidence."[4]

Overlooked in this nicely turned sentence is the possibility that what has been lacking is not evidence but the subjective conditions that would allow the speaker to grasp the evidence as "enough."

> In the ideal detective story the reader is given all the
> clues yet fails to spot the criminal. He may advert to

> each clue as it arises. He needs no further clues to
> solve the mystery. Yet he can remain in the dark for
> the simple reason that reaching the solution is not the
> mere apprehension of any clue, nor the mere memory
> of all, but a quite distinct activity of organizing intel-
> ligence that places the full set of clues in a unique ex-
> planatory perspective.[5]

In a word, it is not evidence that is lacking, but the intelligent act of
placing the evidence in proper constellation. When this is done, the
hitherto missing insight follows as the night the day.

We cannot say that if a tourist is unable to construe a sign
written in a language unknown to him, there must be something wrong
with the sign, nor that a non-literary person's incapacity to construe a
poem, despite having some hold on its every individual word and on
many of its combinations of words, is a sure sign that the poem is a
failure. Most poets would greet the formulas of mathematicized physics
with even blanker incomprehension. What is regularly missing among
the subjective conditions of our understanding of languages, of texts, of
artifacts, of calculations, is mastery of "the code." The code is the key.
In the concrete, however, the referent of the "code" metaphor can turn
out to be less a magic password than a daunting demand for long-term
personal development. One might have to scale a many-storied mountain before reaching the point at which Stravinsky and Shostakovich, or
Rilke and Valéry, or Einstein and Heisenberg, or Russell and Whitehead
begin to become luminously intelligible.

Habitually, we all know this. Selectively, we forget it again
and again, for few of us have entirely let go of our pre-hermeneutical
objectivist heritage. Recently, I reread a particularly fine article designed
to introduce to English-language readers the work of Rudolf Pesch on
the eucharistic words and on the way in which they can be seen to correlate with Jesus' public proclamation of the reign of God. The writer,
Robert Daly of Boston College, concluded his exposition, however, in
a spirit of extreme caution, offering a short but formidable list of items
relevant to Pesch's argument and unfortunately unknowable: "{1} There
is no presently known way of being sure about the genuinity. . .of the
long text of Lk 22:19-20. {2} That the Last Supper was a Passover
meal cannot be proven by historical-critical means. . ." {3} That the
early Christian eucharist was a unified meal celebration remains unprov-

en. {4} Pesch's "genre-critical analysis that Mark is a historical account and not a liturgical text does not contain enough probative force to convince a sceptical mind."[6]

These negative observations, to be sure, are qualified to the extent that Pesch's argument, according to Daly, is "demolished" only if one takes it in "all-or-nothing" terms, the implication being that such terms are unreasonable. One might add to this that the four items in question are knowable in principle, and the fact that they are all disputed is no guarantee of their unknowability. We have deep intractable disagreements on crucial issues in every sphere of human studies without exception. This does not make the truth about all these issues flatly inaccessible. Furthermore, Daly's own indications that the four unknowns may not be absolutely unknowable should be noted. Respecting the long text in Luke, there is "no presently known way" of establishing its genuinity. That the Last Supper was a Passover meal cannot be proven "by historical-critical means." That the early Christian eucharist was a unified meal celebration remains unproven, not necessarily unprovable. Pesch's arguments for his genre-critical conclusions would not convince "a sceptical mind." Though the qualifications are slight or muted, they do take some of the edge off the claim that the right solutions to all four questions are unknowable.

Still, the last point, on what would or would not "convince a sceptical mind," is suggestive. It intimates the writer's conception of what is requisite to knowledge, namely, proof that will sway a sceptic. This has the look of epistemological insurance. What will sway a sceptic should easily be valid for the rest of us.

At this juncture, however, I would offer two observations. The first is that the implied requisite to knowledge is Cartesian overkill. The second is that this overkill is requisite to (and perhaps compensation for) prolongation of the age of innocence. That is, there is a strategy at work here: one makes the test of knowledge excessively rigorous to safeguard the assumption that any proposal passing the test will be generally accepted. To spell the assumption out: the generality of interested parties are reasonable men and women intent on understanding, equipped to understand accurately, and ready to judge in strict accord with evidence.

It is sobering, however, to reflect that even if Rudolf Pesch were to prove all four designated points beyond cavil, there would still be many exegetes of many lands and tongues and cultural communities and confessional allegiances to construe the data otherwise, to contest his arguments, and to reject his conclusions. For, no scholarly community, not even the community of natural scientists, to say nothing of social scientists, of historians, of literary critics and exegetes, is led simply by the careful marshalling and rigorous weighing of evidence.

When we say "sufficient evidence," we do not mean evidence sufficient to win the assent of everyone without exception; we do not mean evidence sufficient to win the assent of a two-thirds majority. We mean evidence sufficient to win the assent of a person of good judgment respecting the points at issue, i.e., of one able, ready, and willing to make his way to the truth. To concede the universality of those conditions was the hallmark of the age of innocence. We have since come to realize that this generosity was ill-advised, misleading, and mistaken. Good judgment is neither universal nor commonplace. We have come to realize, in fact, that the heart of the hermeneutical problem is precisely here, in the categorical need to identify and bring to realization those factors in ourselves that facilitate insight and promote good judgment.

Moreover, when we are dealing with hermeneutics in relation to the Bible, the interpretation of which has generated distinct, separate, sometimes bitterly contentious religio-cultural communities, it is folly to suppose that the issue of what allows one, or positively leads one, to grasp evidence as sufficient (together with all the issues of meaning and value that this settles or at least impinges upon and colors) is squarely met by objectivist considerations of "data" and "argument." It is folly, in other words, to suppose that there is no need to take account of subjectivity, ranging from the habitually perverse to the habitually attentive, intelligent, reasonable, and responsible.[7]

The root of our deepest divisions is not lack of evidence. It is the fact of opposed horizons and, above all, of irreducibly opposed horizons, as a moment's reflection on public controversies will suggest and as sustained reflection will confirm. Irreducibly opposed horizons are a massive human reality labyrinthine in its consequences, leading some sincerely to champion as true and good what others with equal sincerity repudiate as false and evil. In view of this baffling, if common, state of affairs, what is to be done? Since the question comes down finally to "what are we to do about ourselves?" it raises the foundational issue of human authenticity.

II

The most illuminating conclusion to emerge from intentionality analysis in our time is that in virtue of the structures of intentionality the human person is variously self-transcendent and finds his fulfillment in the achievement of self-transcendence of many kinds. As knowledge is intentional self-transcendence, so love is affective self-transcendence, and the peak of self-transcendence is the primacy in one's life of the love of God. Love at its best moves the lover out of the relativizing and distorting reference to self into the freedom to dispose of his life generously. The tendency of the love of God is toward the most radical and thoroughgoing self-transcendence. At the same time, this tendency spontaneously enhances moral, affective, and cognitive self-transcendence. More than any other human impulse, the love of God energizes the wavering but instinctive human dissatisfaction with all that is shabby, shallow, hollow, and destructive. It nurtures the inconstant but deep-seated longing for human authenticity. Finally, religion, though allied with success, is peculiarly powerful amid failure, and so heals as well as fulfills.

As the ineradicable longing for human authenticity and fulfillment is still subject to overlays of illusion and distortion, so this drive to the most radical and thoroughgoing form of self-transcendence is liable to alloys and perversions, flawed forms that nevertheless presuppose and so attest the values they distort. Hence, though religion offers fertile ground for the exacerbation of opposed perspectives, convictions, and commitments, it also and more fundamentally offers great resources for the cultivation of acts and dispositions--self-suspicion and repentance, hope and love--that, if allowed free rein, would sweep away misconstrual and *ressentiment* and expose overblown oppositions for what they are, while bringing truly radical oppositions into focus.

Moral self-transcendence subtly but thoroughly transforms ordinary men and women, making them good. The highest and best form of friendship is uncommon, according to Aristotle, because it supposes good men and good men are rare. But moral excellence not only makes the highest form of friendship possible; it also maintains the social fabric. Its contribution to human sensibility, manners, and taste is personally and socially indispensable. When the free flow of moral self-transcendence is reduced to a trickle, the culture turns into a slum.

The moral conversion that human knowledge and the love of God invite and demand is an effective commitment to values when values and satisfactions conflict. A moral stance of this kind assuredly does not do away with opposed horizons and human conflicts. But, like the self-transcendence that is the love of God, it is bifrontal, dissipating spurious oppositions as well as establishing oppositions crucial to the cause of society.

The intellectual dimension of subjectivity, though unlikely to come to full fruition in philosophic truth without the magnetic pull of religious and moral vitality, nevertheless has its own character and integrity. Its field of operation is the dialectic of sense and intelligence. Sense grounds a childish realism, intelligence an adult realism. Most lives are a symbiosis of the two, for the thousand learning adaptations that we make in childhood often prove to have lifelong staying power.

Russell Baker, the American autobiographer and humorist, offers an illustration and explanation. "O Romeo, Romeo! Wherefore art thou Romeo?" means, of course, "why are you Romeo rather than Silvio or Georgio?" But most educated adults, says Baker, will say it means "Romeo, where are you?" This simplicity is without excuse but not without explanation:

> The explanation of the error has to do with the life-long persistence of misunderstandings which are born in early childhood. Juliet's opening words in the balcony scene are one of the first Shakespearean lines encountered in childhood. To an unformed mind, incapable of grasping subtleties about the irrelevance of names, "Wherefore art thou Romeo?" can only sound like a call for Romeo to tell where he's hiding. . .This tendency of the mind to reject the fruits of its education and lapse back into childhood's happy ignorance may explain the difficulty of rooting out nasty irrational prejudices.[8]

Thus, the child undermines the man. The "childish realism" alluded to above is a shorthand reference to a universal human experience. The primacy of sense life, beginning in infancy, defines the child's sense of the real. This is reflected in his spontaneous recourse to sense-resources for distinguishing his dreams from his waking hours, for keeping the stories he hears in a magic limbo at once held together with and held apart from the everyday world, and for seeing through the jokes, fibs, and subterfuges of his playmates. For the child the real is the live, moving, varied world that is seen, heard, touched, tasted, smelled.

This realism has enough staying power to defeat the efforts of most adults who undertake to ponder the real philosophically. So, Samuel Johnson, when Boswell remarked that Berkeley's idealism, though untrue, could not be refuted, cried, "striking his foot with mighty force against a large stone, till he rebounded from it, 'I refute it *thus.*'"[9] Since the real is what he can see and touch, the child is a realist, and the grown man may reaffirm, like Johnson, the realism of childhood or, like Berkeley, seem to move out of it by appeal to the dependence of primary on secondary qualities and of secondary qualities on perception. In either case perception is king--just as in childhood.

A fundamental alternative to the perceptualism of naive realists, empiricists, and idealists alike comes to light from reflection on human wonder; for, wonder, supervening on perception, reveals itself in and through the questions that make wonder thematic. By contrast with perception, there is no limit on the kinds of objects that questioning may envisage. Whatever limit be posited, one may transcend it by questioning it, asking whether it exists, or what it is, and whether anything lies beyond it and, if so, what. The reach of wonder and, correlatively, the reach of the questioning that thematizes it cannot be restricted at all. Questioning is open *ad infinitum*. Questions intend, not nothing, but everything; not nothing but being; not some modes and spheres of being, but all its modes and spheres. In questioning there is accordingly the possibility of a certain self-transcendence, and whenever a question is satisfactorily (i.e., truly) answered, this possibility is actualized. Without the questioner, to be sure, there is no question; but the truth of a truly answered question stands on its own.[10] Questions intend the real and true answers attain it.

This puts us on the track of fully human knowledge. As the realism of childhood identifies the real with the objects of perception, so a fully human realism identifies the real with the object of true judgment. As one enters the world of the child through the senses, one enters the fully human world through wonder and questioning and question-answering and answer-checking, a process that begins in childhood, that first takes the habitual form of belief and, as time goes on, increasingly takes the form of independently weighing and selectively approving particular answers. Little by little, belief is confirmed or corrected, evidence gains in importance, and there come into view the lineaments of a world known to be real.

We are adverting here to a duality in our knowledge: elementary knowing, which is prior to questions, and fully human knowing, which follows on questions, includes the quest of answers, and culminates in the ascertainment that such-and-such answers are exact. The classic error in the theory of knowledge has been to make elementary knowing the paradigm of fully human knowing, as if, for example, fully human knowing were a high-class kind of seeing.[11] This misleading analogy generates mistaken inferences, e.g., that the object of understanding is clarified by the clearer case of the object of ocular vision. Just as a colored lighted object is a concrete determinant sufficient of itself to actuate sight (supposing that the eye is able to function), so the to-be-understood may be conceived as a concrete determinant sufficient of itself to actuate understanding. But if this were so, it would be difficult to explain why anyone should fail to arrive at a given understanding, or why persons asking themselves the same question do not, in fact, always come up with the same answer. Hence, the juxtaposition of seeing and of knowing turns out to offer clarification not by comparison but by contrast. The to-be-seen is simply there; the to-be-understood, on the other hand, only emerges as it is defined by a question. Further, the to-be-seen is simply seen, whereas the to-be-understood is pondered, clarified by illustration and experiment, readjusted to the question and revised. Finally, when the to-be-seen is seen, sight is fully actuated; but when the to-be-understood is understood, something is still missing in fully human knowing, namely, an answer to the futher question, "is this particular understanding correct?"

"Critical realism" is a descriptive and analytic theory of knowledge designed to differentiate and correlate elementary and fully human knowing. The preceding paragraphs offer illustrations of the theory's descriptive function: upon examination one discovers that the traits of fully human knowing are not to be found in elementary knowing. Sense-knowledge yields neither "reality" nor "appearance," only "data."[12] The salient trait of wonder, on the other hand, as well as of the questions that specify it, is the boundless openness whereby the wonderer/questioner enters into relation not just to data but to reality and, in principle, to the whole of reality. Intending is an immediate relating to the intender to whatever he intends. There is nothing to keep him from intending the real. He could not keep himself from such intending.

The differentiation between elementary and fully human knowing implies no gap between the two, for it is data that give rise to wonder; wonder is objectified in questions; questions call forth answers; answers solicit reflection; reflection culminates in judgment that a given answer is certainly or probably true or false.

Nor is it possible to make the case that fully human knowing may intend or aspire to the real but not attain it, for that is self-reversing. If the case were made that true judgments do not occur, then at least that one true judgment would have occurred. Furthermore, one cannot deny that true ascertainments of matters of fact are recurrent in our lives, for the denial is contradicted by the habitual experience of what is being denied and hence is flatly void of plausibility.[13]

Taking account of the fact of true judgments, the analytic moment in critical realism addresses the issue of the objectivity in virtue of which such judgments occur. Once again, a grasp of the duality of elementary knowing and fully human knowing is indispensable. "Object" in the context of elementary knowing is simply the term of extraverted consciousness: whatever is seen, heard, touched, tasted, smelled. The condition of the objectivity of such knowing is the proper functioning of the senses. But "object" in the context of fully human knowing is whatever is intended by questions and known when the questions are satisfactorily answered. The objectivity of this kind of knowing is accordingly complex. An experiential component lies in the givenness of data. An intelligent component lies in the demand expressed by a question and met by an answer. A rational component lies in the further demand that the answer be true, met by the assembling of evidence and the reflective grasp of it as sufficient.

We can improve this account in the light of Bernard Lonergan's technically adroit formulation of "sufficient evidence" as "the virtually unconditioned"--an understanding the conditions of whose truth are known and known to be fulfilled.[14] Given thus definition, the second and third components of objectivity may be more elegantly conceptualized as follows. Normative objectivity arises when the exigencies of intelligence (namely, for insight in response to a question) and of reasonableness (namely, for the logic relating the insight to the conditions of its truth) are met. Terminal or absolute objectivity results from combining normative with experiential objectivity (the givenness of data), just as, by analogy, a syllogism (if X, then Y; but X; therefore Y) con-

cludes in function of combining the major and the minor propositions.[15]

As the classic epistemological error lies in a confused amalga-
mation that partly reduces object and objectivity in fully human knowing to object and objectivity in elementary knowing, so the epistemological excellence of critical realism lies in the analysis of objectivity
made possible by a clear and consistent differentiation between the two.

What counts for authenticiy, according to Nietzsche, is not
truth but life. Above we have sketched a sequence of philosophic reflections in the contrary conviction that life without regard for truth is
headed away from authenticity toward ruin. And precisely because truth
and a stubborn insistence on truth belong foundationally to human authenticity, we have attempted to highlight an option--critical realism--
that affirms our need for truth and vindicates our access to it. No doubt,
the living-out of truth--for example, in the un-self-regarding generosity
of friendship, loyalty, love--shines with a clarity and immediacy that no
human knowing can match. But to exclude objective knowing from the
world of value is to ensure the ultimate collapse of the world of value.
Authenticity is intrinsically integral. It is a dynamic whole that, though
perhaps never perfect, never ceases to summon and assemble its diverse
but functionally harmonious elements: intellectual, aesthetic, moral,
and religious, individual, personal, and intersubjective, social, cultural,
economic, and political.

Valid interpretation and human authenticity belong to and contribute to each other. Without valid interpretation, human authenticity
is socially and culturally diminished. Without human authenticity, interpretation trails off into the capricious, thwarted by absorption in pretentious or unpretentious trivia *(fascinatio nugacitatis)*. This includes,
on the part of literary scholars who for whatever reason find themselves
with nothing very compelling, or even very definite, to do, a misplaced
hankering to break out into creativity and inventiveness. There follow
declarations of independence from the tyrannies of philology and history, from the merely intended sense of the text, and finally from the text
itself. But faddism, and particularly the faddism that hinges on forms of
alienation, is notoriously ineffective occupational therapy.

An honorable task for those who put a high premium on the
text to be interpreted, interpretation is the three-step process of working
out an understanding of the text, reflecting on and judging how accurate
that understanding is, and presenting what one judges to be an accurate

understanding of the text.[16] Understood in this sense, interpretation is not always necessary, for not every text poses problems of understanding. (If it did, then every interpretation would itself need an interpretation, and so on *ad infinitum.*)

Even where interpretation is appropriate, hermeneutics need not be. If the object of interpretation is to understand the text, the object of hermeneutics is to understand the understanding of texts. When interpretation is luminous, hermeneutics is superfluous. But just as interpretation becomes necessary when the text to be understood is in some way opaque, so hermeneutics becomes necessary when fundamentally diverse interpretations of the same text compete, and especially when the competition threatens to become chaotic. Then the situation calls for a reflective step backward in an effort to discover what has gone awry in interpretation.

We are concerned with the kind of interpretation that will measure up to classic religious texts that decidedly do call for interpretation. In Western civilization no interpretative effort has ever been mounted that would compare qualitatively with the tradition of biblical interpretation. For well over a century this tradition has been cultivated in the philological and historical mode, and for the greater part of this period German Protestant interpreters have taken the leading role. Two schools of theological interpretation (especially of the New Testament) have been successively predominant in Germany: first, liberal theology, which died out in the wake of the first world war, then, kerygma theology, which lost its ascendancy only in the last decade or two.

A conspicuous virtue of both schools was their philological and historical rigor. Both nevertheless exhibited basic shortcomings, as their interpretations of central New Testament themes make clear. For liberal theology the eschatological theme of the *basileia tou theou* (the reign or kingdom of God) was moralized in thoroughgoing fashion, becoming an inner kingdom of repentence *(ein innerliches Reich der Sinnesänderung,* Albrecht Ritschl). Against the liberals, kerygma theologians reaffirmed the centrality of the gospel, but they could not see their way clear to affirm its constituent elements--the expiatory death of Jesus and his resurrection from the dead--at their full value and in their intended sense.

The phrase "intended sense" evokes a theme of the highest relevance at this point, namely, the interpretative ideal. The test of kerygma theology was the "mythological" text, which on the one hand was central to Christianity and on the other was incompatible with scientific modernity. The solution was to transpose the mythical content of the text into existential terms. This procedure was, no doubt, liable to the objection that it made the text intelligible only by eliminating its intended sense. But kerygma theologians could respond that, if the procedure eliminated a superficially intended sense, it did so only to recover thereby the most deeply and authentically intended sense of the text.[17]

This response hinged on a prior thesis having a philosophic and a literary aspect. On the philosophic side, the thesis described knowledge as a symbolic projection from an experiential matrix. Whatever the product of this projection--perhaps a maze of symbol or myth--the act of projecting was a charged self-expression. Among the direct consequences of this view were a hypothesis on myth and a corresponding interpretative strategy. The hypothesis defined myth as an objectified expression of self-understanding; thus, the thrust of all myth was anthropological. The interpretative strategy was to decipher the myth not, so to speak, on its own terms but rather by reference to the existentially grounded, self-revealing and self-defining act that produced it. Interpretation thus became an effort to locate in one's own experience the originating drive producing one's ideas and images, symbols, myths, and other objectifications. In this way Hans Jonas could find the unity behind the diversity of gnostic objectifications, and Rudolf Bultmann could work out a program of saving New Testament eschatology by finding its existential wellsprings.

The drawbacks of the "prior thesis," however, have been coming more and more relentlessly to light. On the philosophic side the gratuitous Neo-Kantian immanentism of its account of knowledge has been exposed by critical-realist critique,[18] and on the literary side the systematizing account of myth as objectified self-understanding has faded in the light of an empirically better grounded analysis of myth.[19]

The successive interpretative failures of pace-setting exegesis over the past hundred years or more--first, of liberal theology, then of kerygma theology--together with the exegetically chaotic scene to which these failures have manifestly contributed attest the deep present need of hermeneutical renewal, if the kind of interpretation most appropriate to the text, theological interpretation, is to flourish again. In the meantime, kerygma theology's failed "prior thesis" on knowledge and the nature of myth strongly suggests that the interpretative ideal is back to where it had been and ought to be: it is the modest, if sometimes arduous, task of clarifying without changing the intended sense of the text.[20]

III

Our question is: What does it take to perform this task well, when the text to be clarified is biblical? Thus far we have answered in the most general terms, broaching the theme of human authenticity and, under the heading of its intellectual component, asserting the full philosophic right to speak of validity, truth, and reality and to insist on their hermeneutical relevance. Having laid this groundwork, we hope now, with a view to the objectivity of interpretation, to get down to particulars on the subjectivity of the interpreter.

No matter how well stocked his resources, the interpreter is truly equipped for his task only if he is "attuned" to it. Normally, this means being attuned to the texts to be interpreted. In view of the devastating alienations of our time, this being in tune cannot be presupposed as standard equipment among interpreters. Graduate schools do not pledge to confer or cultivate it and may never so much as mention it.

We can clarify this not really surprising state of affairs by drawing two distinctions: first, between conditions of possibility (that without which interpretation cannot take place) and conditions of excellence (that without which excellent interpretation cannot take place); second, between kinds or aspects of excellence. For the moment we wish to consider a particular aspect of excellence--not the philological nor historical but the religious and theological aspect--of interpretative excellence. In this specific but spacious context, being attuned to the text is part of being attuned to the world and its maker. In his remarkable phenomenology of festivals and festivity, Josef Pieper made being in tune with the world the condition of "celebration."[21] It is equally the condition of excellence in religious and theological interpretation, inasmuch as the texts to be interpreted, from Genesis to the Apocalypse, are themselves a movable feast, a peerless ongoing celebration that climaxes in witness to the act of God in Christ, reconciling the world to himself.

Nietzsche's idiosyncratic witness is pertinent once again. "The trick is not to arrange a festival, but to find people who can enjoy it"[22] and "to have joy in anything, one must approve everything."[23] Nietzsche felt, as few have, the absence of that comprehensive and permanent festivity that he knew to be somehow deeply right. The classical Greeks in their own way[24] and the Church Fathers in theirs attest its presence. "Our whole lives are a feast day" (Clement of Alexandria).[25] "We have unending holiday" (John Chrysostom).[26] "Festivity is everlasting in the house of God" (Augustine)[27] and "ours. . .is an eternal festival" (Jerome).[28] All these men placed the cross at the heart of Christian life, which removes the suspicion of empty optimism from their statements. More, it divulges the secret of their joy. "Cross" is not just pain, but pain redeemed, and theirs is a "joy that can endure despite the sorrow of failure, humiliation, privation, pain, desertion."[29] Nietzsche knew this splendid paradox only by the hem of its garment. He shrank from and entirely misconstrued it, never dreaming that it was in the pattern of the Isaian Servant and of the Christian kerygma that people were to be found in every era ready for festival. "Festivity" presents itself as a credible candidate for the status of specifically Christian authenticity. As such, it belongs high on the list of the conditions of excellent theological interpretation.

Contrary orientations subvert interpretation. Without having to consider manifest, almost gross, examples of estrangement from the biblical text (the deep ambivalence of Hegel and Schleiermacher, of Friedrich Delitzsch and Adolf von Harnack vis-à-vis the Old Testament; the alienation of Bruno Bauer or Robert Eisler or Arthur Drews vis-à-vis the New), it is enough to adduce evidence of limited or selective estrangement. New Testament scholars, for example, have often tended to lose their poise and touch in the face of specifically apocalyptic themes. From Otto Pfleiderer to the present, efforts to grasp the Pauline theme of the coming resurrection of the dead yield many examples. That Paul harbored apocalyptic conceptions such as the salvation of the quick and the dead at the parousia was too well attested to be denied (e.g., 1 Thess 4:13-17; 1 Cor 15:22-28, 51-57). But exegetes well-disposed toward Paul and ill-disposed toward apocalypticism have repeatedly managed to save him from his lesser self and its immersion in apocalyptic remnants from Judaism such as the parousia and judgment themes.[30] Though Paul strangely clung to conventional images like the descent of a parousiac redeemer, his real thought would be better represented by the image of mystical ascent to the heavenly world.[31] It took some time for him to drop his inherently contradictory idea of resurrection, but he finally did so.[32] Whereas he had once thought of the saved as a tiny remnant, he eventually abandoned the fanatic and intolerant dualism behind this thinking, in favor of reconciliation to "experience."[33] Missionary accommodation led him to a "complete revision" of his apocalyptic eschatology, though he held on to themes like judgment even after they had "ceased to possess any real significance."[34] This whole line of thought, well represented over a period of more than a hundred years, was dependent on a demonstrably false reading of 2 Cor 5:1-10, but, far more important, was sustained by the interpreters' affect-laden recoil from apocalypticism.

    This special and limited example is matched on other fronts. We have long grown familiar with the generic rationalism that finds prophecies and miracles unthinkable and impossible on *a priori* grounds, without regard either to the issue in its contemporary cognitional-theoretical dimension or to the particulars of individual cases.[35] This undiscriminating ideological stance has had a deeply negative impact on the exegetical and historical appropriation of the New Testament. Nevertheless, I would not wish to make the issue of the interpreter's "good will" or "orientation to consent" hinge on resolution of the more than ordinarily complex questions of prophecy and miracle.

    Good will is an antecedent disposition of openness to the horizon, message, and tone of the text. The impersonal curiosity of the physicist is not enough for the interpreter. He does not confront mute nature; he enters into a dialogue, questioning and being questioned. He knows in advance only that without attention and sympathy he may not "hear" the text. The orientation to consent is a condition of such hearing, as Hans-Georg Gadamer, in concert with many others from John Henry Newman to the present, had insisted.[36] Openness to consent is ideally the openness of "basic horizon," the horizon of the thoroughly authentic man.

    As the hermeneutics of consent reflects a prior acknowledgement that the human intentionality objectified in the text is in principle open to the whole of reality, so the hermeneutics of suspicion finds its proper object, not in the self-transcendence of the human spirit, but in the recurrent schemes and patterns of nature.[37] "Consent" goes with interpretation, "suspicion" with analysis. Interpretation deals with the text as text (*parole*, particular utterance); analysis deals with the text as language (*langue*, resources of speech). Insofar as the text is a communication (*parole*), interpretation is prior by nature to analysis. But, if suspicion has no role whatever in interpretation taken strictly as the effort to grasp and mediate what the author has both intended to encode and managed to encode in the text, still suspicion has its place in literary study.

First, it is a stance appropriate to analysis, if not in all its modes, in many of them: those that are in some sense anterior to interpretation (text-critical, form-critical analysis, etc.) and those that bypass or follow upon interpretation (structuralist, psychological, historical, socio-economic, and many other kinds of analysis). Second, suspicion belongs to critique; that is, it belongs to the effort to say, not what the text means (that is the task of interpretation), but how adequately and authentically it means what it means. Critique in this sense includes the thematization of the interpreter's personal encounter with the text.

In bringing these general observations to bear on the concrete effort to read biblical texts well, the main matter is to maximize in oneself what Peter Stuhlmacher has called "the principle of hearing."[38] This, I would say, is first of all an orientation to consent antecedently sensitized by whatever measure of intellectual, moral, affective, aesthetic, religious, and specifically Christian authenticity that one can attain. Second, it is an acquired set of special competences belonging to historical and literary scholarship. In other words, to become attuned to the biblical text is to bring to realization the kind of subjectivity that, measuring up to the text, makes objectivity possible--an enormous challenge.

Suspicion, on the other hand, which is so much easier to hone to a fine edge, is a distinctly secondary matter. In the era since Benedict Spinoza and Richard Simon, suspicion has brought much to light. Inasmuch as it includes the hardy scepticism that is part and parcel of the historian's equipment, it has helped retrieve the common sense of changing societies over the thousand or more years that were the biblical period. Suspicion, moreover, meets the need to spot the traits of propaganda literature, be it from the court of Solomon or from Christian missionary centers in the diaspora of the Greeks.

But the reader must be alert to the distortions of bias not only in the text but in himself. It is the achievement of the masters of suspicion to have placed an array of surgical instruments at his disposal: the analyses of *ressentiment*, of screening devices and defence mechanisms and rationalizing legitimations; and these he may turn on the text to discern its biases and on himself to deconstruct those prejudgments that would block or deflect or otherwise spoil his responding appropriately to the text. This properly locates suspicion in analysis ancillary to interpretation and in the critique that follows upon it.

As Freudian suspicion generated psychoanalysis and Marxian suspicion the critique of ideology, so the suspicions of Reimarus generated the quest of the historical Jesus and those of Strauss and Baur, the inquiries into the nature of the gospel literature and into the drama of early Christian development. Still, all these adepts of suspicion--Freud and Marx, Reimarus, Strauss, and Baur--were reductionists whose work has had to be selectively salvaged by correction from outside their own suspicions. By contrast, the greatness of the great biblical interpreters of the past generation--to mention two, Gerhard von Rad and Joachim Jeremias--lay in the acuteness that informed their capacity to listen and to hear. It was greatness *ex auditu*.

NOTES

1. Bernard Lonergan, "The Ongoing Genesis of Methods," in **A Third Collection. Papers by Bernard J. F. Lonergan**, ed. F. E. Crowe (New York/Mahwah: Paulist, 1985) 146-165, p. 147.

2. Oswald Spengler, **The Decline of the West. Vol. 1: Form and Actuality. Vol. 2: Perspectives of World History** (London: George Allen & Unwin, 1926-28). See the review by R. G. Collingwood, *Antiquity* 1 (1927) 311-325.

3. Rudolf Bultmann, "The Problem of Hermeneutics," in **Essays Philosophical and Theological** (London: SCM, 1958) 234-261, p. 239. Adding the crucial modifier "authentic" to "subjectivity," Bernard Lonergan, **Method in Theology** (London: Darton, Longman & Todd, 1972) 162-165.

4. See Nathan Glick, "Sidney Hook, Embattled Philosopher," *Encounter* 75 (June, 1985) 28-32, p. 30, note 6.

5. Bernard Lonergan, **Insight: A Study of Human Understanding** (New York: Longmans, 1958) ix.

6. Robert J. Daly, "The Eucharist and Redemption: The Last Supper and Jesus' Understanding of His Death," *Biblical Theology Bulletin* 11 (1981) 21-27, p. 26.

7. On the transcendental precepts (be attentive, be intelligent, be reasonable, be responsible), which accord with the four levels of human intention-

ality (experience=data, understanding, judgment, decision), see **Method in Theology** 53-55, 231f.

8. Russell Baker, "Why Art Thou Romeo?" *International Herald Tribune*, May 18, 1984.

9. James Boswell, **The Life of Samuel Johnson** (London: Macmillan, 1922) 162.

10. Bernard Lonergan, "The Subject," in **A Second Collection. Papers by Bernard J. F. Lonergan**, eds. W. F. J. Ryan and B. J. Tyrrell (London: Darton, Longman & Todd, 1974) 69-86, p. 70, on how, ontologically, truth resides only in the subject, but intentionally is independent of the subject.

11. See **Insight**, 252f. on the distinction between elementary knowing and fully human knowing; 422f. on how failure to make and maintain the distinction (a failure epitomized in the tag "knowing is like seeing") generates the component of aberration in the dialectical development of philosophy. As Lonergan elsewhere puts it, the notions of knowledge and reality that are formed in childhood (i.e., the reduction of knowing to analogy with seeing and of the real to what is there to be seen) "down through the centuries have provided the unshakable foundations of materialism, empiricism, positivism, sensism, phenomenalism, behaviorism, pragmatism. . ." **Method in Theology**, 213f.

12. See Bernard Lonergan, "Cognitional Structure," in **Collection. Papers by Bernard Lonergan**, ed. F. E. Crowe (New York: Herder & Herder, 1967) 221-139, p. 235.

13. See **Insight**, 281-283 on the character and undeniability of true ascertainments of concrete matters of fact.

14. **Insight**, 280f., 343-345; **Method in Theology**, 102.

15. **Insight**, 280f. and "**Insight** Revisited," in **A Second Collection**, 263-278, p. 275.

16. **Method in Theology**, 155.

17. James M. Robinson, "Hermeneutic Since Barth," in **The New Hermeneutic**, eds. James M. Robinson and John C. Cobb, Jr. (New York: Harper & Row, 1964) 1-77, p. 34: ". . .demythologizing does 'eliminate' the inadequate mythical conceptualization for the sake of stating more adequately the myth's meaning, such meaningless arabesques are not to be 'eliminated.'"

18. Frederick Lawrence, "Method and Theology as Hermeneutical," in **Creativity and Method, Essays in Honor of Bernard Lonergan**, ed. Matthew L. Lamb (Milwaukee: Marquette University Press, 1981) 79-104, see pp. 86-89, 96-100.

19. Walter Burkert, **Structure and History in Greek Mythology and Ritual** (Berkeley: University of California Press, 1979) 1-34, 143-158.

20. "Intended sense" throughout this paper refers to the author's in-

tention only insofar as it is intrinsic to the text, i.e., expressed or encoded or objectified in the text. (The "intended sense" would fall under the strictures evoked by the catch-phrase "intentional fallacy" only if it is conceived as extrinsic to the text.)

21. Josef Pieper, **In Tune With the World. A Theory of Festivity** (New York: Harcourt, Brace & World, 1965).

22. Cited by Pieper, **In Tune**, 10.

23. Cited by Pieper, **In Tune**, 20.

24. Pieper, **In Tune**, 38, cites Pythagoras on life as a festival, and Plato's **Laws** on every day a festival.

25. Clement of Alexandria, **Miscellanies**, 7, 35, 5.

26. Chrysostom, "De sancta Pentecoste," Migne, **Patrologia Graeca** 50, 454.

27. Augustine, "Enarrationes in Psalmos," 41, 9; Migne, **Patrologia Latina** 36, 470.

28. Jerome, **Epistola ad Algasiam** 121, cap. 10; Migne, **Patrologia Latina** 22, 1031. The patristic texts are cited by Pieper, **In Tune**, 38.

29. Lonergan, "Theology and Man's Future," **Second Collection**, 135-148, p. 145.

30. Otto Pfleiderer, **Paulinism**, 2 vols. (London: Williams and Norgate, 1877) vol. 1 261-276.

31. Ernst Teichmann, **Die paulinische Vorstellungen von Auferstehung und Gericht** (Frieburg-Leipzig: Mohr, 1896) 72-74.

32. R. H. Charles, **A Critical History of the Doctrine of the Future Life in Israel, in Judaism, and in Christianity** (London: Black, 1899) 394f.

33. C. H. Dodd, "The Mind of Paul: II" (1934) in C. H. Dodd, **New Testament Studies** (Manchester: Manchester University Press, 1953, repr. 1967) 83-128, pp. 121, 126, 108.

34. Wilfred L. Knox, **St. Paul and the Church of the Gentiles** (Cambridge: Cambridge University Press, 1939) 128, 141.

35. See B. F. Meyer, **The Aims of Jesus** (London: SCM, 1979) 99-102.

36. Hans-Georg Gadamer, **Truth and Method** (New York: Seabury, 1975) 245-274.

37. John C. Robertson, Jr., "Hermeneutics of Suspicion vs. Hermeneutics of Goodwill," *Studies in Religion/Sciences Religieuses* 8 (1979) 365-379.

38. Peter Stuhlmacher, **Historical Criticism and Theological Interpretation of Scripture** (Philadelphia: Fortress, 1977) 85-87.

PART TWO

APPLICATION TO EXEGESIS,
HISTORY, AND THEOLOGY

V

DID PAUL'S VIEW OF THE
RESURRECTION OF THE DEAD
UNDERGO DEVELOPMENT?

"Is it not a remarkable thing that you should have started the idea--and the word--Development, as the key to the history of church doctrine, and since then it has gradually become the dominant idea of all history, biology, physics, and in short has metamorphosed our view of every science, and of all knowledge?" So wrote Mark Pattison to John Henry Newman in 1878,[1] thirty-three years after the publication of Newman's **Essay on the Development of Christian Doctrine**.[2] Rarely had a single idea so rapidly and thoroughly transformed a whole culture's field of vision. This implies, to be sure, that Newman had had predecessors and allies of sorts as well as kindred and alien successors.

Among the predecessors was G. W. F. Hegel, whose triad of thesis, antithesis, and synthesis impinged on biblical history and exegesis especially through the work of Ferdinand Christian Baur.[3] By the end of the century "development" had established itself in biblical studies as an indispensable heuristic resource. Likewise, by century's end Richard Kabisch and Johannes Weiss had discovered "eschatology" as the very form of early Christian consciousness, aspiration, and reflection.[4] Soon Albert Schweitzer would so effectively thematize the issue of eschatology as to make it foundational for the exegesis of the New Testament, the history of religions (Judeo-Christian sector), and New

Testament theology. Moreover, these two thought forms, "development" and "eschatology," inevitably intersected. Kabisch was the first to bring development to bear on eschatology grasped as a controlling principle, and Schweitzer offered the first real appreciation of this effort as well as the sharpest critique of its shortcomings.[5]

It soon became clear that eschatology--pervasive in the texts, but for long centuries overlooked by their readers--and development--burked in the texts, but highly conscious among nineteenth-century scholars after Baur--were not only great but intoxicating discoveries. Just because the eschatological consciousness had been a vital experience in earliest Christianity, but lay outside the experience of modernity, and just because the consciousness of development had been a stunning advance since the mid-nineteenth century, but was by and large alien to the whole of late antiquity, the combination of the two generated the most uninhibited hypotheses and far-ranging, free-wheeling reconstructions of early Christian thought.

Here I propose, first, to recall the main lines of the discussion of development in one sphere of Pauline eschatology, namely, the theme of the coming resurrection of the dead; second, to question whether the Pauline texts (1 Thess 4; 1 Cor 15; 2 Cor 5; Phil 1) support the maximalists or the minimalists in the debate on the "development" of Paul's view. Maximalists argue that he moved from a relatively crude, conventional affirmation of resurrection to a more refined conception of survival, and often enough they have characterized this as a transition from Jewish to Greek categories. Minimalists doubt or deny a change of categories, but often enough have acknowledged the appearance of new, if minor, doctrinal elements in the later texts, or at least some variation in Paul's personal attitude toward the prospect of death and resurrection. Third, I propose to reflect on the context in which this debate has a significance beyond antiquarian, or even historical, curiosity. Therefore, Part 1 is history; Part 2 is exegesis; Part 3 is hermeneutics.

I

It was Baur who initiated this kind of investigation, and Otto Pfleiderer who, prior to the realization that eschatology was not only an aspect but the very horizon of early Christian consciousness, framed the first influential hypothesis of development in Paul's eschatological thought.[6] The pattern of Pfleiderer's view of Paul went well with the dominant weave of Liberal theology. Tutored like many Liberals first by Baur, then by Hermann Lüdemann's study of Pauline anthropology, Pfleiderer saw distinct "branches," Jewish and Hellenistic, in the Pauline "doctrinal system."[7] Paul, moreover, had shifted from the one to the other. If the first branch grew out of the expiatory death of Jesus and formed "the negative part of the Pauline Gospel in opposition to the Jews or the Jewish Christians," the second branch grew out of Christ's risen life in the radiant element of *pneuma*, far beyond "transitory and unclean *sarx*.[8] "Life" here was eschatological, but "the *transcendent eschatological idea* became of necessity an *immanent ethical* one," for the Christian's future share in "resurrection life" depended on his having died with Christ in baptism and so on his having already participated in Christ's "*pneuma* life." Baptism, accordingly, marked the moment of entry "into mystical communion with Christ and of the reception of his *pneuma*. [9]

The great development in Paul was, then, away from the sphere of the eschatological into that of the mystical. The messianic *zōe* was thus "stripped of its one-sided, supernatural, apocalyptic character" and became ethical and spiritual. This transition followed "one of the deepest laws of development in the history of religion": profound mysteries are concealed and protected in the calyx of apocalyptic imagery "until they are capable of flourishing alone. . . ."[10]

Let this sketch suffice to suggest the tenor and style of Pfleiderer's thinking about Paulinism. Though differing in detail from Baur and Lüdemann, Pfleiderer reflected ideas from both and specifically reflected the tendency to reduce a many-faceted faith to a fairly breezy history of ideas--a besetting defect of the Liberal movement.[11] The sketch may also serve to provide some measure of context for Pfleiderer's retrieval of Pauline eschatology.

"Development" in Pfleiderer's view did not exclude inconsistencies and unresolved antinomies. Rather, it hinged on them. All through "the Apostle's dogmatic teaching" there ran a duality reflecting the trajectory of Paul's own career: "from a Pharisee and a zealous upholder of the law," he had become "a chosen instrument of the gospel of the favour of God in Christ."[12] To the two phases divided by this turnabout belonged the two categories of Pauline thought: "remnants from Judaism" and "Christian gospel." Ranged under the rubric of Jewish remnants were the ideas of final judgment eternally distinguishing the saved and the lost on the basis of "just due"; the parousia as the decisive moment of the resurrection and redemption of the body; the messianic reign, beginning with the parousia and the resurrection of those in Christ and ending with the reduction to impotence of the last enemy, death (=the resurrection of all) and the handing over of the reign to the Father (1 Cor 15:24-26). Ranged under the specifically Christian gospel were salvation by the pure *charis* of God, the indwelling *pneuma*, shaping in the believer the image of Christ's death and resurrection, and for those in Christ the unhindered union with the Lord--clothed with a heavenly body--immediately upon death (2 Cor 5:1-10; Phil 1:23). Pfleiderer abstained from all effort to reconcile these two quite "incompatible" sets of ideas; for that, he thought, could be done only by recourse to "arbitrary criteria."[13]

Pfleiderer was undeterred by the flat impossibility of finding significant Greek analogies for (to say nothing of Greek attestation of) any part or aspect of the specifically Christian gospel, be it the pure gift of righteousness by faith, or the indwelling, energizing, patterning *pneuma* of God/Christ, or entry into immortality with a radiant *doxa*-body prepared in heaven. In 1887, fourteen years after his two-volume work on Paulinism, he returned to the theme of Paul's Hellenized eschatology in **Primitive Christianity**.[14] Here Paul's development away from Jewish thinking into Alexandrian Platonizing was attested by 2 Cor 5:1-10, supplemented by Phil 1:21f. and 3:8f. Paul, in a word, drew on Hellenistic resources to spiritualize the Christian hope of salvation and, incidentally, to provide a neat exit out of the dilemma of the delayed parousia. As Albert Schweitzer remarked of this confident, comprehensive view,

> Pfleiderer believes also that he can show the course of the development by which the new conception was arrived at. In 1 Thessalonians, he thinks, the Apostle still rested unquestioningly in that notion of a corpo-

> real resurrection which primitive Christianity shared
> with Judaism. But in the explanations of I Cor. XV
> the influence of the Greek ideas become observable,
> while in 2 Corinthians and Philippians it becomes
> dominant.[15]

Pfleiderer's Paul--who moved back and forth between Judaic resurrection and Greek immortality, without being conscious of the divergence between the two sets of ideas, yet without ever mingling them--was unmasked as an exegetical illusion by the superior (if still quite fallible) synthesis of Richard Kabisch.[16] In opposition to Kabisch, Ernst Teichmann in 1896 produced a monograph in the form of twin essays on the Pauline conceptions of resurrection and judgment.[17]

According to Teichmann's reconstruction, Paul's thought on the resurrection of the dead registered a movement from Jewish apocalyptic spirituality to Hellenistic Wisdom spirituality. Like Pfleiderer, Teichmann argued that this evolution could be traced through three stages. In the first stage (1 Thess 4:13-17) Paul affirmed a resurrection of the dead in the sense of a resuscitation of the corpses of the faithful, an event to take place at the parousia. In a second, mediating stage (1 Cor 15:50ff.) he affirmed the annihilation of everything earthly, including the earthly body, and the appropriation of a new, spiritual body--still, however, to take place at the parousia. In a third and final phase, represented by 2 Cor 5:1ff. and, still better, by Phil 1:21ff., resurrection has been abandoned, or abandoned in all but name, in favor of the bestowal of a new body at the moment of death.[18]

This scheme of development drew attention to the intermediate stage represented by 1 Cor 15:50ff. In this passage Paul introduced the notion of transformation. In 1 Thess 4 resurrection had no more implied "transformation" than had, for example, the story of Elijah swept up to heaven in a fiery chariot. But now transformation must make its appearance as a consequence of the Pauline antithesis of *sarx* and *pneuma*. Moreover, for Teichmann "transformation" really meant "total annihilation."[19] *Sarx* would be annihilated and man created anew. Hence Paul's maintenance of the idea of *resurrection* was incoherent with the real character of his thought. By the time of 2 Cor 5 it had been dropped; for here the new *sōma*, which had existed in heaven since the creation, has "replaced" the earthly body.[20]

On the text of 2 Cor 5:1-10 Teichmann made five points: {1}

the earthly body, destined for decay, is an obstacle to our union with the Lord; {2} but for every individual believer God has prepared a heavenly body to clothe him at the moment of his death; {3} "nakedness" images the *pneuma* stripped of its earthly body and separated from Christ; {4} this fate, however, will not befall the believer; {5} the subject of old and new life is the *pneuma*, which appears before the tribunal of Christ immediately after death. We accordingly have here a sharp change from the parousia-oriented thought of 1 Cor 15. Resurrection, as Teichmann observes, has not become "entirely unnecessary."[21] Still, he finds it "interesting" that, despite this stunning development, Paul hangs on to the traditional term (2 Cor 1:9; 4:14; Phil 3:11).[22]

The basic idea in Teichmann's account was derivative from Pfleiderer: the "Spirit" of God bestowed in baptism was the seed of personal survival. At one time the Apostle's eschatological thought had been well represented in the image of the glorious return of Christ to earth; but, without ever abandoning this now empty image, Paul arrived finally at an eschatology better represented as the believer's ascent into the heavenly world. True, Paul never managed to shake off the hope of being united to Christ without having to die. But that merely betokened the inescapability of biographical limits: Jewish-Greek syncretism was the Apostle's daily bread.[23]

The Pfleiderer-Teichmann line has had unlikely success in England. R. H. Charles, in his 1899 study of "future life" according to Israel, Judaism, and Christianity,[24] maintained that 1 Cor 15 argued incoherently (a) for corporeal continuity between the dead and the risen, and (b) for the postponement of the resurrection to the parousia. When writing 1 Cor 15, Paul "does not seem conscious" of the contradiction, but by the time he wrote 2 Cor 5 he had "become conscious of the inherent inconsistencies of his former view" and abandoned it in favor of the resurrection of the righteous following immediately on death.[25]

H. A. A. Kennedy in 1904[26] observed that Paul's eschatological conceptions, though by no means worked into a systematic account *de novissimis,* had

> a far greater mutual congruity than some recent investigators have been willing to recognize. But *in an age when the notion of development is regarded as the key to all problems,* it is perhaps natural that scholars should use it in explaining

certain phenomena which look like antinomies in the
Pauline Epistles. This view has been worked out to
its furthest limit by Sabatier, Pfleiderer, Teichmann,
and others.[27]

Kennedy resisted it. First, he offered an account of 1 Cor 15 that was remarkable for the treatment given to vv. 50ff. Here he formulated the
question to which the text was an answer, as follows: now that his readers could form some conception of the experience of their deceased
friends, what of themselves? How were the survivors, the living, to
pass into the final kingdom of God?[28] The answer was, "we shall all be
transformed" {51b}. That is, "the dead shall rise incorruptible, and we
[the living] shall be transformed" {52bc}. Second, he turned to 2 Cor 4-
5. In the first verses of chapter 5 Kennedy interpreted the issue as that
of survival to the Parousia (*stenazomen* in vv. 2 and 4 had a striking
parallel in Rom 8:23). But his recoil from the opinion that between 1
Cor and 2 Cor Paul had changed his mind about resurrection did not allow him to acknowledge that Paul might have meant what he said
about dying and being "at home with the Lord" (vv. 6-9). Kennedy concluded at most to a negative result: for Paul death could not bring the
believer into separation from his Lord.[29] Paul's yearning (vv. 2-8) was,
as before, "for the immortality of the *sōma pneumatikon*" at the parousia.[30] Kennedy accordingly referred the two states contrasted in 2 Cor
5:6-9--"being at home in the body and absent from the Lord"/"being absent from the body and at home with the Lord"--to life in the natural or
fleshly body and life at the parousia in the spiritual body.

Now, there is no argument over the sense of the first limb in
this contrast: but, whereas there appears to be no visible support for
Kennedy's reading of the second limb ("being absent from the body and
at home with the Lord" = parousia), the parallel of Phil 1:23 positively
militates against it. Respecting the latter text, Kennedy cited Paul
Wernle's interpretation without making it any more cogent: "[Paul's]
yearning overleaps all between death and resurrection, and hurries to its
goal for reunion with Jesus."[31]

Albert Schweitzer's survey, **Paul and His Interpreters**
(1911), ET 1912) traced the views of Paul especially from F. C. Baur
to Schweitzer's own time. On the issue of development he noted that
Auguste Sabatier had been the first to differentiate phases in Paul's development;[32] that Pfleiderer, inspired perhaps by Lüdemann's study of

Paul's use of *sarx*, had fixed on Pauline eschatology as the privileged sphere of development;[33] that what Teichmann added to Pfleiderer was merely an overconfident extremism.

> Not one of [Teichmann's] "results" can be proved
> from the Apostle's letters. . . . He asserts, for in-
> stance, that in Thessalonians those who arise from the
> dead enter the kingdom of God in their earthly bodies.
> But from the Jewish Apocalyptic and from the teach-
> ing of Jesus it clearly appears that the resurrection in-
> cluded within itself a transformation of this creaturely
> corporeity into a glorified corporeity.[34]

Several factors have combined to keep Schweitzer's straightfor-ward, devastating critique from delivering the *coup de grâce* to the Pfleiderer-Teichmann line. First, Schweitzer was unable to match his critique with a plausible positive retrieval of Pauline eschatology.[35] Second, the modern hankering to convert variations into "developments" meshed with the modern recoil from apocalyptic escha-tology. As scholars yielded to both impulses, Paul became ever more dynamic and rational.

In C. H. Dodd's account of "the mind of Paul" the dynamism and rationality were attested by a many-sided evolution of attitudes.[36] The mature Paul--the Paul that matured between First and Second Co-rinthians--"has become reconciled to experience."[37] He has found a new value in human institutions, particularly the state and its magistrates, and, correlatively, a new distance from apocalypticism and its parousias. In Dodd's view, apocalypticism was "a form of compensation in fantasy for the sense of futility and defeat,"[38] its hallmark "a radical devaluation of the present world-order in all its aspects."[39] The newly mature Paul has broken with this. Whereas he had earlier thought of the saved as a tiny remnant,[40] he now foresaw the winning over of "all Israel" and, in-deed, the redemption of the whole human race[41] and the whole material creation.[42] What brought about the "decisive change"[43] by which Paul suddenly "outgrew" his "harsh dualism"?[44] Apart from naming it a "second conversion," in which "the traces of fanaticism and intolerance disappear,"[45] Dodd did not say. This left room for others to come up with an answer.

To Wilfred L. Knox the answer lay not in a second conversion but in Paul's missionary strategy of accommodation to Hellenistic culture.[46] Knox observed that "the conception of a new age which had already begun and was shortly to be completed by the appearance of the Lord was fairly prominent in Christian preaching."[47] Paul kept to this in 1 Cor 15, but he did so in a spirit of accommodation to the Hellenistic readership. For example, the resurrection of the dead was no longer to a material but to a spiritual body.[48] This, however, was not enough to meet the difficulties of the Corinthians, rooted in their acceptance of popular Hellenistic philosophy. So, in 2 Cor 5 Paul took missionary accommodation to Greek categories further, to the "complete revision" of his eschatology.[49] He made the body the garment that the soul "was anxious to cast aside, the burden from which it longed to be delivered."[50] Present possession of the Spirit (2 Cor 5:5) could be equated with "the divine afflatus of Hellenistic belief."[51] Paul adopted the conception that the soul did not simply lay aside the body, but put on a new and glorious one. In imagery drawn from Babylon but at home in the mysteries and indeed everywhere in Hellenistic syncretism, Paul converted eschatology into "an accepted Hellenistic view of the life to come" (2 Cor 5:1-5).[52] Though he had substituted the immortality of the soul for the resurrection of the body and the gradual spiritualization of the soul for the great assize at the end of time, he strangely failed to abandon all talk of judgment (2 Cor 5:10), despite its having "ceased to possess any real significance. . . ."[53]

W. D. Davies has offered a detailed analysis of Knox's treatment of 2 Cor 5, but, though he accepted the view urged since Pfleiderer that Pauline eschatology underwent notable development between 1 Cor 15 and 2 Cor 5, he refused to accept Knox's answer to the question of what the change consisted in and what brought it about.[54]

Davies focused on three factors. First, the change consisted in rescheduling the acquisition of a heavenly body from the parousia to the death of the individual believer. Second, the occasion of this doctrinal development was partly psychological ("he himself had been at the gates of death"[55]) and partly pastoral ("the problem of Christians who died was becoming a pressing one"[56]). Third, the condition of the possibility of the change lay in the early Christian and Pauline consciousness of realized eschatology: the "conception of the Age to Come as having already dawned."[57] In 1 Cor 15 Paul's mind had been "centered on the ᶜōlām habā' as the End of all history." In 2 Cor 5:1f., however, "it is not resurrection as characteristic of 'the End' that concerns him;"

his mind turns, rather, to what lies immediately beyond death.[58] In short, 1 Cor 15 corresponded to the Judaic notion of the age to come as reserved for the eschatological resurrection of the dead following the messianic age; 2 Cor 5 corresponded to the Judaic notion of the age to come as eternally existent: "it always IS in the heavens and we awake to it at death."[59]

In 1955 Joachim Jeremias espoused and developed an undeveloped indication in Adolf Schlatter's exegesis of 1 Cor 15:50.[60] Neither the living *(sarx kai haima)* nor the dead *(hē phthora)* could inherit the reign of God (that is, the existence proper to salvation in the age to come) as they were; rather, the condition of entry into the age to come, whether for the living or for the dead, was a divinely wrought transformation to take place at the parousia: "we shall not all sleep, but we shall all be changed."[61]

Jeremias not only championed this exegesis against the interpretation that took 1 Cor 15:50 to signify the flat incompatibility of the earthly or bodily with final salvation; he also explicitly related his reading of the text to Teichmann's reconstruction of Paul's thought on the resurrection of the dead. If in this reconstruction 1 Cor 15:50ff. was the link in an alleged transition from Jewish apocalyptic notions to Greek sapiential notions, Jeremias could argue that with the loss of this link the whole construct collapsed.

Jeremias's interpretation has been not only influential but decisive in its main point. Joachim Gnilka reported some years ago that the Teichmann reconstruction, setting immortality in opposition to resurrection, "is nowadays rightly without supporters."[62] Nevertheless, Gerd Luedemann has recently reasserted the views of Teichmann at three points. First, at the time Paul founded the Christian community of Thessalonica, he conceived of salvation at the parousia without reference to the resurrection of dead Christians. Second, when Paul did integrate the resurrection of the dead with the salvation of the living at the parousia (1 Thess 4), he conceived of resurrection as a mere revivification of corpses. Third, Pauline dualism (spirit versus flesh) grounded Paul's view that the sphere of "flesh and blood" will be "destroyed" at the parousia.[63] From this it would seem that for some few, at least, the question of Paul's view of the resurrection of the dead is back to square one, i.e., to where it was roughly a hundred years ago.

Meantime, the opening lines of 2 Cor 5:1-10 continue to be a *crux interpretum*. Whereas Jacques Dupont found clues to the hope of

the parousia in these first lines, Paul Hoffmann offered a detailed counterpart to Rudolf Bultmann's exegesis; that is, he deciphered the text as
mirror writing, on the supposition that it reflected, by opposition, the
eschatology of gnostic opponents.[64] Friedrich Lang has surveyed the
variety of recent scholarship on 2 Cor 5:1-10.[65]

If Gnilka's assurance that the Teichmann line "is nowadays. . .
without supporters" is no longer quite exact, still that particular line is
a dead letter for the vast majority today. The influence of kerygma theology, however, is not quite so passé. Though it is notoriously difficult
to say what will finally prove to have been going forward in our own
time, it is nonetheless tempting to hazard a comment on the rich har-
vest of works dealing with 1 Cor 15 since 1970, namely, that special
importance attaches to the analysis of parallels to 1 Cor 15 in ancient
Jewish texts on the resurrection of the dead. The quest of such parallel
material was of distinctly secondary interest to Barth, Bultmann,
Schniewind, and their generation. Yet no small part of the scholarly literature designed to consolidate or resolve issues framed by these thinkers and exegetes has now been rendered all but obsolete by just such analytic work. An example of the latter is the series of articles, reflecting
a Strasbourg dissertation, that Rodolphe Morissette published in
1972.[66]

Current opinion on the relevant texts resists consensus. Still,
it seems to me possible that a contribution to greater order might well
lie in locating and addressing the strategic exegetical issues that generate
diverse opinion on "development" in Paul's eschatology.

II

For present purposes there is no need to offer (indeed, within
the limits of a single essay there would be no excuse for offering) a fully detailed exegesis of the Pauline texts. I shall allow the main forms of
the hypothesis of development to define the crucial points and shall
limit my interpretative efforts to them. The hypothesis may be set out
in three main propositions.

1. In 1 Thess 4 Paul affirmed salvation, at the parousia, of not
only the living but the dead. Here he conceived of salvation in primitive

Judaic terms: the dead return to the conditions of this life; then the living "will be swept up together with them on clouds into the air to meet
the Lord" (Pfleiderer, Teichmann, Jeremias, G. Luedemann. et al.). Crucial question: Does Paul understand the dead to return by resurrection to
the conditions of the present life?

    2. In 1 Cor 15 Paul affirmed salvation at the parousia of both
the living and the dead, but by now he had arrived at the insight that

> *sarx kai haima basileian theou klēronomēsai ou dyna-*
> *tai oude hē phthora tēn aphtharsian klēronomei* (v. 50)

This means that Paul's affirmation of "resurrection"--which supposed
some continuity between, on the one hand, "flesh and blood/the perishable" and, on the other, "the kingdom of God/imperishability"--was incoherent with his deepest soteriological thought (Pfleiderer, Teichmann,
Charles, Dodd, W. L. Knox, et al.). Crucial questions: (a) Does 1 Cor
15:50 rule out corporeal participation in final salvation? (b) What does
the *mystērion* (secret) of 1 Cor 15:51 refer to?

    3. In 2 Cor 5:2-4 Paul reduced this incoherence by affirming
that a foreordained heavenly body would be bestowed on the believer
immediately upon death. This was an adoption of Greek categories
(Pfleiderer, Teichmann, Knox, et al.) or a deployment of Judaic categories (W. D. Davies). Finally, in Phil 1:21-23 he supported this revision, establishing a certain primacy of the Greek theme of immortality
(Pfleiderer, Teichmann, Knox, et al.). Crucial questions: (a) Does 2
Cor 5:2-4 refer to the parousia or to the acquisition of a resurrection-
body immediately upon death? (b) Is 2 Cor 5:6-9 concerned with the
parousia, or with an intermediate state after death? (c) What light, if
any, does Phil 1:23 throw on the matter?

    Jeremias's 1955 essay all but put an end to the idea that "flesh
and blood" (interpreted as the corporeal principle itself) had no part in final salvation. After 1955 that particular reading of the text of 1 Cor
15:50 was largely abandoned, few today being ready to follow Teichmann in suppressing the prima-facie sense of "change" ("we shall all be
changed") in favor of making it mean annihilation and new creation[67]
With the loss of 1 Cor 15:50, the full-blown hypothesis of "development"--a complete trajectory with visible point of departure (1 Thess 4),
apogee (1 Cor 15), and arrival at a new eschatology (2 Cor 5)--did indeed collapse.

Still, lesser developments could be maintained. Jeremias himself maintained a forward move from 1 Thess 4 to the mature Paul of the later correspondence. In 1 Thess 4, according to Jeremias, something was missing: the idea of transformation. In this one particular he agreed with Teichmann and, in common with Teichmann, argued from. . .silence.[68]

But the notion that transformation from earthly to heavenly corporeity was in no way supposed by the resurrection theme in 1 Thess 4 is burdened with improbable consequences. First, this would not accord with the evidence of late Old Testament texts and Jewish noncanonical literature. Dan 12:2f. is a keynote passage actualizing the destiny of the Servant in Isa 52-53 as the resurrection of the righteous (v. 3) and assimilating the resurrected righteous to the angels (cf. the equation of "stars" and angels in Dan 8:10). See also Isa 26:19; lQH ll:l0-14; **Pss. Sol.** 3:16; **2 Bar.** 49-51, 61-63. Transformation belonged to resurrection even when, as in **2 Bar.** 50:1-3, transparent apologetic considerations motivated a brief temporal dissociation of the two. Second, this view would not cohere with the indissoluble connection between transformation and resurrection in the tradition of Jesus' words (Mark 12:24f.; parr. Matt 22:29f.; Luke 20:34-36) as well as in the Resurrection narratives (e.g., Luke 24:31, 36-53; John 20:19-23; Mark 16:12). Third, it is difficult to believe that Paul or any other early Christian could conceive of the resurrection of the dead in total abstraction from the resurrection of Jesus, which in the light of all available evidence was itself invariably conceived in terms of utter uniqueness respecting the past and prototypal status respecting the future (cf. pre-Pauline formulas correlating Jesus' resurrection with the exaltation of the Isaian Servant, such as 1 Cor 15:3-5; Rom 4:25; 8:34; Pauline and para-Pauline formulations such as 1 Cor 15:20, 45; Rom 8:29f.; Acts 26:23). All the material on Jesus' resurrection, early and late, quite unambiguously supposed a transformed corporeity from which, for example, the prospect of death was definitively banished. In short, nothing positively favors the view that in 1 Thess 4 resurrection signified merely the reconstitution of the earthly body, whereas several considerations tell decisively against it.

We return, then, to 1 Cor 15, the keystone in the hypothesis of development. The first part of the text is organized as follows: vv. 1-11; kerygmatic foundation; vv. 12-34 respond to the assertion *anastasis nekrōn ouk estin* (there is no raising of dead men). The question of how

the rest of the text is organized has been diversely answered. Johannes
Weiss proposed that vv. 35-57 were ranged under the rubric of the question *pōs* (how?).[69] Jeremias modified this by attributing a chiastic de-
sign to the text.[70] He first differentiated two questions in v. 35. *Pōs
egeirontai hoi nekroi?* (How are the dead raised?) inquired after the event
of resurrection; *poiǭ de sōmati erchontai?* (with what kind of body do
they come [from the tomb]?) inquired after the new corporeity of the risen. In Jeremias's reading, the questions were answered in inverse order.
Vv. 36-49 offered an answer to "with what kind of body?" and vv. 50-
57 answered the "how?"

　　　　This beguiling view might well impose itself, if in vv. 50-57
we were to find some verifying particular, however, slight, showing
that the text had been consciously conceived in relation to the *pōs*?
(how?) of v. 35. But no such verifying particular occurs in the text.
Moreover, the *pōs* of v. 35 is explicitly concerned with "the dead,"
whereas the passage opening in v. 50 is concerned with the living and
the dead; indeed, it highlights the living ("we shall not all fall asleep,
but we shall all be changed"). Again, the phrase in v. 50, *touto de phē-
mi, adelphoi* (this I tell you, brothers), seems to open a new, if related,
topic (cf. 1 Cor 7:29). It would seem likely, then, that in v. 35 the
words *poiǭ de sōmati?* (with what kind of body?) do not pose a question
distinct from *pōs*, but simply specify the intended thrust of *pōs*. (This,
in fact, is how the great majority of interpreters take it.) With v. 49,
Paul's answer to *pōs* and to *poiǭ de sōmati* is concluded. But this generates a new question: How are vv. 50-57 related to what precedes
them?

　　　　In quest of an answer, we might ask what the *mystērion* (secret) of v. 51 refers to. The text furnishes an immediate answer: we
shall not all fall asleep, but we shall all be changed. Fair enough; but
what is it in these words that up to this point is still secret, i.e., that
has not hitherto been dealt with by Paul? I shall proceed by a process of
elimination.

　　　　First, it was hardly a secret among Paul's Christian contemporaries (for it was no secret in the eschatological instructions whether of
Paul or of other early Christian teachers[71]) that not all would die.
Though some had already died and others, including Paul himself,
might still die, nevertheless the Christian faithful (and Paul hoped to be
among them) would live to see the parousia. The secret, accordingly,

was not future preservation of Christians from death, nor was it a differentiation of two classes at the parousia, the living and the dead.[72]
          Was the secret, then, the fact of the transformation of those ri-
sen from the dead? Hardly. Earlier, Paul had alread said:

> speiretai en phthora, egeiretai en aphtharsia;
> speiretai en atimia, egeiretai en doxe;
> speiretai en astheneia, egeiretai en dynamei;
> speiretai sõma psychikon, egeiretai sõma pneumati-
> kon.
> The sowing takes place in decay, the raising in immu-
> nity to decay;
> the sowing in humiliation, the raising in glory;
> the sowing in weakness, the raising in power;
> a natural body is sown, a spiritual body is raised.
>   1 Cor 15:42b-44a

Was the secret, then, that (unlike **2 Bar.** 50:1-3) the transformation of
the newly risen would take place simultaneously with their resurrection,
namely, at the parousia? Not likely. For Paul resurrection was always
transformative resurrection (vv. 42-49), and it had already been ascribed
to that moment, in v. 23 (*en te parousia autou*, at his coming).
          The secret, then, must be this: *although those still living at
the parousia would not die, they too--like those raised from the dead--
would at that same moment be transformed.*
          The sense of the passage as a whole is clarified in the light of
this interpretative option. The living would indeed not pass through
death, but, like the dead and at the same moment as the dead, they
would be "changed." Christ's victory over the last enemy, death, would
be effected by the transformation of all. Neither *sarx kai haima* nor *he
phthora* could enter into life without being changed.
          Here we should emphasize that Archibald Robertson and Alfred
Plummer,[73] Adolf Schlatter,[74] and Joachim Jeremias[75] were completely
right in observing that *he phthora* in the second line of the distich of v.
50 is not synonymous with *sarx kai haima*; for, contrary to the RSV
and the NEB, *he phthora* does not mean "the perishable";[76] it means
"corruption" (NAB) or "decay" (Goodspeed). In context this must be an
abstractum pro concreto referring to "the dead." The distich, then, states
a predicament: neither the living nor the dead can enter the reign of God

as they are. But with the triumphant announcement "we shall all be changed," the "secret" following the distich addresses and disposes of this predicament. The living as well as the dead will be transformed. Verses 53f. accordingly celebrate the entry into the reign of God respectively of the dead (*to phtharton*, this being of decay) and the living (*to thnēton*, this mortal being).

The whole passage (50-57) was occasioned (as H. A. A. Kennedy had said as long ago as 1904[77]) by an implicit response and final question of the addressee: "We can now form some conception of the resurrection of our dead friends, but what of ourselves? How are those to enter into life who will live to see the parousia?" Just as Paul had insisted (in 1 Cor 15:35-49) that the dead would not return from the grave in earthly bodies, so he now taught (1 Cor 15:50-57) that those living at the parousia would not remain in their earthly bodies either. "We shall all be changed." Thus the duality of the living and the dead at the parousia commands the triumphant conclusion of 1 Cor 15, just as it had commanded the text of 1 Thess 4. Indeed, this duality is also a key to 2 Cor 5.

Of this passage W. D. Davies has asserted that "there is nothing in the text to suggest Paul's hope of surviving to the parousia."[78] Nevertheless, there are in the text two classes of specific indices to just that hope.

The first is a class of linguistic indices which connect 2 Cor 5:2-5 with two passages on final salvation at the parousia, namely, Rom 8:18-27 and 1 Cor 15:50-55. (a) The *stenazein* ("sighing" or "groaning") motif of 2 Cor 5:2-4 is paralleled by the sighing or groaning of Rom 8:22f., which bears on "the redemption of our bodies" at the parousia; (b) the *pneuma-arrabōn* (Spirit-pledge) motif of 2 Cor 5:5 is paralleled by the *pneuma-arrabōn* passage of Rom 8:23 (cf. Rom 8:26f.) In the passage in Romans the presence of the Spirit as foretaste or first installment looks ahead to the final bodily redemption and the consummation of sonship at the parousia; 2 Cor 5:5 is structurally similar. (c) The combined motifs of *thnēton, endysasthai,* and *katapothēnai* in 2 Cor 5:4 are paralleled by the parousia passage of 1 Cor 15:53f.:

> this being of decay [the dead] must put on *(endysasthai)* immunity to decay and this mortal being *(thnēton:* the living) must put on *(endysasthai)* immortality

and when this being of decay puts on immunity
   to decay
and this mortal being puts on immortality,
then the word of Scripture will come true:
"Death has been swallowed up *(katepothē)* in
   victory. . ."

Is there indeed nothing in the text to suggest Paul's hope of surviving to the parousia? In 2 Cor 5:4abc Paul expresses recoil from being stripped (of his earthly body) and desire of being able to "put on (his heavenly body) over" *(ependysasthai)* his earthly body. This "putting on over" evokes the secret of 1 Cor 15:51, we shall not all die but we shall all--the living as well as the dead--be changed at the parousia. The transformation of the living, that is, will not involve disembodiment. In 2 Cor 5:4d, moreover, Paul follows this with phrases inescapably reminiscent of 1 Cor 15:53f., "so that this mortal being [*to thnēton:* the expression is applied, in 1 Cor 15:53f., to the class of those still living at the parousia] may be swallowed up *(katepothē)* by life."

The second class of indices to hope of survival to the parousia in 2 Cor 5:2-5 is not linguistic so much as conceptual. The key ideas are antithetical: being "clothed" (=embodied) versus being "naked" (disembodied), these two states corresponding respectively to the living and to the dead; at the parousia those still living will "put on" a heavenly embodiment "over" their earthly embodiment. This was substantially established by J. N. Sevenster in a 1953 essay which, though sometimes unidiomatic and infelicitous, was a remarkable exegetical achievement.[79] Sevenster not only established the probable sense of *gymnos* (naked=disembodied); he went further, to trace the way in which the text, supposing three states (this life, the disembodied state of the dead, and the consummation-event of resurrection/transformation at the parousia), gave expression to two comparisons. In 2 Cor 5:1-4 the prospect of the third state is far more desirable than the prospect of the second; in 2 Cor 5:6-9 the second state, insofar as it means "being with the Lord," is simply superior to the first. The second state, when set against the third, is far from desirable (vv. 2-4); but, when compared with the first, it is objectively and subjectively preferable (vv. 6-9).

I would add two observations to those of Sevenster. First, the object of the *stenazein* (and *baroumenos*) motif is twofold; recoil from nakedness and longing for the parousia; but the second of these objects

must not be overlooked, for it may be the more fundamental of the two
(cf. Rom 8:22f.). Second, the three states are successive, but not in
fixed universal fashion, for those living at the parousia will miss the
second. From Paul's personal standpoint the best possibility of all
would accordingly be immediate parousia (2 Cor 5:1-4), bringing the
state that outstrips all others.

On the face of it, the text of Phil 1:23 simply confirms that
Paul entertained the conception of an intermediate state between the
present life and the parousia, entered into by death and aptly characterized as being "with the Lord." Those who deny that Paul harbored any
such conception generally find themselves constrained to discover the
parousia motif here. But in this text, at least, there really is not so
much as a hint that the parousia is intended.[80]

Let me summarize our results by repeating and responding to
the "crucial questions." Apropos of 1 Thess 4, did Paul understand resurrection as the return of the dead to the conditions of the present life?
No; nothing in the text or context supports this reading, whereas numerous considerations tell against and exclude it.

Apropos of 1 Cor 15:50-57, does v. 50 rule out the notion of
corporeal participation in final salvation? No, the issue is not "body
versus spirit" but "body in the present age--be it the flesh and blood of
the living or the decayed body of the dead--versus body transfigured and
immortal in the reign of God." Second, what does the *mystērion* (secret) of vv. 51f. refer to? It refers to the destiny of the living at the Parousia: They, too, like those risen from the dead, will be transformed at
the parousia.

Apropos of 2 Cor 5, do vv. 2-4 refer to the parousia or to the
acquisition of a resurrection-body immediately upon death? Linguistic
and conceptual indices point to the parousia. Are vv. 6-9 concerned with
the parousia or with an intermediate state after death? They bear on an
intermediate state, just as Phil 1:23 does.

Final result: there is a total lack of persuasive evidence that
Paul's teaching on the resurrection of the dead underwent significant development either between 1 Thess 4 and 1 Cor 15, or between 1 Cor 15
and 2 Cor 5. Allusion to "the intermediate state" occurs at least in 2
Cor 5 and Phil 1, apparently without entailing any change in Paul's
conception of the resurrection of the dead and transformation of the living at the parousia.

III

Anyone who treats the charged expressions encoun-
tered in cultural history exclusively from the
'historical standpoint' is in that very measure incapa-
ble of genuine interpretation.

Josef Pieper[81]

I have offered above a swift survey of the generations-long debate between maximalists and minimalists on whether Paul's view of
the resurrection of the dead underwent significant development. I have
concluded that the case of the minimalists is much stronger than that of
their adversaries from Pfleiderer to the present day. But what is the significance of the debate itself and of the admittedly swiftly-sketched resolution thereof that I have just presented?

The debate has hermeneutical significance, and can perhaps be
made to yield a hermeneutical lesson.

Hermeneutics bears on the understanding of texts. A basic feature of such understanding is the triangular structure of reader, text, and
referent.[82] The reader understands the text by understanding what it is
about, and he understands what the text is about by understanding the
text. If in form this circle is vicious, in fact it is broken upon by acts
of insight which, alternating between text and referent, spiral toward an
ever clearer and firmer understanding of both.

Hans-Georg Gadamer recalled Luther's statement of the issue:
"whoever does not understand the things cannot draw the sense from the
words: *(qui non intelligit res non potest ex verbis sensum elicere).* [83]
There are more positive formulations of essentially the same principle:
(a) "preunderstanding" of the text is given in independent access to its
referent *(die Sache:* not "the subject matter," but the referent in its integral relevant reality), and (b) an appreciative understanding of the text
supposes a "life-relationship" to the referent and hence to the text.[84] It
follows that there is nothing so futile as positivistic objectivism, with
its "principle of the empty head,"[85] according to which the less the interpreter has in his head, the more likely he is to avoid "reading into the
text" his own opinions and prejudices. To understand a lecture on color,
it is no advantage to be free of prejudices by having been born blind.

On the contrary, the blind man finds discussion of color obscure precisely because he lacks independent access to the referent, i.e., to color.

It may be worth our while, then, to pause over the referent or *die Sache*. And in the present instance this is--what? The resurrection of the dead, an event conceived as belonging to a climactic future, when the risen and glorified Christ will destroy the last enemy, death.

What can be our access to an as yet nonexistent event? It is not empirical in the sense that our access to the everyday events of our lives is. Nor is it well exemplified by access to history, though history, too, intends events nonexistent in our own present. The access to history is through a reconstructive activity of intelligence working on data variously mediated to us, but we cannot construct the future as we reconstruct the past. The past, however, is not irrelevant here, for in the texts on the resurrection of the dead the past event of the resurrection of Jesus grounds the eschatological future:

> Now the truth is that God has raised Christ from
> the dead,
> the first-fruits of those who have fallen asleep;
>
> for, just as through a man there came death,
> so the more surely through a man there shall come
> the resurrection of the dead;
>
> . . .just as we have borne the image of the man
> of dust,
> so the more surely shall we bear the image of the
> heavenly man as well (1 Cor 15:20f., 49)

What is the carrier of meaning here, if not the correlatives, promise and hope? In the light of the election-historical mission of Jesus, the promise is fused with his victory over death; he is accordingly the ground of hope. So the texts are expressions of hope, suffused with hope, an intelligent hope that insists on coherent claims to truth (1 Cor 15:12-34).

Now, that ancients observed that interpretation belongs to the arts that do not impart wisdom, for the object of interpretation is not what is true but only what is said.[86] Formally, no doubt, this is true, but it is an ambiguous truth and can turn into a trap. For if the interpreter who wrestles with the truth of the text may easily find himself wringing from it just what he himself takes to be true, the interpreter who stands aside from the struggle over truth may just as easily, and perhaps more fatefully, trivialize the text, missing the drama of its depths.

This is the point of the above epigraph taken from Josef Pieper. The deadliest evasion of all, Pieper seems to be saying, is the assumption of a closed, impermeable "observer viewpoint," from which one may spend one's whole interpretative effort busily tracing "influences" and "derivations," "developments" in the writer and his record of subsequent impact *(Wirkungsgeschichte).* [87]

Here, it seems to me, lies the hermeneutical lesson of the last hundred years of disconcertingly shallow interpretation of Paul on the resurrection of the dead. In dealing with the Pauline texts, Teichmann, Dodd, and Knox (for example) practiced trajectory criticism. Each posited a distinctive sort of trajectory, but behind all three hypotheses lay a common repugnance toward apocalypticism as intrinsically perverse and illusory. None of the three pushed through this self-imposed barrier to *die Sache.* The upshot in each case was casual dismissal of the scenario which Paul presented as the central message of Christian hope.

The error common to the line that started with Pfleiderer did not lie simply in the assumption of an "observer viewpoint" and of an exclusively historical conception of the interpreter's task, nor did it lie simply in a too facile appeal to the category of "development." The main seeds of error were sown in estrangement from particularities of the text and, above all, from the referent itself *(die Sache).* This controlling estrangement--the chronic vice of one great wing of biblical scholarship since Spinoza--converted the observer viewpoint into an alienated viewpoint and the historical task into the construction of chimerical trajectories, from supernatural Judaic fantasies to a reasonable Hellenistic wisdom (Teichmann), from harsh and fanatic dualism to maturity of experience (Dodd), from fumbling efforts to fairly effective efforts of accommodation to the Gentile mind (Knox). As *die Sache* disappeared from view, "development" dominated interpretation. Moving in a diametrically opposite direction, let me conclude with some positive considerations bearing on recovery of *die Sache.*

Peter Stuhlmacher has made the point that, as a pre-Christian theme, the resurrection of the dead was far more firmly rooted in the life of postexilic and postbiblical Israel than has generally been acknowledged.[88] With the Christian gospel, however, a new and unique hope was born in the world. It lay at the heart of the Christian movement, indissolubly bound to the risen Jesus, a fundamental facet of the Christ-event.

"Every historical event," wrote Heinrich Schlier in one of his later essays, "presses toward its text and has its text. Otherwise, it is not an 'event' in the full sense of the word. The complete text of the event we are considering--the resurrection of Jesus--is the New Testament."[89] If the text corresponding to the resurrection of Jesus is the New Testament, this text has peak passages, where hope founded on the risen Christ finds powerful and eloquent expression. Among them is chapter 15 of Paul's first letter to the Corinthians. Though the past few generations have shown intense interest in the retrieval of Christian eschatology, this particular text has repeatedly proved to be among the most vexatious and opaque, for subjective reasons such as I have just evoked.[90] On the other hand, since the Second World War the West has witnessed the flowering of a rich if extremely diverse literature--psychological, phenomenological, philosophic, and theological--on human hope: its role in the establishment of personality, in effecting the transition from absorption with "having" to communion with "being," its reference to personal fulfillment, its irreducibility to the this-worldly, its finally transcendent reference.[91] This literature is a resource for finding access to *die Sache,* the referent of the great hope-passages of the New Testament, preeminently including those on the resurrection of the dead.

Among the striking ascertainments to emerge from contemporary explorations of hope is the linguistic distinction between "to hope to" or "to hope that" and "to hope" simply.[92] Paul, for example, tells the Corinthians: "I hope to spend some time with you, if the Lord permits" (1 Cor 16:7). Here is hope that belongs to the vast category of human hopes *(espoirs);* it is not hope simply and absolutely *(espér-ance),* as in the words "if we have hoped in Christ for this life only, we are the most pitiable people of all" (1 Cor 15:19).

In one of his penetrating treatments of hope, Pieper alluded to the phenomenological studies of Herbert Plügge, a clinical physician who observed among his patients that these two classes of hope--everyday hope and fundamental hope--stood in paradoxical relationship to one another. Fundamental hope--not directed toward anything that one could "have," but bent on "being" and "selfness," on "salvation of the person"--emerged at the very moment that everyday hopes collapsed. "Out of the loss of common, everyday hope true hope arises."[93]

In Pieper's view, the test case was the situation of the martyr, for whom the last wisp of human hope was gone. "We can hardly speak of hope, if none exists for the martyr."[94] Indeed, this is precisely the level at which Paul pitched his passionate expositions and expressions of hope. He dealt with fundamental hope, having to do with being, with salvation of the person. What Paul added to the mysterious human phenomenon of such hope was reference to the gospel, that is, to the news of God's act on behalf of every human being in the death and resurrection of Jesus, made Christ and Lord. This gave a unique grounding to "fundamental hope" and, by adding certain dimensions to it through reference to Jesus' own resurrection, it gave this hope the profound and permanent form that it has in the Pauline letters.

I asked above why recognition of *die Sache* (which we may now characterize, shorthand-fashion, as fundamental hope transvalued by the gospel) was so fitful and dim in the tradition that began with Otto Pfleiderer's gratuitous guesswork. I first answered that hardly anything undermines interpretation more grievously than strict limitation to the stance of the outside observer. In the instance that we have been considering, this invited a too facile recourse to the heuristic category "development." I added that a deeper, more potent factor had been alienation vis-à-vis aspects of the text and its referent. Finally, I should remark that the fundamental hope of 1 Thess 4, 1 Cor 15, and 2 Cor 5 is among those "things of God" that according to Paul no one understands except by the Spirit of God (1 Cor 2:11; cf. Mark 4:11; parr. Matt 13:11; Luke 8:10; Matt 16:17; 11:25-27; par Luke 10:21f.; John 6:44; 15:5, etc.). This is more than a home truth repeatedly verified by experience. It is sheer hermeneutical realism, founded on a requisite proportion between the knower and the known.[95]

NOTES

1. See Owen Chadwick, **From Bossuet to Newman: The Idea of Doctrinal Development** (Cambridge: Cambridge University Press, 1957) x.

2. John Henry Newman, **An Essay on the Development of Christian Doctrine** (Garden City: Doubleday, 1960). The Essay first appeared in 1845; a revised edition appeared in 1878.

3. This is not to say that Baur was above all and nothing but a Hegelian, nor that the Hegelianism of Baur was pure Hegel. It is to say that the pattern of Hegelian evolutionism had an impact on studies of early Christianity and that this was more through Baur than through any other single 19th-century biblical scholar (e.g., D. F. Strauss, Bruno Bauer, et al.).

4. Richard Kabisch, **Die Eschatologie des Paulus in ihren Zusammenhängen mit dem Gesamtbegriff des Paulinismus** (Göttingen: Vandenhoeck & Ruprecht, 1893); Johannes Weiss, **Jesus' Proclamation of the Kingdom of God** (Philadelphia: Fortress, 1971) [German original, 1892; revised and expanded version, 1900]).

5. Albert Schweitzer, **Paul and His Interpreters: A Critical History** (London: Black, 1912 [German original, 1911]) 58-63.

6. Otto Pfleiderer, **Paulinism: A Contribution to the History of Primitive Christian Theology** (2 vols.; London: Williams and Norgate, 1877 [German original, 1873]).

7. Herman Lüdemann, **Die Anthropologie des Apostels Paulus und ihre Stellung innerhalb seiner Heilslehre** (Kiel: Universitätsbuchhandlung, 1872); Pfleiderer, **Paulinism** 1, 18.

8. Ibid. 1, 18.

9. 121121121 Ibid. 1 19.

10. Ibid. 1, 20.

11. See Franz Schnabel, **Deutsche Geschichte im neunzehnten Jahrhundert. 4: Die religiöse Kräfte** (Freiburg: Herder, 1936, 31955.

12. Pfleiderer, **Paulinism** 1, 276.

13. Ibid. 1, 259; see also 260-71.

14. Otto Pfleiderer, **Das Urchristentum, seine Schriften und Lehren in geschichtlichem Zusammenhang** (Berlin: Reimer, 1887).

15. Schweitzer, **Paul and His Interpreters**, 71.

16. See n. 4 above. For a summary see Schweitzer, **Paul and His Interpreters**, 58-63.

Auferstehung und Gericht und ihre Beziehungen zur jüdischen Apokalyptik (Freiburg-Leipzig: Mohr, 1896).

18. Ibid. 33-62.

19. Ibid. ("Die völlige Vernichtung") 53.

20. Ibid. 62.

21. Ibid. 65-67.

22. Ibid. 67.

23. Ibid. 74.

24. R. H. Charles, A Critical History of the Doctrine of a Future Life in Israel, in Judaism, and in Christianity (London: Black, 1899).

25. Ibid. 394f.

26. H. A. A. Kennedy, St Paul's Conceptions of the Last Things (London: Hodder and Stoughton, 1904).

27. Ibid. 24; my emphasis.

28. Ibid. 261.

29. Ibid. 269.

30. Ibid. 270.

31. Ibid. 272.

32. August Sabatier, L'Apôtre Paul, esquisse d'une histoire de sa pensée (Paris: Fischbacher, 1870).

33. See Pfleiderer, Paulinism 1, 259, 265f.; Schweitzer, Paul and His Interpreters 69-72.

34. Schweitzer, Paul and His Interpreters 76.

35. For his attribution to Paul of an elaborately detailed eschatology, see Albert Schweitzer, The Mysticism of Paul the Apostle (New York: Holt, 1931) esp. 65-68. The main lines of this solution appear as a heuristic scheme in Paul and His Interpreters, 240-45.

36. C. H. Dodd, "The Mind of Paul: I"(1933) and "The Mind of Paul: II" (1934), in C. H. Dodd, New Testament Studies (Manchester: Manchester University Press, 1953, repr. 1967) 67-82, 83-128.

37. C. H. Dodd, "The Mind of Paul: II" 108.

38. Ibid. 126.

39. Ibid. 113.

40. Ibid. 121.

41. Ibid. 123f.

42. Ibid. 124.

43. Ibid. 125.

44. Ibid. 126.

45. C. H. Dodd, "The Mind of Paul: I," 81.

46. Wilfred L. Knox, St Paul and the Church of the Gentiles (Cambridge: Cambridge University Press, 1939) 1-26. Hereafter, Paul

tiles (Cambridge: Cambridge University Press, 1939) 1-26. Hereafter, **Paul and Gentiles.**

47. **Paul and Gentiles** 126. Knox's phrase "fairly prominent" understates the matter. The concrete form of realized eschatology in early Christianity was the kerygma of Christ's resurrection, to which the supposition of "imminent parousia" long remained firmly attached. C. H. Dodd, in chapters 2 and 3 of his **Parables of the Kingdom** (London: Nisbet, 1935), presented a brilliant piece of detective work in explanation of the origins of this scheme. A deftly corrected version of Dodd's hypothesis appeared in a review essay by Joachim Jeremias, "Eine neue Schau der Zukunftsaussagen Jesu," *Theologische Blätter* 20 (1941) 216-22. This recovery of Jesus' own eschatology and its transformation in early Christianity had been presaged by Wilhelm Weiffenbach, **Der Wiederkunftsgedanke Jesu nach den Synoptikern kritisch untersucht und dargestellt** (Leipzig: Breitkopf und Härtel, 1873). For a summary of the whole, see B. F. Meyer, **The Aims of Jesus** (London: SCM, 1979) 202-9.

48. **Paul and Gentiles** 127.

49. Ibid. 128.

50. Ibid. 137.

51. Ibid. 140.

52. Ibid. 136.

53. Ibid. 141.

54. W. D. Davies, **Paul and Rabbinic Judaism: Some Rabbinic Elements in Pauline Theology** (Philadelphia: Fortress, 1948, 41980) 311-20.

55. Ibid. 311.

56. Ibid.

57. Ibid, 314.

58. Ibid. 317.

59. Ibid. 316.

60. Joachim Jeremias, " 'Flesh and Blood Cannot Inherit the Kingdom of God' (1 Cor. XV. 50)," in **Abba: Studien zur neutestamentlichen Theologie und Zeitgeschichte** (Göttingen: Vandenhoeck & Ruprecht, 1966) 298-307.

61. Ibid. 298-302.

62. Joachim Gnilka, "Contemporary Exegetical Understanding of the Resurrection of the Body," in **Immortality and Resurrection,** ed. Pierre Benoit and Roland Murphy (New York: Herder and Herder, 1970) 129-41; see 131 on Teichmann's thesis that hope of immortality undermined belief in resurrection.

63. On the first agreement with Teichmann, see Gerd Luedemann, **Paul Apostle to the Gentiles: Studies in Chronology** (Philadelphia:

Fortress, 1984) 212; on all three agreements, see G. Luedemann, "The Hope of the Early Paul: From the Foundation-Preaching at Thessalonika to 1 Cor 15:51-57." *Perspectives in Religious Studies* 7 (1980) 195-201; cf. 195f. on the first point, 197 on the second, 200 on the third. To be sharply distinguished from Luedemann's work is the proposal of Joseph Plevnik, "The Taking Up of the Faithful and the Resurrection of the Dead in 1 Thessalonians 4:13-18," *Catholic Biblical Quarterly* 46 (1984) 274-83. Plevnik argues that the transformative moment is present in 1 Thess 4, but located in the "taking up" of the still living and of the resurrected dead "to meet the Lord." If Plevnik is correct, it follows that there is a development between 1 Thess 4 and 1 Cor 15: transformation is located in the very resurrection of the dead and in the simultaneous and parallel change of the living. This seems to me possible, but somewhat less likely than the view that I propose: Paul always conceived resurrection as transformative, but in 1 Cor 15 he added the "secret" that the living, too, would be transformed.

      64.   Jacques Dupont, **SYN CHRISTOI: L'Union avec le Christ selon saint Paul** (Louvain: Nauwelaerts; Paris: Desclée, 1952) 135-53; Rudolf Bultmann, **The Second Letter to the Corinthians** ed. E. Dinkler (Minneapolis: Augsburg, 1985); Paul Hoffmann, **Die Toten in Christus** (Münster: Aschendorff, 1966, 31978).

      65.   Friedrich Lang, **2 Korinther 5, 1-10 in der neueren Forschung** (Tübingen: Mohr, 1973).

      66.   Rodolphe Morissette, "L' Expression SOMA en 1 Cor 15 et dans la littérature paulinienne," *Revue des sciences philosophiques et théologiques* 56 (1972) 223-39; "La condition de ressuscité, 1 Corinthiens 15:35-49: Structure littéraire de la péricope," *Biblica* 53 (1972) 208-28; "L'Antithèse entre le 'psychique' et le 'pneumatique' en 1 Corinthiens, XV, 44 à 46," *Revue des sciences religieuses* 46 (1972) 97-143; "Un midrash sur la mort (I Cor., XV, 54c à 75)," *Revue biblique* 79 (1972) 161-88. Perhaps the most striking exploitation of ancient Jewish parallels is found in the article published in *Biblica*. One result is the improbability that Paul's opponents in Corinth argued for a resurrection as having already taken place.

      67.   Luedemann, as we have noted (see n. 63 above), is among the exceptions.

      68.   Jeremias, "Flesh and Blood," 307. This *faux pas* was occasioned, it seems clear to me, by Jeremias's defective specification of the referent of "secret" in 1 Cor 15:51f. Having drawn a sharp conceptual distinction between "resurrection" and "transformation," Jeremias referred the "secret" to the timing of the latter. But, as we shall see, there is no evidence that Paul himself diferentiated resurrection and the transformation that was part and parcel of resurrection. If in 1 Cor 15:35-49 he had already thematized resurrection precisely as transformative, Paul must have referred the "secret" of v. 51, not (as Jeremias

maintained) to the idea that the change of the living and the dead is to take place immediately at the parousia (rather than after the judgment, as in **2 Bar** 51), but simply to the transformation of the living at the Parousia (as the counterpart of the transformative resurrection of the dead). Günther Bornkamm, ""*mysterion, myeo,*" **Theological Dictionary of the New Testament** 4, 802-28, at 823: the secret in question is "what Paul tells the Corinthians about the change which will overtake Christians still alive at the parousia." This I take to be exact.

69. Johannes Weiss, **Der erste Korintherbrief** (Göttingen: Vandenhoeck & Ruprecht, 1910) 345, 353, 380.

70. "Flesh and Blood" 304f.

71. Regularly assumed in Matthew, Mark, and Luke is an apocalyptic thesis according to which the Son of man will come to gather his own before they are exterminated in the eschatological ordeal. Two examples out of many: "But when they persecute you in one town, flee to the next; for truly I say to you, you will not have gone through all the towns of Israel before the Son of man comes" (Matt 10:23); "there are some standing here who will not taste death before the Son of man comes" (Mark 9:1: parr. Matt 16:28; Luke 9:27).

72. It should be remembered that in writing to the Thessalonians Paul's point was not that those still living would not die (that was taken as settled), but that the dead would not fail to join them in salvation at the parousia.

73. Archibald Robertson and Alfred Plummer, **A Critical and Exegetical Commentary on the First Epistle of St. Paul to the Corinthians** (Edinburgh: Clark, 21914) 375f.

74. Adolf Schlatter, **Paulus der Bote Jesu: Eine Deutung seiner Briefe an die Korinther** (Stuttgart: Calwer, 1934) 441f.

75. "Flesh and Blood," 299-301.

76. In Paul the sense of *phthora* as decay/corruption is usually quite clear; where a sense approximating "perishability" is required, it is expressed by combining *phthora* with some other term; see, e.g., Rom 8:21, "bondage to decay" *(he douleia tēs phthoras).*

77. **Last Things**, 259.

78. **Paul and Rabbinic Judaism**, 311.

79. J. N. Sevenster, "Some Remarks on the GYMNOS in II Cor V 3," in **Studia Paulina in honorem Johannis de Zwaan septuagenarii**, ed. J. N. Sevenster and W. C. van Unnik (Haarlem: Bohn, 1953) 202-14.

80. See the treatment of Dupont, **SYN CHRISTOI** (note 64 above) 171-84.

81. Josef Pieper, **Was heisst Interpretation?** Rheinisch-Westfälische Akademie der Wissenschaften, Vorträge G 234 (Opladen: West-

deutscher Verlag, 1979) 21.

82. See Emerich Coreth, **Grundfragen der Hermeneutik: Ein philosphischer Beitrag** (Freiburg: Herder, 1969) 64f., 116f., 123-27.

83. See Hans-Georg Gadamer, **Truth and Method** (New York: Seabury, 1975) 151.

84. In biblical scholarship the widespread use of the term "preunderstanding" is attributable to the influence of Rudolf Bultmann, "The Problem of Hermeneutics," in **Essays Philosophical and Theological** (London: SCM, 1958) 234-61, at 239. On the sense of *die Sache,* cf. Coreth, **Grundfragen** (page references as above, n. 82); on "life-relation" see Bultmann, "The Problem of Hermeneutics," 241-43, 252f., 255f.

85. See the analysis of Bernard Lonergan, **Method in Theology** (London: Darton, Longmann & Todd, 1972) 157.

86. **Epinomis** 975c (Platonic dialogue of doubtful authenticity).

87. Pieper, **Was heisst Interpetation?** 21f. Pieper refers to C. S. Lewis's brilliant evocation of the theme in **The Screwtape Letters.** See **The Screwtape Letters and Screwtape Proposes a Toast** (London: Bles, 241966) 121: "The Historical Point of View, put briefly, means that when a learned man is presented with any statement in an ancient author, the one question he never asks is whether it is true."

88. Peter Stuhlmacher, "Das Bekenntnis zur Auferstehung Jesu von den Toten und die biblische Theologie," *Zeitschrift für Theologie und Kirche* 70 (1973) 365-403; see 383-89.

89. Heinrich Schlier, **Über die Auferstehung Jesu Christi** (Einsiedeln: Johannesverlag, 1968, 41975) 6.

90. For evidence of the acute discomfort that this chapter caused Rudolf Bultmann, see the citations in James M. Robinson, "Hermeneutic since Barth," in **The New Hermeneutic,** ed. James M. Robinson and J. B. Cobb Jr. (New York: Harper and Row, 1964) 1-77, esp. 31-33.

91. A few representative works in which these themes have come to expression: Joseph Pieper, **On Hope** (San Francisco: Ignatius, 1986) [German original, 1935]; Gabriel Marcel, **Homo Viator: Introduction to a Metaphysics of Hope** (Chicago: Regnery, 1951); Ernst Bloch, **Das Prinzip Hoffnung** (Frankfurt am Main: Suhrkamp, 1959, rev. 1970); Herbert Plügge, **Wohlbefinden und Missbefinden: Beiträge zu einer medizinischen Anthropologie** (Tübingen: Niemeyer, 1962); Robert O Johann, "The Meaning of Hope," *The Theologian* 8 (1952) 21-30; Pierre Teilhard de Chardin, **The Future of Man** (London: Collins [Fontana], 1959); Jürgen Moltmann, **Theology of Hope: On the Ground and the Implications of a Christian Eschatology** (London: SCM, 1967).

92. See, e.g., Joseph Pieper, **Hope and History** (New York: Herder and Herder, 1969) 21-25.

93. See the account in Pieper, **Hope and History** 24-26; the last citation is from 26.

94. Ibid. 32.

95. Proportion in this context signifies, first, a broad isomorphism of structures of knowing and structures of being: see Bernard Lonergan, **Insight: A Study of Human Understanding** (New York: Longmans, 1958) 115, 499-502; second, a narrower correlation of knowing and being, which evokes the related themes of horizons, conversions, connaturality: see Lonergan, **Method in Theology** 235-93. As the break with cognitional myth (or, in other words, intellectual conversion) is requisite to an adequate account of cognition, so "moral knowledge is the proper possession only of morally good men" (**Method** 240) and real grasp of "the things of God" supposes religious conversion. As Pieper put it in **Was heisst Interpretation?** 29: "So wenig ein amusischer Mensch ein Gedicht zu verstehen und zu interpretieren vermag, so wenig kann es einen ungläubigen Theologen geben--wofern man. . .unter Theologie den Versuch versteht, Offenbarung gültig zu interpretieren."

VI

OBJECTIVITY AND SUBJECTIVITY

IN

HISTORICAL CRITICISM OF THE GOSPELS

Over the past decade or so there has been no lack of publications treating the criteria for historicity judgments on gospel traditions.[1] This is not to say that a solid consensus has begun to heave into view. The present situation is characterized rather by confusion and disagreement. Confusion has been the legacy of the night battle, now petering out, between biblicists and methodical sceptics. Disagreement bears partly on which criteria are most cogent and which most regularly apposite,[2] partly on whether any of the criteria are in fact up to the task for which they have been devised.[3]

The purpose of this study is, first, to offer an account of the bases on which judgments of historicity and non-historicity are properly made; second, to consider an objection, namely, that in light of the subjectivity with which indices to historicity are applied, it seems to follow that they are ineffective; third, to offer a response to this objection, which takes account of subjectivity as component and condition of objectivity.

I

By and large, treatments of criteria for establishing the words of Jesus as historical have been content to pass over in silence such

questions as how exactly the criteria fit into the total process of con-
ducting a historical investigation, whether the criteria have a limited object or are supposed to bear decisively on every act of historical judgment, and how the criteria of historicity relate to the distinction
between early and late literary traditions.

Having now used the word "criteria" many times, I shall
henceforward abandon it in favor of the more modest term "indices."
None of the so-called criteria of historicity are in the strict sense norms
or standards invariably relevant and requisite to the inference of historicity. That Jesus had disciples, that he affirmed the authority of the scriptures, that he shared in the life of synagogue and temple, that he understood God (whom he called Father) as the God of Abraham, Isaac, and
Jacob, of Moses and David and Isaiah, all this is historical, though it
all accords with the Judaism of the time. Again, that he proclaimed the
reign of God, that he often taught in parables, that he addressed God as
Abba, that he "cleansed" the temple, that he suffered crucifixion under
Pontius Pilate, all this is historical, though it all accords with the faith
of the earliest Church. Since all these data, regardless of their accord
with Judaism and Christianity, are by common consent historical, we
might quietly drop the hard-line language of "criteria" as well as the
doctrinaire sophistry of "methodical scepticism" (data must be taken to
be unhistorical till proved otherwise by the ascertainment of their simultaneous discontinuity with Judaism and early Christianity). This is
mock-rigor, which does not hold in practice. On the contrary, in the
cases listed above it is historicity that holds, and is all but universally
acknowledged to hold, despite the lack of discontinuity with the post-
Easter Church or the lack of originality vis-à-vis Judaism.

The error lay in misconceiving two distinct indices to historicity as a single acid-test failing which any given datum must be methodically branded non-historical. In other words, the question of these two
indices has been thoroughly confused by their having been, first, mistakenly understood in terms of criteria in the strict sense; second, mistakenly amalgamated (by Ernst Käsemann)[4] so as to make up a single criterion; third, mistakenly represented (under the catch-phrase "methodical
scepticism") as the only effective test of historicity. It is of course true
that discontinuity with the post-Easter Church on the part of various
traditions on Jesus, or the originality of various traditions vis-à-vis Judaism, are precious indications of historicity. Indeed, discontinuity with
the post-Easter Church, of itself and without the need of simultaneous

originality vis-à-vis Judaism, is a particularly solid index to the historicity of data. But both indices function *in sensu aiente* and not *in sensu neganti:* their presence positively tells in favor of historicity, but their absence does not positively tell against historicity. By denying that the absence of these indices positively tells against historicity, or justifies the methodical ranging of data in the non-historicity column, one breaks cleanly with the grounding of historicity judgments on mere assumption.

In the allotting of a large role to assumption the school of methodical scepticism was matched by that of methodical credulity. If the first group assumed non-historicity till proved otherwise, the second, under the banner *in dubio pro tradito,* assumed historicity unless it was ruled out by flatly contradictory data or data so contrary and unharmonizable as to infringe on the presumption of Jesus' psychological unity.

This kindly attitude toward assumption has many roots, and in the above-mentioned two schools it doubtless has some disparate roots, but we should not overlook a common root, namely, the critic's recoil from acknowledging that he does not know. All too human, the recoil is understandable but hardly justifiable. Why should assumption be allowed to dispose of residues, disguising the critic's actual state of knowledge? The naive biblicist, though readily believing that literary doublets regularly reflect repeated historical events, can hardly claim to know this. He merely believes it. Likewise, the methodical sceptic cannot fail to be aware that if authentic materials contrary to Church tendencies were conserved in the gospel tradition, authentic materials in accord with Church tendencies were *a fortiori* conserved. This means taht there are traditions which in fact are historical but which, since they fail the acid-test of discontinuity with early Christianity, cannot be identified as historical. And though the methodical sceptic dutifully ranges in the non-historicity column all traditions that are in continuity with early Christianity (e.g., the Last Supper accounts), he knows that he does not know which of them are historical and which are not. In short, he knows that he does not really know whether there was a Last Supper. Why then systematically range the Last Supper accounts in the non-historicity column rather than acknowledge that in terms of his own actual knowledge the historical question remains moot? In form his negative conclusion is sham knowledge. It adds, not to real knowledge, but to the sludge of gratuitously opaque or misleading procedures.

In the context of historical investigation there is point in distinguishing between data and conclusions. Data belong to the premises, conclusions to the results, of such investigation. Both involve judgments on historicity. If judgments on data are more fundamental, those that constitute conclusions are more significant, for the point of the historical enterprise is reconstruction. New questions, especially if they are satisfactorily answered, move historical inquiry forward.

The allusion to "new questions" implies a quarrel with the assumption that legitimate historical questions are somehow to be found preformed, if not ready-made, in the sources. Intelligent men, observed R. G. Collingwood, do not ask themselves questions that they do not think they can answer;[5] but granted that sensible limit, all questions are fair game. Among numerous New Testament critics, however, a certain phobia respecting such "new questions" seems to hang on, neurosis-like, from the era of positivism. Kerygma theologians, for example, winced not only at the religious significance that their Liberal predecessors attached to Jesus' "personality," but also at the very idea of posing a question (namely, about the personality of Jesus) that went beyond the concerns of the sources. Consistency, happily, did not inhibit these same critics from posing their own new questions.

Historicity is one dimension of a satisfactory answer to a new historical question, but here the judgment of historicity is immediately guieded, not by indices to the historicity of data, but by the argumentation that organizes and illuminates data by giving satisfactory answers to questions about the understanding of data.

Moreover, the network of relations that comes to light in the course of an investigation is likely to modify some of the inquirer's initial judgments on data, supplying new grounds for confirming or reversing them. Thus, Suetonius provided a notice to the effect that Nero at one time intended a Roman evacuation of Britain. Collingwood rejected this, not because some better authority contradicted it, but because his reconstruction of Nero's policy, based on Tacitus, would not allow him to think that Suetonius was right.

> And if I am told that this is merely to say I prefer
> Tacitus to Suetonius, I confess that I do; but I do so
> just because I find myself able to incorporate what
> Tacitus tells me into a coherent and continuous pic-
> ture of my own, and cannot do this for Suetonius.[6]

Let us consider a testimony from New Testament literature that, unlike Suetonius's notice, finds confirmation elsewhere in the sources. The *apo*-formula used by Paul in 1 Cor 11:23 indicates the intention to specify Jesus as the originator of the eucharistic tradition.[7] If, in addition to this, Paul can be thought to be knowledgeable on the matter and free of the suspicion of deceit, one may infer historicity. Though this direct pattern of inference is rare, owing to the rarely concrete indication that historicity is specifically conprehended within the intention of the text, it nevertheless illustrates the non-monopoly of oblique patterns of inference (indices like discontinuity and originality, which make no appeal to evidence of historical intention) on the establishing of the historicity of data.

Finally, we should fill out the account of indices that pertain to oblique patterns of inference. None of these indices are of themselves decisive, i.e., decisive in principle and so invariably decisive. Their usefulness, however, is evident; or, rather, their usefulness is evident once one had satisfied oneself that the account of the gospel tradition offered by the first form critics is simply inadequate and misleading. For it should be acknowledged that, if the first Christian communities produced the gospel tradition largely with reference to their own concerns and largely without concern for the actual memory of Jesus, then discussion of these indices is superfluous. It may be well, then, to entertain at least briefly the prior question: does the gospel tradition provide us with data, and abundant data, on Jesus?

The faith-formulations of the earliest Church (pre-Pauline formulas conserved by Paul, e.g., 1 Cor 11:23-25; 15:3-5, and archaic motifs such as occur in Acts 10:34-40) illuminate the structure of the earliest Christian faith as a faith that intends actual historical events.[8] Early faith-formulations accordingly offer heuristic guidance for a judgment on the hypothesis that, as penetrated by the faith of the earliest Church, gospel traditions dispensed with the memory of Jesus, or freely and radically revised it to serve new communitarian purposes. Since the earliest Christian faith-formulations point in an altogether different direction, namely, to a faith that intends historical events and to the collective witness of the Jerusalem community gathered around "Cephas and. . .the twelve" (1 Cor 15; 5), we should positively expect gospel traditions to be filled with the memory of Jesus. This expectation hinges on a generic continuity between two liturgical and catechetical traditions: the earliest faith-formulas and their contemporary narrative counterpart, the gospel tradition. To suppose the contrary is, moreover, to overlook major data: first, that the disciples of Jesus could hardly have undertaken a mission to Israel unless they could plausibly claim to be presenting, in the light of the scriptures, an eye-witness account of Jesus;[9] second, that the reference back to Jesus--the account of the gospel tradition implicitly offered by the gospel tradition--is massively commended to us by the tradition-oriented character of the ancient world, specifically including the world of Palestinian Judaism.[10] In this light and only in this light can discussion of multiple and multiform attestation and of linguistic indices to historicity make positive sense.

Multiple attestation figures in the discussion insofar as "multiple" points to "early" and "early" to "historical." Both links should be understood to hold with statistical generality, neither being guaranteed in individual cases; hence, multiple attestation functions as an effective index only in conjunction with other indices. The same holds for the multiform attestation of a tradition (e.g., in narrative material and sayings material, or as parable and as saying, etc.). The operative assumptions are, first, that a datum from early tradition is more likely than one from late tradition to have found attestation in independent lines and forms of tradition; second, a datum from early tradition has a greater probability of historicity than one from late tradition. Caution is obviously in order: multiple attestation of itself cannot guarantee a given tradition as early, nor is early tradition by that mere fact guaranteed as historical. Since the most authoritative witnesses to the career of Jesus did not immediately disappear form the stage of history and the ongoing life of the Church, later traditions could have arisen, and no doubt did arise, to correct or clarify earlier traditions in historically valid fashion. We cannot then exclude the possibility that a later tradition might be historically better than a more primitive tradition. Finally, there is nothing to prevent the most primitive form of a tradition from appearing in a late, even the latest, redaction.

Linguistic indices pioneered over the past century reached remarkable refinement in the gospel criticism of Joachim Jeremias and are epitomized in the first chapter of his New Testament theology.[11] They include "ways of speaking preferred by Jesus" (the use of the divine passive, antithetic parallelism, rhythmic patterns in two-beat, three-beat, four-beat, and *qina* metre, alliteration, assonance, paronomasia, use of hyperbole and paradox) and--of particular value as indices to historicity--irreducibly personal idiom (distinctive form and content of riddles and parables, new coinages respecting "the reign of God," a distinctive use of *'amen*, the use of *'abba'* as an address of God).

Since the burden of proof falls, as Willi Marxsen argued some years ago,[12] neither on historicity nor on non-historicity, but on whoever wishes to pronounce either way, there should be three columns for judgments on historicity (historical, non-historical, and question-mark), and a full treatment of indices should include indices to non-historicity.

David Friedrich Strauss presented an early treatment of this issue. Though his criteria were partly ideological (e.g., the "impossibility" of disturbing "the chain of secondary causes"), and though ideology ultimately commanded his whole historical effort, Strauss made a beginning with his methodical observations on "plausible historical sequence" and "psychological credibility."[13] He was little interested, however, in reconstructing positive history; hence, the attempt to retrieve Jesus' horizons, perspectives, and purposes, and precisely in the light of this retrieval to raise the question of historicity respecting gospel traditions out of harmony with them, fell outside Strauss's purview. Nor did he concern himself with the history of the first Christian communities, which might have allowed him, not only to suspect (as he often did), but actually to establish, the correlation of distinctive post-Easter concerns with particular gospel traditions.

Contemporary efforts to do just these two things have so far provided the most secure way of ranging gospel traditions in the non-historicity column without methodical reliance on assumption. If, for example, it is possible to recover the eschatological schema supposed by the words of Jesus and if according to this schema there was a material coincidence of the day of the Son of man (resurrection, exaltation, parousia) with the last judgment and the reign of God,[14] then gospel texts, in the measure in which they reflect the expectation of an interim between, say, the glorification of Jesus and the last judgment (in accord with the whole of post-Easter Christian eschatology) are non-historical. Closely related to this is the distance between two conceptions of the entry of the gentiles into salvation: by the eschatological pilgrimage and by the world mission.[15] Gospel texts, in the measure in which they reflect the expectation of a world mission, are unhistorical. A positive reconstruction of the origins of the world mission leads correlatively to the same result. Despite multiple and multiform attestation, both the supposition of the world mission and the explicitly universalist missionary mandate of the risen Christ are unhistorical.[16] Linguistic indices to non-historicity are available for study especially in parables research and, in particular, in Jesus' "explanations" of his parables.[17]

If the hypothesis could actually be established, rather than merely posited, that early Christian prophets speaking in the name of the exalted Christ supplied the Church with sayings that were finally assimilated to the synoptic tradition, this too might be made to generate some concrete indices to non-historicity.[18]

In any case, gospel criticism of immediate relevance to historical research would be immensely improved by a steep reduction in the role of assumption and a correlative insistence that the critic offer a reasoned account of all judgments on historicity, laying out the full argument for his historical conclusions, and specifying the indices that he appeals to respecting the historicity and the non-historicity of data.

II

The survey of issues offered above has been swift and schematic, but we can take time now to reflect on objections and, in view of them, to reconsider whether the indices to the historicity of gospel data are in fact up to the task for which they have been devised. In two widely noticed essays M. D. Hooker has made a series of trenchant observations on this topic.[19]   The following is a summary of the first essay.

The knowledge that historical investigation of Jesus aims at is of what is characteristic of him, whereas "the tradition-historical method" (discontinuity with early Christianity and originality vis-à-vis Judaism) yields only what is unique to him. The method is effective, moreover, only on condition of "a fairly confident knowledge of both areas" (early Christianity and the Judaism contemporary with it), a condition quite imperfectly fulfilled. To say that there is no known parallel in Judaism and Christianity to some datum of the gospel tradition is an argument from silence and should be regarded as such. Further, the method dictates its own conclusions, inevitably producing a picture (e.g., an unmessianic Jesus) in keeping with the assumption of dissimilarity. The application of the method is bound to be subjective, especially when a rider is attached to dissimilarity, namely, that to be historical a datum must not only differ from Judaism and Christianity but also be "at home" in first-century Palestine.

The addition of the principle of "coherence" (data that cohere with authentic material may themselves be accepted as authentic) to that of "dissimilarity" invites a further exercise of subjectivity: it may well be that our judgments of coherence and incoherence fail to reflect accurately the mentality of first-century Palestine, which is what counts here. Again, any errors in the results obtained by the "dissimilarity" principle are liable to be magnified by the principle of "coherence." Finally, practitioners of these methods apply them selectively, so that the real criterion of judgment is the critic's particular way of construing the data in question.

Debate about "the burden of proof" is appropriate only on extremist suppositions (e.g., that the gospels give us straightforward historical reports of Jesus' words, or that Jesus himself said nothing sufficiently memorable to have come down to us). More appropriately, the burden of proof lies on each scholar who offers a judgment on any part of the material.

The conclusion of the article is a plea against "dogmatism" and an argument, first, in favor of acknowledging other principles in addition to dissimilarity and coherence (multiple attestation and what we have called above "linguistic indices"); second, in favor of applying criteria positively, not negatively (whereas the presence of an index counts in favor of historicity, its absence does not of itself count against it); third, in favor of putting a premium on convergence; fourth, in favor of insisting on a reasonable "pedigree" for gospel material (a historically plausible account of its origin), whether it be adjudged historical or not. The article ends with a word suggesting that Jesus himself used the expression "Son of man" and questioning the assumption that he made no direct messianic claims.

The second essay, though it eventually goes over the same matter and makes the same points, begins differently and especially ends differently. It begins by focusing on the failure to observe how severely limited form criticism is as a tool of inquiry into the origin and historical reliability of gospel materials; and it ends by focusing on the failure of New Testament scholars to "draw the logical conclusion" from "the inadequacy of their tools."

What is this logical conclusion? It is this: the answers that the New Testament critic gives to his historical questions about Jesus

are very largely the result of his own presuppositions

> and prejudices. If he approaches the material with the
> belief that it is largely the creation of the early Chris-
> tian communities, then he will interpret it in that
> way. If he assumes that the words of the Lord were
> faithfully remembered and passed on, then he will be
> able to find criteria which support him.[20]

To be sure, we need working hypotheses, but they "are only hypotheses," and as for "assured results," "there are none."

Recently, E. E. Ellis has confirmed that the indices to historicity can produce no "assured results," as "the devastating critique of M.
Hooker has shown."[21] Some years earlier a more discriminating comment was made by J. B. Muddiman: "it is not clear whether [Dr. Hooker's] complaint is against the criterion of dissimilarity as such, or
against its misapplication."[22] Indeed, this ambiguity pervades both articles, and even if it seems to be resolved by the uncompromisingly negative conclusions of the second article (the scholar's tools are
"inadequate" to his purposes and there are no "assured results"), it is not
completely disposed of even here, for the wholesale theoretical repudiation of "assured results" has by no means led the writer to abandon personal assessments ("if my own assessment tends to be a more traditional one. . .").[23] And there is, if not ambiguity, then simple oversight as
well as rhetorical overkill in the final conclusion; for, although it is
true that the critic's historical judgment is settled not by obedience to
some "criterion" but by his "own understanding of the situation," and,
above all, true that conclusions on the historical Jesus are bound to cohere with premises on the origin and character of the gospel tradition, it
is obviously untrue that to have one's "own understanding of the situation" is inevitably to indulge in prejudice or wishful thinking, and that
any set of premises on the origin and character of the gospel tradition is
mere assumption, one set being no better nor worse than another. The
good observations in both articles remain good, but their effect is somewhat offset by disregard of the last-mentioned home truths.

The result, then, is ambiguous. Some critical assessments are
proposed as preferable to others; on the other hand, all of them are taken
in the end to be "highly speculative" and hypothetical. The chaotically
divergent opinions in the scholarly community "cannot all be right--
though they may well all be wrong."[24]

At the root of the troubled consciousness barely disguised by this bleakly negative conclusion lies the omnipresent and unelucidated issue of "subjectivity," one of the few topics on which New Testament scholars sound almost unanimous. Everyone warns against subjectivity. The trouble with "the traditio-historical method" is that "its application is bound to be subjective,"[25] and when we turn to the principle of coherence "subjectivity is even more of a danger."[26] We should try, tentatively, to locate the most plausible *Sitz im Leben* for each text, but "always remembering the danger of subjectivity."[27] Again, "subjectivity" is the flaw in Bultmann's suggestion "that authentic teaching can be guaranteed by the presence of 'the distinctive eschatological temper which characterized the preaching of Jesus.' "[28] Though Muddiman picked out the ambiguity that ran through the critique of dissimilarity, he nonetheless heartily commended the cautionary notes frequently sounded against "the practical danger of subjectivism."[29] The situation, then, appears to be this: for over a hundred years New Testament scholars, conscious of the need for objective historical judgments, have been devising historical "criteria" and trying to make judgments in accord with them. Some critics have acutely observed how imperfect, if not futile, this ostensible escape from subjectivity has turned out to be. They have concluded, at least in theory and often against the better judgment evidenced in their practice, that the critical enterprise is riddled to its foundations with prejudice and powerless to produce solid results. If the tools of even the most rigorous critics fail to eliminate subjectivity, what other conclusion can there be?

III

Another conclusion becomes not only possible but necessary as soon as objectivity is brought into relation with its conditions. Central among these conditions is a subject capable of cognitional self-transcendence: capable, that is, of going beyond image and symbol, supposition and conjecture, wishful thinking and peer-group thinking, to the act of affirming what is so. Admittedly, once truth is reached, it is intentionally independent of the subject that reached it: that is self-transcendence and the goal of inquiry. But the ontological home of truth is the subject. The goal is not reached apart from a demanding process, as the drive to truth reveals itself in wonder, converts wondering into questioning and questioning into question-answering, solicits reflection on the answers, and climaxes in the act of judging them to be certainly or probably true or false. All of these are activities of the subject and there is no objectivity without all of them. Truth, in fine, ripens on the tree of the subject, and objectivity is the fruit of subjectivity at its most intense and persistent.

Why have we ever thought otherwise? No doubt, because objectivity is relative to the actual process of knowing, and to the everyday world of common sense this process is far from transparent. Still, intelligence is not limited to the perspectives and procedures of common sense. With help,[30] we can learn to catch ourselves in the act of knowing, and so come to the realization that knowing is a structured manifold having an empirical component (data), an intelligent component (questioning, construing, defining), and a rational component (marshalling evidence, reflecting, judging). If the process of coming to know is manifold, so correspondingly is objectivity. Its empirical component is the givenness of data; its intelligent component is insight, or rather the demand expressed by a question and answered by an insight; its rational component is the further demand for sufficient evidence that the answer is true, met by the assembling of evidence and the reflective grasp of it as sufficient.

If one's suppositions about knowing correspond to the views of empiricists or positivists, objectivity will be reduced to its empirical component. Then the big danger will be "subjectivity"; and if despite heroic effort subjectivity cannot be eliminated, it will appear that great projects (historical critique, for instance) must, unhappily, surrender their claims. If one's suppositions about knowing correspond to the views of idealists, objectivity will be reduced to its intelligent component (e.g., the internal coherence of insight). Only if one's views tally with those of critical realism will objectivity be acknowledged as the achievement of a full and ordered subjectivity, subjectivity that attends to data but goes beyond data to questions, that cherishes insight but goes beyond insight to truth.

If the conversion of "subjectivity" from a boo-word to a hurrah-word is new to New Testament criticism, this only betrays the durable underground attachment of New Testament studies to positivism. But the suppositions of positivist theory and the practice of historical criticism do no correlate. Regardless of what theoretical hunches may be

lurking in his subconscious, the practicing critic shows by his performance how well he knows that success hinges not just on data, but on
"his own understanding of the situation." He is somehow aware, even if
he fails to bring it to thematic articulation, that everything he knows--
his whole fund of experience and range of understanding and hard-won
equilibrium of judgment--is quite properly at the beck and call of all his
critical endeavors.

Indices to the historicity of data do not change this; they illustrate it, for these indices are just heuristic resources epitomizing dis-
creet, more or less useful, patterns of observation and inference. They
function in criticism not entirely unlike the way proverbs function in
common sense. Faced with an issue that must quickly be settled one
way or another, one might wonder which of two proverbs fits the situation: "He who hesitates is lost"? Or "Look before you leap"? If added
insight is needed to know which piece of wisdom is relevant here and
now, so in the criticism of historical data, when the indices offer mixed
signals, added insight is required to know which factors tip the balance.
This added insight is not a misbegotten intrusion of subjectivity; it is
that without which a true judgment is simply impossible. And just as
it is no defect in the indices to historicity that they sometimes offer
mixed signals, so it is no defect in the critic that he should refuse to
treat indices as rules to be obeyed. The defect lies rather in the theorizing that establishes this illusory dilemma: either the burden of objectivity must be borne by "criteria" expected to eliminate the bothersome
business of the historian's "subjectivity," or we must stoically admit
that answers are just products of presupposition and prejudice, assured
results are fictitious, and all parties to the critical debate may be wrong.

The positivism of a hundred years ago called on "the sources"
to turn the trick. A hankering after "objective sources," nourished on
the illusion that access to history should be mediated not by the intelligence of the historian but by sources equipped to do his job for him,
dominated the quest of the historical Jesus from the 1860s to the First
World War. The disillusionment that followed was eventually relieved
by a new faith in "method"; and though the earlier critical reaction
("blame the sources") has now given way to a new critical reaction
("blame the methods"), the fact is that the deep problem has lain neither
in New Testament sources nor in historical-critical methods, but in
some cumbersome philosophical luggage--a medley of inadequate and
misleading views of knowledge and objectivity. Bernard Lonergan has

identified the core of the problem as

> an exceedingly stubborn and misleading myth con-
> cerning reality, objectivity, and human knowledge.
> The myth is that knowing is like seeing, that objec-
> tivity is seeing what is there to be seen and not seeing
> what is not there, and that the real is what is out there
> now to be looked at.[31]

But, as knowing is not seeing, so the criteria of objective knowing are
not those of successful seeing. Objectivity is not a matter of keeping
"subjectivity" from interference with seeing what is there and not seeing
what is not. It is a matter, rather, of bringing subjectivity to full flow-
er, i.e., to the point of cognitional self-transcendence. This, to be sure,
is a challenge. Objectivity is the fruit not just of subjectivity but of authentic subjectivity. Owing to the heritage of human bias--unconscious
motivation, individual and group egoism, the illusory omnicompetence
of common sense--subjectivity is easily inauthentic. But whereas positivist theory is at a total loss here and can only urge that we all avoid
dogmatism, critical realism has something both profound and useful to
say.

Profound: for, the intentionality analysis at the heart of critical realism brings to light the unity of the human spirit, namely, its
eros for self-transcendence. The distinct dimensions of self-transcendence
--intellectual, moral, religious--are so interrelated that, when they occur
within a single subject, the moral sublates the intellectual dimension,
and the religious dimension sublates the moral.[32] Genetically, on the
other hand, the order will often be just the opposite. The self-
transcendence that is the love of God opens up the whole sphere of values; these include the value of believing religious truths; and in such
belief lie impulses not only for the moral life but for the break with
cognitional myth.

Useful: for, the same intentionality analysis grounds an effective hermeneutic of suspicion respecting bias, evasions, screening devices, and the ideological rationalizing of alienations--not only in others
by in oneself.[33] This will not banish the perspectivism of history, but
it is the beginning of a constructive response to subsurface inauthentici-
ty in historical scholarship.

NOTES

1. A selection of discussions since 1971: C. F. D. Moule, "The Techniques of New Testament Research: A Critical Survey," in **Jesus and Man's Hope II**, edited by D. G. Miller and D. Y. Hadidian; Pittsburgh: Pittsburgh Theological Seminary, 1971, 29-45. D. G. A. Calvert, "An Examination of the Criteria for Distinguishing the Authentic Words of Jesus," *New Testament Studies* 18 (1971-72) 209-218. R. S. Barbour, **Traditio-Historical Criticism of the Gospels** (London: SPCK, 1972). D. Lührmann, "Die Frage nach Kriterien für ursprüngliche Jesusworte--eine Problemskizze," in **Jésus aux origines de la christologie** (ed.) J. Dupont (Gembloux: Duculot, 1975) 59-72. Robert H. Stein, "The 'Criteria' for Authenticity," in **Gospel Perspectives. Studies of History and Tradition in the Four Gospels**, (eds.) R. T. France and David Wenham (Sheffield: JSOT Press, 1980) 225-263. Heinz Schürmann, "Kritische Jesuserkenntnis. Zur kritischen Handhabung des 'Unähnlichkeit-kriteriums'," *Bibel und Liturgie* 54 (1981) 17-26. E. Earle Ellis, "Gospels Criticism. A Perspective on the State of the Art" in **Das Evangelium und die Evangelien. Vorträge vom Tübinger Symposium 1982**, (ed.) Peter Stuhlmacher (Tübingen: Mohr, 1983) 27-54.

2. Holding the field as "most cogent" and sometimes proposed as "exclusively cogent" is the criterion of dissimilarity, formulated along the lines urged by Ernst Käsemann. The "only case," according to Käsemann, in which we have "somewhat firm ground under our feet" is when a tradition for whatever reason is unattributable either to Judaism or to Christianity; see "Das Problem des historischen Jesus" (1954) in **Exegetische Versuche und Besinnungen I** (Göttingen: Vandenhoeck & Ruprecht, (1960) 187-214, p. 205. That other criteria are "more regularly apposite," however, has been proposed on occasion, e.g., "the recovery of the historical milieu," e.g., Maria Trautmann, **Zeichenhafte Handlungen Jesu** (Würzburg: Echter Verlag, 1980) 115f., or even "multiple attestation," e.g., Harvey K. MacArthur, "Basic Issues. A Survey of Recent Gospel Research," *Interpretation* 18 (1964) 39-55. cf. 47.

3. See especially the articles of M. D. Hooker cited below, note 19.

4. See above, note 2.

5. R. G. Collingwood, **The Idea of History** (Oxford: Oxford University Press, 1946) 281.

6. Ibid. 245.

7. See Joachim Jeremias, **The Eucharistic Words of Jesus** (London: SCM, 1966) 202f.

8. See B. F. Meyer, **The Aims of Jesus** (London: SCM, 1979) 60-69.

9. See Birger Gerhardsson, **Memory and Manuscript** (Lund: Gleerup, 1961) 330.

10. Ibid. 19-32, 324-335.

11. Joachim Jeremias, **New Testament Theology I. The Proclamation of Jesus** (London: SCM, 1971) 1-37.

12. Willi Marxen, **The Beginnings of Christology** (Philadelphia: Fortress, 1969) 8.

13. David Friedrich Strauss, **The Life of Jesus Critically Examined** (London: SCM, 1972) 87-91.

14. See Meyer, **The Aims of Jesus**, 202-209.

15. See Joachim Jeremias, **Jesus' Promise to the Nations** (London: SCM, 1958).

16. See especially Anton Vögtle, "Die ekklesiologische Auftragsworte des Auferstandenen," in **Das Evangelium und die Evangelien. Beiträge zur Evangelienforschung** (Düsseldorf: Patmos, 1971) 243-252.

17. See, for example, Joachim Jeremias, **The Parables of Jesus**, (London: SCM, 1963) 77-79.

18. Thus far, however, the case has not been made. See David Hill, "On the Evidence for the Creative Role of Christian Prophets," *New Testament Studies* 20 (1974) 262-274. See also the verdict of *non constat* in David E. Aune, **Prophecy in Early Christianity and the Ancient Mediterranean World** (Grand Rapids: Eerdmans, 1983) 142-145.

19. M. D. Hooker, "Christology and Methodology," *New Testament Studies* 17 (1970-71) 480-487; "On Using the Wrong Tool," *Theology* 75 (1972) 570-581.

20. "On Using the Wrong Tool," 581.

21. E. E. Ellis, "Gospels Criticism," (see above, note l) 31.

22. J. B. Muddiman, "Jesus and Fasting. Mark ii. 18-22," in **Jésus aux origines** (see above, note 1) 271-281, p. 271.

23. "On Using the Wrong Tool," 580.

24. "On Using the Wrong Tool," 581.

25. "Christology and Methodology," 482; "On Using the Wrong Tool," 576.

26. "Christology and Methodology," 483; "On Using the Wrong Tool," 576.

27. "Christology and Methodology," 487.

28. "On Using the Wrong Tool," 576.

29. Muddiman, "Jesus and Fasting," 271.

30. See Bernard Lonergan, **Insight. A Study of Human Under-standing**, (New York: Longmans, 1958}; **Method in Theology**, (New York: Herder & Herder, 1972) 3-25, 57-99.

31. Lonergan, **Method in Theology**, 241-243.

32. See Lonergan, **Method in Theology**, 241-243.

33. Bernard Lonergan, "The Ongoing Genesis of Methods," *Studies in Religion/Sciences Religieuses* 6 (1976-77) 341-355, cf. 349-353.

VII

LONERGAN'S "BREAKTHROUGH"

AND

THE AIMS OF JESUS

The immediate aim of **The Aims of Jesus** was "to understand the Jesus of ancient Palestine."[1] Why should this aim, so obviously and thoroughly historical, have involved or invited the accompaniment of philosophic and theological considerations? Is history of itself so defective that it cannot arrive at its own destination without help from other disciplines?

According to **Aims**, the essential answer is no. The book affirmed the spontaneity and autonomy not only of historical interest and historical encounter but of technical historical inquiry and reconstruction, as well. Nevertheless, a qualifying observation is in order, which will raise a new question.

Cognitional theory has a generic relevance to history as theory to practice, and in particular cases this theory of history may be indispensable to a sorting out of baffling practical issues. The essential service thus rendered is hit off in the phrase *removens prohibens* ("removing what prohibits"). The task of theory is to discover in historical practice intrusions that are alien to history, and to eliminate them.

The "new question" that this raises is whether, and how, theology (which like faith itself, has an important stake in history) might impinge on historical inquiry without distorting it.

Philosophy and the History of Jesus

R. G. Collingwood (1889-1943) brilliantly performed the task of detecting and demolishing intrusions alien to history. Indeed, it was Collingwood who made the classic case for the autonomy of historical thought. In **The Idea of History** he traced the long story of the growth of history to maturity and so to the full consciousness of its autonomy.[2] The fault that Collingwood found with positivism, for example, was its undiscriminating deference to science. If science defined knowledge, history had to be some sort of science, and if not elegant, exact, first-rate science, then a prosaic, inexact, second-rate imitation. But history, Collingwood argued, was a first-rate original, not a second-rate mimic. By recovering both historically and analytically the independent character of historical thinking, Collingwood rendered a service of "removing what prohibits." He repeatedly uncovered alien encumbrances in historical thinking and argued for their elimination. Thus, he urged that history was not at all a matter of discovering laws at work in human events. It concentrated rather on human intentionality, perspective, purpose--what Collingwood called "the thought of the agent." This is what gave a human event its characteristic density and constituted, as he put it, "the inside of the event," the real goal of historical inquiry.

Many cite Collingwood but few follow him in the effort to free history from irrelevant baggage. This is a pity, for the work of purification ought to be going forward full steam to the benefit especially of the history of religions, where ideological dead-weight is especially evident and counterproductive. Since the heyday (1890-1920) of the German history-of-religions school and under its immediate influence, historians of earliest Christianity in particular have saddled themselves with inhibitions and prohibitions that tacitly undermine the autonomy of history.

Let the post-Bultmannian "new quest" of the historical Jesus illustrate. This was a movement that ran from the 1950s to the 1970s under the sponsorship of existentialist theologians (e.g., Ernst Käsemann, Günther Bornkamm, Ernst Fuchs) who rightly feared that their existentialism, unless room were made in it for the historical reality of Jesus, might result in a disastrous docetism, dissolving the identity of the earthly and the heavenly Lord.[3] But the history that they begrudgingly allowed themselves was mined by artificial limitations.

First of all, the new questers shared with Bultmann and his

history-of-religions-school mentors the Enlightenment conception of history as a closed cause-and-effect continuum *(ein geschlossener Wirkungs-Zusammenhang).*[4] This view, which was systematized by Ernst Troeltsch's principles of criticism, analogy, and correlation,[5] not only removed from the sphere of intelligible reality a whole series of central Christian doctrines (e.g., the incarnation of the Word, the sending of the Spirit), it also established--on a non-historical *a priori* basis--a negative historical verdict on, for example, miracles without analogy today (especially nature miracles) of the corporeal dimension of the Easter appearances.

Second, in accord with Bultmann's methodically sceptical style of bringing form criticism to bear on gospel materials, the new questers adopted Ernst Käsemann's principle of gospel criticism: a gospel tradition recounted words or acts of Jesus could be adjudged historical only if it was unparalleled both in Judaism and in early Christianity.[6] Thus, inasmuch as the early Church's eucharistic practice paralleled the Last Supper accounts (and so might conceivably have served as the source of the Last Supper accounts), the Last Supper was methodically classified as unhistorical.[7]

Third, the new questers forbade themselves any inquiry that might be construed as a hankering after historical support for the kerygma. Determination to keep the purity of faith intact ruled out as theologically irrelevant and unwelcome whatever historical ascertainments would make kerygmatic affirmation credible. On this issue the new questers functioned as an alert Inquisition, each keeping a gimlet eye on the existentialist orthodoxy of the other with repeated corrections and calls to order.

So here was a group of existentialists who decided that for theological reasons they were obliged to enter into historical inquiry and research on Jesus. But what happened, in their historical practice, to the autonomy of history? First, the historical process was cut down to rationalist dimensions, as "the closed universe" of Enlightenment propaganda was allowed to settle questions of historicity on a non-historical basis. Second, an implausible postulate on the creativity of anonymous Christian communities was allowed to dictate a criterion (Käsemann's principle) on the basis of which the bulk of the gospel tradition was methodically reduced to non-historicity. Third, an illusory fear that too much history might, in the words of Gerhard Ebeling, "render the decision of faith superfluous"[8] drove the would-be historian away from any historical data, inquiry, or conclusion that might illuminate historically the truth of the gospel.

Is this history? Here, I would say, history has lost the freedom to be itself, namely, an autonomous form of knowledge. For years Bultmann and his followers indulged in the habit of citing Collingwood on history. This is ironic, for virtually nothing of Collingwood's drive to free history of alien inhibitions and prohibitions passed into their practice.

With this foil in place, I am ready to answer the question I was asked to deal with in these pages: how did Lonergan's "breakthrough" in cognitional theory and epistemology relate to my efforts of historical reconstruction in **The Aims of Jesus**?

The answer is that Lonergan decisively confirmed me in an account of history-as-knowledge that allowed me to deal with historical questions historically. I saw no reason for appropriating, and several reasons (to which Lonergan contributed a final cogency) for not appropriating, the Enlightenment conception of history as a closed continuum. I rejected methodical scepticism as gratuitously suppositive[9] and made four revisions in Käsemann's principle.[10] I did not recoil from historical inquiry relevant to the kerygma and, in fact, found no gospel tradition theologically uncongenial, much less dangerous. I accordingly found myself in a position to consider all gospel traditions as potential historical data and to consider all actual historical data as open without reservation to historical treatment.

Lonergan, it seemed to me, offered the most trenchant contemporary follow-up on Collingwood. Collingwood in the last years of his life proved to be no mean cognitional theorist himself, but it cannot be said that he ever worked out a truly satisfactory theory of knowledge. Lonergan did, in his masterwork, **Insight**;[11] and though **Insight** did not make of history a leading theme, it did treat the issues crucial to the understanding of history-as-knowledge.

First, and this is a matter of general and remote relevance to history, **Insight** demystified the conflicting epistemologies of the modern era (naive realism, empiricism, idealism), tracing them to a common root, namely, the fallacy that knowing is like seeing, that knowing the real is, or would be, akin to seeing it. Lonergan's alternative turned first of all on the negative observation that, just as understanding is not perceiving nor like perceiving, so the object of understanding is not an object of perception nor like an object of perception.

It is not some new sort of datum added to the data of sense and of consciousness. Intelligibility is no more "like" a datum than wondering and questioning and question-answering and answer-checking are "like" seeing or hearing or touching. In Lonergan's account, knowledge is equally irreducible to the pseudo-objectivity of "seeing what is there to be seen" and to the defective subjectivity or projecting merely pragmatic order onto the chaos of the real.

Second, **Insight** offered a remarkable treatment of world process as "emergent probability." This broke cleanly with both the classical cosmologies of Aristotelian ancestry and the modern cosmologies that began with Galileo. The most striking feature of emergent probability were its transposition of scientific laws of the classical type from the status of necessity to that of verified possibility, and its provision of a dynamic context (namely, schemes of recurrence operative in accord with statistical frequencies) for the actual functioning of laws of the classical type. Emergent probability thus spelled an end to the cult of necessity characteristic of modern as well as Greek cosmology. The durable thesis of the "closed universe" may well turn out to be the last gasp of this now clearly obsolete necessitarian cosmology.

Third, **Insight** provided a rather full treatment of commonsense knowledge, of which history is a sophisticated specialization. Moreover, Lonergan's later work, **Method in Theology**, followed this up with an explicit account of history-as-knowledge, culminating in a brilliant, rapid-fire treatment of heuristic structures proper to historical inquiry.[12]

The impact of adequate theory is to reinforce the autonomy of historical thinking. But however excellent, theory cannot guarantee successful practice. Inasmuch as the immediate resource and inspiration for my own practice was the line of historical work that passed from Gustaf Dalman (1855-1941) to Joachim Jeremias (1900-1979), questions about my practice correlate in part with questions about theirs (to be posed below, under the heading "theology"). In any case, Lonergan's cognitional theory did not supply me with anything convertible into a shortcut in practice. On the contrary, the freer the historian from alien intrusions, the more demanding his task becomes. He cannot loftily dismiss whole complexes of material as *a priori* unhistorical, nor even begin with the supposition that non-historicity holds until proved otherwise.[13]

The question of miracles is a touchstone. In **Aims** the treatment of miracles is cautious, since I was unable to work out a satisfactory way of dealing with the historicity of individual miracle narratives.[14] But once I saw that the tie between exorcisms and apocalyptic eschatology was unique to Jesus,[15] I could find a way of approaching miracles through the sayings material.[16] The point is that for me the question of Jesus' miracles remained strictly historical. Even where I was unable to resolve questions of historicity (say, for scenes like the stilling of the storm or the various raisings of the dead), I kept the historicity of such events an open question--something on which two of my reviewers, Dennis Nineham and Michael Goulder, gagged.[17]

Theology and the History of Jesus

Theology has an inalienable stake in history and stands to profit from relevant historical advances. But can theology impinge on historical inquiry without distorting it? Van Harvey answered with a faintly qualified negative.[18] Lonergan answered with a distinction.[19] On the one hand, there was pre-critical history, which might well, even now, have an honorable place in the life of a nation or a church or a corporation of what-have-you; but, since this kind of history was artistic and popular, apologetic and ethical, it easily suffered "the evangelical consequences" of serving two masters.[20] On the other hand, there was critical history, which alone could serve as a functional specialty in theology. Its aims were austere. They did not typically include the refutation of calumnies (apologetic) or the apportioning of praise and blame (ethics). Rather, they bore on retrieving the past "as it actually was" *(wie es eigentlich gewesen)* .[21]

Now, as Collingwood insisted, the questions of the historian, be his history ever so critical, are entirely his own choice. Since at this point he is completely free, it follows that he may choose questions that reflect religious and theological interests, and theology, by providing historical inquiry with penetrating questions, may thereby play a creative rather than obstructive role in history. But willing as I am to acknowledge this and even insist on it, I confess to having found that historical questions directly and immediately drawn from theology have repeatedly tended to distort the apprciation of data.[22] Nothing, however, promotes the cause of theology better than the drive to truth, and this drive may well be fueled by religious and theological values, interests, motives.

Consider Dalman and Jeremias. Both broke new ground in philological and environmental research and in stylistics. As with every historian without exception, their practice also exhibited limits, lacunae, and errors. Neither matched his practice with comparable achievements in theory, nor even with a deft account of just what it was that he was doing. In both cases theological motives powered historical achievements that would hardly have been thinkable apart from a vital personal relationship to the New Testament world of meaning. (This was the hermeneutical home-truth to which Harvey's book was blind.) Dalman, nurtured from boyhood in Pietism, had been intent on the conversion of the Jews. Jeremias resolutely sought to recover the only voice that "can invest our message with full authority."[23] For my part, I do not share the Pietism from which Dalman's missionary ambitions arose, nor Jeremias's reduction of "authority" to the voice of the historical Jesus; but so far as I can judge, neither in the case of Dalman nor in that of Jeremias did historical conscience give way to, much less collapse under, theological pressure. All in all, religious motive was crucial to their historical practice and, so far from corrupting it, boosted it to a level of brilliance.

The question about the aims of Jesus is not formally theological.[24] But just as encounter with Caesar and his aims is an invitation to politics, and encounter with Socrates and his aims, an invitation to inquiry and wise ignorance, a taste for measure and a stomach for standing one's ground, so encounter with the aims of Jesus is an invitation to faith, hope, love. The question of Jesus' aims is neutral, but the answer to the question is theologically charged, and this, of course, was to be foreseen. Jeremias argued that precisely because Jesus took the end to be near, "it had to be his purpose to gather God's people of the time of salvation. . . .Indeed, we must put the point even more sharply: the *only* significance of the whole of Jesus' activity is to gather the eschatological people of God."[25] I take this to have been a great insight, although it remained isolated, unexplained, and unproven in Jeremias's book. One way of stating the theological concern of **Aims** is to say that it sought to supply evidence designed, at best, to make Jeremias's insight historically compelling and, at least, to make it historically plausible. By his will to bring into being the eschatological people of God, Jesus himself laid the foundations of the christology that defined him as the copestone of the new sanctuary (Mark 12:10; parr. Matt. 21:42; Luke 20:17; Eph 2:20f.; 1 Pet 2:6f.) and the first-born of many brothers (Rom 8:29; Col

1:18; Rev 1:5; Heb 2:10-18).

To conclude: wide reading in historical-Jesus research seems of itself not to settle whether, as Albert Schweitzer thought, hatred is a positive factor in historical research[26] or whether, as Van Harvey thinks, belief has an inevitably distorting effect on historical inquiry.[27] But for reasons that Lonergan has given at length,[28] I find his view immeasurably more persuasive than either of theirs: faith is the eye of love, and reveals the value of believing; in religious belief lie the seeds of intellectual conversion; and the great bulk of what we know is not immanently generated but intelligently believed.

Granted the pivotal importance of faith, there is a place in the life of faith for immanently generated judgments of credibility. If critical history, for example, shows that Jesus in fact lived out his career in the conviction of fulfilling a distinctive messianic role affecting the destinies of Israel and of the nations, it becomes more credible than it would otherwise be that he really was the Messiah, as Christian faith has always affirmed. Though judgments of credibility may seem meaningless to the fideist, who rejoices exclusively in a faith which, he believes, is unsupported by reason of any sort, they are very meaningful indeed to those who affirm a symbiosis of faith and reason (which obtains in fact, whether one knows it or not, or likes it or not) and who are accordingly intent on living the life of faith in a fully responsible and fully human way. For them it follows as the night the day that history done competently and honestly has a role of importance to play in the lives of Christians, and this never more clearly and crucially than today, as the life of reason comes under unprecedented assault by ideologists and absurdists and is unwittingly subverted by both ends of the spectrum, from the fideists at one end to the empiricists, positivists and behaviorists at the other.

NOTES

1. B. F. Meyer, **The Aims of Jesus** (London: SCM, 1979) 19.

2. R. G. Collingwood, **The Idea of History** (Oxford: Oxford University Press, 1946) 14-204.

3. Ernst Käsemann, "The Problem of the Historical Jesus," in **Essays on New Testament Themes** (London: SCM, 1964) 33-34, 45-47; also Käsemann's essay, "Die neue Jesus-Frage," in **Jésus aux origines de la christologie**, ed. J. Dupont (Gembloux: Duculot, 1975) 47-57, esp. 55-57.

4. Rudolf Bultmann, "Is Exegesis Without Presuppositions Possible?" in **New Testament and Mythology and Other Basic Writings** ed. S. M. Ogden (Philadelphia: Fortress, 1984) 145-53, esp. 147-48.

5. See Ernst Troeltsch, "Über historische und dogmatische Methode in der Theologie," in **Gesammelte Schriften**, vol. 2 (Tübingen: Mohr, 1922) 729-53, esp. 730-35. See also Troeltsch'e article, "Historiography," in Hastings' **Encyclopedia of Religion and Ethics** (New York: Scribner's, 1914) 716, 720.

6. Käsemann, "The Problem of the Historical Jesus," 37.

7. **Aims**, 84.

8. Gerhard Ebeling, **Word and Faith** (Philadelphia: Fortress, 1963) 56.

9. **Aims**, 82-83.

10. **Aims**, 85-86.

11. Bernard Lonergan, **Insight. A Study of Human Understanding** (New York: Longmans, 1957).

12. Bernard Lonergan, **Method in Theology** (New York: Herder & Herder, 1972) esp. 224-33.

13. **Aims**, 81-85.

14. **Aims**, 158.

15. Cf. Gerd Theissen, **The Miracle Stories of the Early Gospel Tradition** (Philadelphia: Fortress, 1983) 277-86.

16. **Aims**, 154-58.

17. Dennis Nineham, *Epworth Review* 7 (1980) 91-93; Michael Goulder, *Theology* 83 (1980) 57-60.

18. Van A. Harvey, **The Historian and the Believer** (New York: Macmillan, 1966).

19. **Method**, 185-96.

20. **Method**, 185.

21. Leopold von Ranke, from the preface to his **History of the Romanic and Germanic Peoples from 1492 to 1535** (1824).

22. See **Aims**, 19 on Liberal theology; 52 on the sharp difference between the control of ideology in Jeremias's practice and its encroachments on the practice of the new questers; 175 on Christian apologists of the early twentieth century, etc.

23. Joachim Jeremias, **The Parables of Jesus** (London: SCM and New York: Scribner's, 1954) 9.

24. **Aims,** 111, 174-75.

25. Joachim Jeremias, **New Testament Theology I:** The **Proclamation of Jesus** (London: SCM and New York: Scribner's, 1971) 170.

26. See **Aims,** 258, note 12.

27. **The Historian and the Believer,** passim.

28. See **Insight,** 703-18; **Method,** 41-47; 115-124; 243; 283-84.

VIII

THE "INSIDE" OF THE JESUS EVENT

What can history do for christology? Or, rather, with reference to christology, what can history do for us?

A telling answer would take account of past and present, old and new. History done competently and honestly offers the kind of entrée to tradition that accords with the critically differentiated consciousness of the contemporary West. We have become aware that the very act of inheriting demands that one's heritage be translated into one's own cultural language; and this perhaps more than anything else is what has brought about developments in doctrine.

Long before the rise of the historical consciousness this process of translation had proceeded apace. It generated the worlds of christological meaning that came to expression in early Christianity, e.g., when the Easter faith of the Jerusalem Church was translated into a thematization of the pre-existence of Christ on a par with God (cf. the Philippians hymn, Phil 2:6-11). This was a startling translation but (as Gregory Dix recognized)[1] still a merely adequate translation of the original Easter faith into another range of wondering and questioning, a new conceptual idiom and aesthetic pattern.

For centuries this process of translation or transposition was carried on not only without benefit of an accompanying theory of development but without even the hint that something new was taking place and that some account of it was in order. Safely relocating the most innovative aspects of their own historic experience in God's original act of revelation, ancient and medieval Christians overlooked or disavowed the novelty regularly emergent in the transpositions that allowed each culture and each age to appropriate its religious heritage.

In our own changed situation it is history that allows whoever among us is able to enlarge and enrich the old with the new *(vetera novis augere et perficere)* to discern what the old really was so that the new might enlarge and enrich rather than just displace, diminish, or destroy it. Bernard Lonergan has persuasively commended this principle by realizing it in practice.[2] Though his words on the *vetera* and *nova* had the ring of a consciously and reassuringly traditional formula, they have made room for a problem barely entertained and a solution barely hinted at in classical Catholic tradition.

The problem is summed up in the conditionedness of acts of meaning by historical contexts of meaning. True, St. Thomas "was quite accurate on the matter of eternal truths. They exist, but only in the eternal and unchanging mind of God"[3] (S. T. I, q. 16, a. 7). Still, neither Thomas nor, much less, the Renaissance scholasticism prolonged by manuals down to our own time drew the conclusion that theology, if it was to make our religious heritage truly and thoroughly intelligible to us, would have to undertake the vast historical task of recovering the contexts in which religious formulations were originally embedded, of tracing through subtly shifting semantic centers of gravity the transpositions of religious themes from one context to another, and of thereby helping to meet the conditions for distinguishing between successful and failed transpositions in the past as well as for effecting successful transpositions in the present, with both the new developments they entail and the concomitant sloughing off of untransposable "period trash."[4]

Shorn suddenly of the protection of its conceptualist premises, of the illusion of meaning without context, objectivity without subject, truth without mind and so without time, Catholic theology is newly and finally positioned to capitalize on the discovery that, far from being the enemy of the truths of philosophy and religion, the swelling tide of historical knowledge is a condition of their transposability from context to context and hence of their lasting validity. What history can do for us with reference to christology is nothing less than to allow us to enter into our rightful christological heritage in the recognition that this very act of inheriting recurrently requires an enlarging and enriching of the old with the new.

The present essay, I hasten to add, does not itself ambition anything so grand. It remains at the level of determining what the old really was. It is an effort to recover a single but crucial moment in the emergence of christological meaning. It undertakes to consider Christ as subject, not at that threshold where one conducts the inquiry into "subject" and "consciousness" (and where Lonergan realized in a particularly striking way the ideal of enlarging and enriching the old with the new)[5] but beyond that threshold in the properly historical sphere, where Christ is the subject of horizons, perspectives, purposes, and purposeful words and acts.

II

The central act of the Jerusalem Church was to interpret the Easter vindication of Jesus as messianic enthronement. But how did this interpretation relate to the historic career of Jesus? Was messiahship tacked onto the figure of Jesus after the fact? Or was it inevitable, in the light of his historic words and acts, that divine vindication should be construed in just this way? In either case the resourceful historian of religions may make the interpretative act of the Jerusalem Church historically comprehensible. But this must not be allowed to conceal the chasm between messianic enthronement as one interpretative option out of many, and messianic enthronement as the uniquely coherent, the "inevitable," interpretation of Jesus' vindication.

Clearly relevant to this issue (the resolution of which cannot but determine in large part how one will understand both Jesus and the Jerusalem Church) is the question of where to locate the beginnings of thematic christology. On this there ae two positions in contemporary scholarship, one locating these beginnings in the Easter experience of the disciples, the other positing the historicity of the disciples' pre-Easter confession of Jesus as Messiah (cf. esp. Mark 8:27; Matt 16:16; Luke 9:20; John 6:68f.; 1:41f.) and, still more fundamentally, the messianic self-understanding of Jesus himself (Mark 8:27c, 29; Matt 16:13c, 15; Luke 9:18c, 20; Mark 14:62; Matt 26:64; cf. Mark 15:2; Matt 27:14; Luke 23:3; John 18:37;). These two views represent a complete disjunction: thematic christology either did or did not originate earlier than Easter. Between these contradictory alternatives there can be no middle ground or third position.

Nils Alstrup Dahl, to be sure, has presented in his well-known essay "The Crucified Messiah"[6] what at first looks like a third position.

But in fact it is a combination in which pre-Easter thematic messiah-ship is affirmed but in so weak a sense as to be left virtually unaf-firmed. At Jesus' trial before the Sanhedrin (if there actually was a trial before the Sanhedrin) and at his trial before Pilate, "Messiah" (or "king") figured in an accusatory question. Out of a willingness to ac-commodate to the categories of the questioner (for he "could not deny the charge that he was the Messiah without thereby putting in question the final eschatological validity of his whole message and ministry"),[7] Jesus acknowledged, either by a word "extorted" from him or at least by silence, that he was the Messiah.[8]

Dahl, it should be noticed, did not ask precisely why it was that Jesus thought he would put his whole ministry in question unless he were to accept a title that he did not otherwise find appropriate. Moreover, one cannot but wonder whether this supposed dilemma of Je-sus is coherent with the view that "Messiah" in the Judaism of Jesus' time was merely one among many parallel figures and by no means "the necessary contemporary expression" for "eschatological bringer of salvation."[9] Dahl's view had the merit of insisting once again on the great significance of the *titulus* on the cross by attesting that there had indubitably been some messianic thematization of Jesus, whoever grounded and by whomever sponsored, in the pre-Easter period; that it played a key role in Jesus' condemnation; and that this itself was of lasting significance for the post-Easter Church. Nevertheless, his view as it stands neither represents a genuine third position between the two we have distinguished nor exhibits the internal coherence of an histori-cally plausible account. Leaving it aside, then, we shall consider only the clearly stated alternatives; thematic christology either did or did not originate earlier than Easter.

For either of these views the price of probability is to concede meaning and importance to the data on which the opposing view is based. For, even should it be made plausible that prior to the Easter event Jesus himself deliberately elicited from his disciples acknowledg-ment as "the Messiah" *(mĕšîhā' = ho christos)* or that he was referring to his own future destiny and role in evoking "the Man" *(bar 'ĕnāšā' = ho huios tou anthrōpou)* foreordained to bring the eschatological ordeal to an end (see, e.g., Luke 17:22-30), it nevertheless remains implausi-ble that, as it stands, the gospels' presentation of the use of such titles literally transcribes the pre-Easter past. There are some indisputably non-historical uses of the titles (on "Messiah" or "Christ" see Mark

9:41; Matt 23:10; on "Son of Man" see, e.g., Mark 2:10; Matt 9:6; Luke 5:24; Mark 2:28; Matt 12:8; Luke 6:5; Matt 8:20; Luke 9:58); there are still more instances in which historicity is doubtful; and, in any case, those who find the beginnings of thematic christology in the time of Jesus' ministry must still acknowledge that the Easter even triggered a christological explosion. Conversely, even if it should be plausibly argued that thematic, titular christology dates only from the Easter experience of the disciples, it is still altogether implausible that the dramatic emergence of such christology lacked solid roots in the pre-Easter career of Jesus.

This is not to minimize the significance of the debate or the difference between the two stands it has brought to light. In terms of the history of religions the debate is significant both as history and as the history of a religion. It is the function of history to settle matters of fact and the condition of historical achievement is a passion for getting things straight. But the question of who and what stood at the beginnings of thematic christology not only bears on a matter of fact but on a hinge fact of great significance to Christianity as a religion. For, the history of Christianity is the history of a people bonded not by blood but by meaning, and struggling to achieve its own summoning selfhood by finding its way to the center of that meaning. the relation of christological confession to the Jesus of history and, indeed, to his self-understanding belongs inalienably to that center. As Franz Mussner once put it, this is a *Schicksalsfrage* for Christianity. If christology has no roots at all in the consciousness of the historical Jesus, how in the end could it vindicate its claim to be other than and much more than mere ideology?[10]

Behind myth, urges one school of research, stands ritual. But behind the Christ myth--that is, behind the affirmation of Jesus as messianic Lord--stands not just ritual but a disruptive flesh-and-blood figure, a man with a public career and definable mission, a charismatic hero to the depressed elements of the society he addressed, a defendant accused of a political crime and executed by a known official. How one answers the question of whether the Jerusalem Church's interpretation of him as Messiah reflects Jesus' own understanding of his mission or is a wholly independent conception of his person and work tends to settle how one will answer such ulterior questions as whether Christianity originated with Jesus or his disciples, whether public events in the history of Israel pertained to its foundations, whether the categories ap-

propriate to understanding Christianity in its origins and root structures
are supplied by Torah and prophets (Messiah, covenant, remnant, etc.)
or by gnosis or the mysteries or other cults of Hellenistic Egypt,
Greece, and Rome. If these are matters of moment, they only underscore
the importance of accurately locating the beginnings of thematic christology. Obviously, this project is far too large to be undertaken here in
its full scope. In what follows we shall be obliged to do no more than
indicate in summary fashion certain grounds for locating these beginnings in Jesus himself. With particular reference to the temple riddle
(Mark 14:58 par.) we shall correlate the aspects of weal *(Heil)* and woe
(Unheil) in Jesus' conception of his mission. Finally, we shall return
to the issue of whether or not there is an intrinsic connection between
thematic christology and Jesus' actual career.

III

The complexity of the question "did the historical Jesus understand himself to be the Messiah?" derives, ironically, from the disciples'
Easter proclamation of his messiahship, for this proclamation grounds
the possibility that the Easter Church might have merely retrojected
messiahship and messianic consciousness to the days of Jesus' public
life. The methodical sceptic (that is, the critic who argues that, of words
and acts attributed to Jesus, only that is historical which contradicts
practices or convictions of both Judaism and the early Church) immediately infers from the continuity between the Easter proclamation and the
messianic texts of the gospels the impossibility of showing historically
that Jesus understood himself to be the Messiah. The restrictive or negative side of the methodical sceptic's principle ("*only* that is historical
which. . .") is arbitrary and invalid[11] and no historical critique consistently observing it could be anything but self-defeating.[12] In its positive
moment, however, and in the following formulation, the principle is
valid: those words and acts attributed to Jesus that are discontinuous
with the practices and convictions of the early Church do derive from
him. It follows that the critic interested in the issue of Jesus and messiahship should pay particular attention to traditions that relate to messiahship but fail to correlate with the early Church's own characteristic

messianic themes.

The leading candidate for such status may well be the riddle apparently taken up out of the Jesus tradition with mortal effect by Stephen and the *hellēnistai* (cf. Acts 6:14). Approximating the formulation which it receives in the account of Jesus' own trial, we have:

> Destroy (or I will destroy) this sanctuary
> and within three days I will build another.[13]

Limitations of space do not permit here a full-dress review of scholarship on this saying from Dalman to the present day. Let it suffice to make three remarks on this exegetical history and to follow them with a few further observations on the interrelation of the themes of weal and woe.

First, it is an extraordinary fact that scholarly opinion since Dalman is practially unanimous in favor of historicity. Given this or that qualification on the wording, the critics are almost all at one in attributing the saying to Jesus himself.

Second, the effort to locate in the history of religions the field of meaning to which the saying is related has been at least partly successful. But the hope of finding a pre-Jesus model in which the motifs of destroying and building the sanctuary were already conjoined has not been met. Neither the proposal of Reitzenstein,[14] accepted by Bultmann[15] and Goguel,[16] on a background in the eschatological myth of the primaeval man (= "Son of man") nor the proposal of J. G. H. Hoffmann,[17] following Engnell's studies in divine kingship,[18] on a background in Canaanite ritual (and thence in the royal messianism of the Bible) has proved out. In both cases something is lacking either in the data or in the argument or in the two together.[19] That classical messianism, on the other hand, offers a relevant background for the motif of building the sanctuary has several times been noticed, beginning with the observations of Dalman and culminating in those of Otto Betz.

Dalman made the fundamental observation that Jesus "spoke of the building of the temple (cf. Matt 26:61, Mark 14:58) in the same sense in which the Messiah is the builder of the temple according to Zech 6:12, 13."[20] The building of the temple was the task of the son of David (i.e., Solomon) according to the oracle of Nathan (2 Sam 7:13f., repeated in 1 Chron 17:12f.) and this motif was actualized by prophets (Hag 1:1f.; 2:20-23; Zech 6:12f.) intent on the post-exilic rebuilding of the temple. But was Jesus' adoption of the temple-building motif meant "in the same sense" as that of Zech 6? Was he to build a physical temple? The latter question Dalman left unanswered; but he did show that the riddle of Jesus may well have had a scripturally grounded messianic significance.[21]

Betz pointed to the fact that the text of Nathan's oracle had been interpreted messianically by the Essenes (4QFlor 1-13), admittedly without a messianic interpretation of the precise words "he shall build a house for my name" in 2 Sam 7:13).[22] He articulated the correlations in the Christian reading of the oracle between the motifs of Davidic Messiah, Son of God, resurrection, enthronement, and the building of the temple. He rooted the crucial tie between messiahship and the building of the temple in the historical Jesus' own symbolic actualization of biblical tradition. Betz was thus able to recognize the significance of age-old biblical tradition for understanding both the Markan trial-scene before the Sanhedrin (esp. Mark 14:58-62) and the celebrated "Thou art Peter" pericope (esp. Matt 16:16-19).

Third, the effort to say how the motifs of destroying "this sanctuary" and building another fit in with other data on Jesus' view of the future was crowned with success--a success largely overlooked by subsequent scholarship--in the work of C. H. Dodd and Joachim Jeremias. Dodd found that he could easily fit the phrase on destroying the sanctuary into the framework of Jesus' vision of events destined to take place in history (all of which belonged to "the eschatology of woe"); but, finding himself unable to fit into the same historical framework the phrase on building another sanctuary, he posited a complementary framework of post-historical "apocalyptic" events (Jesus' "eschatology of bliss") to which it must have been meant to refer.[23] These events would be opened by the day of the Son of man: at once resurrection, enthronement, and parousia. Dodd's achievement was thus to set the temple saying in the fully coherent context of a two-phase vision of the future: first, woe, rooted in the response to Jesus' ministry and epitomized in the destruction of the temple; then bliss, inaugurated by the day on which the Son of man is revealed (Luke 17:30) and epitomized in the new temple.

Jeremias offered a critical appreciation of this analysis.[24] The critical aspect was evident in his disengaging the reconstruction from Dodd's one-sided system of "realized eschatology." But the positively appreciative aspect was evidenced by the way in which Jeremias added the high gloss of technical precision to Dodd's insightful reconstruction.

The eschatological scheme of early Christianity differentiated perforce between resurrection and parousia, for the consummation of history did not take place with the resurrection. The "three days" sayings, on the other hand, supposed an eschatological scheme in which "the third day," the great turning point, was a global undifferentiated whole. This, together with the motif of Jesus as the destroyer of the temple, made the temple saying problematic to the early Christian community. Since the triumph imaged in the new temple had not come with Jesus' resurrection, the promise to build it in three days looked like unfulfilled prophecy. (The fourth gospel solved the problem by reinterpreting the new temple as the body of the risen Christ; cf. John 2:19-21).

Jeremias had never doubted the messianic sense of the temple saying or its transcendent and symbolic perspective.[25] And thirty years after his article on Dodd's reconstruction of Jesus' vision of the future, he completed the analysis by offering a convincing treatment of the three-days motif as designating the interval between the climax of the eschatological ordeal and its resolution with the coming of the reign of God.[26]

The end-result of research and reflection on the temple riddle from Dalman to the present day is to have vindicated its historicity; to have located at least one element of its background in the history of religions, namely, in biblical texts identifying the Messiah as that son of David/Son of God (2 Sam 7:13f.; 1 Chron 17:12f.; Ps 2:7; 89:27; 110:3; cf. 4 Q Flor 11) who is appointed to build God's house (2 Sam 7:13f; 1 Chron 17:12f; Hag 1:1f.; 2:20-23; Zech 6:12f.); and, finally to have set the saying in the context of the historical Jesus' own view of the future as divided between the eschatological ordeal (here epitomized in the destruction of the temple) and its swiftly following ("in three days") resolution (here epitomized in the building of the new temple, i.e., the transfigured community of Jesus' followers).

The saying is a consciously enigmatic disclosure of Jesus' mission as comprehending both weal and woe. The enigma lies in the antithesis "destroy/"build," which correlates with Israel's divided response to him, seen now as settled. The antithetical structuring recalls two images from the classic tradition of the prophets. The first is that of Jerusalem, the temple city set high on the mountain, under attack by the nations but inviolable under the protection of Yahweh (Isa 8:9f.; 17:12-14; 14:26f.; Joel 2:1-20; Zech 12:2-4). The second is that of Yahweh bringing the nations up against Jerusalem (Zech 14:2; Ezek 38:14-17) or himself laying siege to the city (Isa 29:2f.; Zeph 3:8b).[27] The basic theme is that Yahweh protects Jerusalem; Yahweh against Jerusalem is a thematic reversal grounded in the prophetic conviction that the inviolability of the city was conditioned on its allegiance to God (e.g., Isa 7:9b; 14:32; 28:16). This is simply a variation on the basic thematic reversal effected by the prophetic movement as a whole: far from being an unconditional guarantee of security, the day of Yahweh would see his judgment turned against Israel itself.

The riddle of Jesus gave this thematic legacy a new shape. In the ordeal about to break out unbelieving Jerusalem would go under. But at the center of Jesus' eschatology stood the messianic remnant, the unique beneficiary of God's saving act. This surely is the key to the remarkable phenomenon of Jesus' consistent *application to the disciples* of the imagery of the city on a mountain (Matt 5:14;[28] cf. Thomas, 32), the cosmic rock (Matt 16:18; cf. John 1:42), and the new sanctuary (Mark 14:58; Matt 26:61). *Here* was the inviolable city streaming light onto the world; here was the temple built on rock, secure against the assaults not of the nations but of death; here was the sanctuary to be built by the newly enthroned king.

IV

R. G. Collingwood distinguished between the "outside" and the "inside" of an event.[29] The outside is what can be described in terms of time, place, and movement. The outside of the Jesus event is easily summarized: a public figure in his mid-thirties, Jesus was itinerant in the regions of Galilee and Judea in the days of the Roman prefect Pontius Pilate (A.D. 26-36) at whose command he was executed by crucifixion on the charge of claiming to be a king.

This summary is not historical knowledge in the proper sense but data for historical knowledge. Knowledge adds to data the effort to understand the data and the effort to secure that understanding as correct. Such efforts entail the quest of ever fuller data, deeper understanding, more detailed and circumstantial cross-checking. The result, inevitably, is to discover something of the "inside" of the event under investigation; that is, to grasp it as motivated in some way, moving in some direction, significant in some context. This internal factor, which gives the event its human and historical density, can only be described in terms of meaning. The meaning of the event--the meaning intrinsic to and constitutive of it--has two sources: the intention of its author(s) and the context of its actualization.

Prescind from their differences and actions are all the same. But consider actions, not abstractly in their physical reality alone, but concretely in their properly human integrity, and they are all unique. This concrete approach to action, typical of history as distinct from science, is equally the key to the historian's scepticism of "laws" purporting to explain a given action and to his interest in recovering the particular perspectives and purposes that account for the coming to be of the action and its unique contour. Thus, the historian is positively concerned with action not only as taking place in a given context and having a given impact on it but also as a revelation of the agent. For, action is symbolic. Its meaning is irreducible to its pragmatic effect--what Michael Novak, echoing William James, has called its "cash value." Every action, argued Novak, "also means what the agent intends it to mean, i.e., what he is symbolizing by it. . . .Action is like speech: each life utters a unique word."[30] This corresponds to the category of "incarnate meaning" and is obviously central to "the inside of the event."

At this point we might recall, for purposes of illustration, the novelty of Jesus' initiative toward notorious sinners (*hamartōloi;* cf. e.g., Mark 2:14; Matt 9:9; Luke 5:27; cf. 19:5). Apart from the cleansing of the temple, no other feature of his public career so startled his contemporaries. To the sinners themselves his free entry into contact and communion (cf. "dining" in Mark 2:15f.; Matt 9:10f.; Luke 5:29f.; cf. 5:2) with them was irresistible (cf. "friend" in Matt 11:19; Luke 7:34; cf. Mark 2:14c; Matt 9:9d; Luke 5:27c; 7:37f.) but to the upright *(dikaioi)* it was indefensible (e.g., Mark 2:16; Matt 9:11; Luke 5:30; Matt 11:19; Luke 7:34; 7:36-50; 15:1f.). Now, Jesus no more intended to write off the upright than he did the sinners; hence a set of memorable words, several of them in the form of "I have come" sayings, addressed to the upright and meant to explain, justify, and commend his initiative toward the sinners. These texts present Jesus' behavior toward the sinners in the images, first, of the physician:

It is not the healthy but the sick who need the physician
(Mark 2:17a; Matt 9:12; Luke 5:31),

second, of the messenger (cf. Luke 14:16f.) commissioned by his master to tell the invited guests that the banquet is ready:

I have not come to summon the righteous but the sinners
(Mark 2:17b; Matt 9:13; Luke 5:32),

and third, of the shepherd who, having counted his sheep and found one
missing, sets out in search of the straggler:

The Son of man has come to seek and to save the lost
(Luke 19:10).

Now, the point of the images of physician, messenger, and shepherd is
to make the "inside" of Jesus' actions intelligible: to reveal the purposes that fill them and to present them in a swiftly sketched parabolic setting designed to illuminate and commend them. As the physician goes
to the sick because they need him, as the messenger summons the
guests at his master's bidding, as the shepherd for whom every sheep
counts sets out for the straggler--so I go to the sinners. The images un-
ravel an enigma; no enigma remains in Jesus' behavior toward sinners if
one takes account of the sinners' need (Mark 2:17a; Matt 9:12; Luke
5:31), of the claim on God of every child of Abraham (Luke 19:9f.; cf.
13:16) and, finally, of God's own will, benevolence, good pleasure
(Mark 2:17b; Matt 9:13; Luke 5:32; cf. Luke 15:11-32; *thelein* in
Matt 12:7; 20:14f.; *thelēma* in Matt 18:14; *chara* in Luke 15:7, 10).
The images are designed to offer the explanatory perspectives in which
Jesus' startling, enigmatic comportment toward sinners suddenly becomes transparent, a luminous epiphany of divine love.

If we allow these explanatory images to function as patterns
on which to understand "Messiah," the question arises: what action of
Jesus is "Messiah" meant to explain?

The answer lies half-hidden in traditions we have already alluded to: the confession at Caesarea Philippi (Matt 16:13-20; John 1:41f.;
cf. John 6:68f.; Mark 8:27-30; Luke 9:18-21) and the trial before the
Sanhedrin (Mark 14:57-62; Matt 26:60-64). For these suggest, as we

have noted, that "Messiah" should be defined in accord with the most classical biblical messianism as that Son of David and Son of God who is appointed to build God's house; second, that we should understand the whole mission of Jesus, divided between a present earthly and future heavenly phase, as the building of the new sanctuary or (to translate the metaphor) the bringing into being of the eschatological covenant and people of God.

The point at which all the words and acts of Jesus' public career converged was the eschatological restoration of Israel. "Messiah" in the sense of the above texts adds nothing to this except to specify it, under the image of the new sanctuary, as the appointed task of the messianic Son of David/Son of God. "Messiah," in short, is explanatory. As "physician" or "messenger" or "shepherd" explains Jesus' initiative to sinners, "Messiah" explains the totality of his words and acts and affirms their interconnectedness as facets of one purpose. To predicate "Messiah" of Jesus in the sense he himself intended is to grasp the "inside" of the Jesus event as the single task of re-creating Israel--and the nations by assimilation to Israel--in fulfillment of the Scriptures. To this messianic mission belonged, above all, Jesus' death as "ransom" (Mark 10:45; Matt 20:28; cf. Isa 43:3f.), expiatory offering (Mark 14:24c; Matt 26:28b; Luke 22:20c; John 6:51; cf. Isa 53:10), and covenant sacrifice (Mark 14:24b; Matt 26:28a; Luke 22:20b; cf. Exod 24:8; Jer 31:31-34), not only for Israel but for the nations (Mark 10:45; Matt 20:28; Mark 14:24; Matt 26:28b; cf. John 6:51; Isa 52:13-53:12).

If Jesus himself thus saw to it that his messiahship be defined by his destiny, a like intention imposed itself in the confessions of the post-Easter Church. "Messiah" had originally provided the heirs of the biblical tradition with a world of meaning taken over by Israel from "sacral kingship" and thematizing enthronement, restoration of temple and cult, judgment, and the universal reign of justice and peace. Messiahship did not lose its sacral and royal aura everywhere in early Christianity, witness the gospels. But the death and resurrection of Jesus established the new soteriological pattern that early defined the messiahship of Jesus and so dominantly that the predicate "Christ" became rather the *subject* of predication, a cognomen, a name. At the springs of this development, however, stood the historic figure whose real task, despite appearances, was caught parabolically and comprehensively in the royal images of master-builder and temple (Matt 16:18;

Mark 14:58; Matt 26:61; John 2:19).

NOTES

1. Dom Gregory Dix, **Jew and Greek: A Study in the Primitive Church** (Westminster: Dacre Press, 1952) 77-81.

2. **Insight** and **Method in Theology** are the outstanding but not the only examples. For Lonergan's statement of the ideal, see the end of the *verbum* articles and the end of **Insight; Verbum: Word and Idea in Aquinas,** 220; **Insight: A Study of Human Understanding,** 748.

3. Bernard J. F. Lonergan, "Philosophy and Theology," **A Second Collection,** 193-208, p. 193.

4. The phrase in inverted commas is borrowed from Austin Farrer, **Finite and Infinite: A Philosophical Essay** (Westminster: Dacre Press, 1943; repr. 1964) ix.

5. Bernard J. F. Lonergan, **De constitutione Christi ontologica et psychologica** (Rome: Gregorian University Press, 1964) 83-148. See also "Christ as Subject: A Reply," **Collection,** 164-97.

6. N. A. Dahl, "The Crucified Messiah," **The Crucified Messiah and Other Essays** (Minneapolis: Augsburg, 1974) 10-36.

7. Ibid., 33.

8. Ibid.

9. Ibid., 26.

10. F. Mussner, "Wege zum Selbstbewusstsein Jesu. Ein Versuch," *Biblische Zeitschrift* 12 (1968) 161-72, p. 161.

11. See B. F. Meyer, **The Aims of Jesus** (London: SCM Press, 1979) 81-84; p. 277 n. 8.

12. See M. D. Hooker, "On Using the Wrong Tool," *Theology* 75 (1972) 570-81.

13. For the various textual forms see Mark 14:58; Matt 26:61; Mark 15:29; Matt 27:40; John 2:19; cp. Acts 6:14. Aramaic retroversion, slightly revised from G. Dalman, **Orte und Wege Jesu** (Gütersloh: Mohn, 41924; repr. Darmstadt: Wissenschaftliche Buchgesellschaft, 1967) 324.

'ănā' sātar hĕkĕlā' hādĕn
ûlitĕlātā' yômîn nibnê ḥôrānā.

14. R. Reitzenstein, **Das Mandäische Buch des Herrn der Grosse und die Evangelienüberlieferung** (Heidelberg: Winter, 1919) 63-70.

15. R. Bultmann, **The History of the Synoptic Tradition** (Oxford: Blackwell, 1968) 120f., p. 401.

16. M. Goguel, "La parole de Jésus sur la destruction et la reconstruction du Temple," **Congrès d'histoire du christianisme I**, ed. P. L. Couchoud (Paris: Rieder and Amsterdam: Van Holkema & Warendorf 1928) 117-36, pp. 135f.

17. J. G. H. Hoffmann, "Jésus messie juif," **Aux sources de la tradition chrétienne** [M. Goguel Festschrift] (Neuchâtel/Paris: Delachaux & Niestlé, 1950) 103-11, p. 105.

18. Ivan Engnell, **Studies in Divine Kingship in the Ancient Near East** (Oxford: Blackwell, [3]1967; original: Uppsala, 1943) 150.

19. M. Lidzbarski, **Das Johannesbuch der Mandäer** (Giessen: Töpelmann, 1915) 242 n. 4, was probably right in the first place that the Mandaean text is dependent on Jesus' saying. The key word *hêkělā'* differs, however, in meaning in the two texts. In Jesus' saying it is the sanctuary of the Jerusalem temple; in Enoš's word it is 'palace' as symbol of the world. Again, Engnell has attempted to reconstruct the Canaanite pattern for the Sukkot festival. But even if the reconstruction were more certain than it is, its relevance to Jesus' word remains doubtful. Thus, Hoffman can appeal to a vague and uncertain parallel but can offer no textual support for it.

20. G. Dalman, **The Words of Jesus** (Edinburgh: Clark, 1902) 307.

21. Dalman also took notice of the scripturally grounded (Ps 2 and 110) identification of "Messiah" and "Son of God," ibid.

22. O. Betz, "Die Frage nach dem messianischen Bewusstsein Jesu," *Novum Testamentum 6* (1963) 20-48; also, **What Do We Know About Jesus?** (Philadelphia: Westminster, 1968) 83-112. On the one hand, the Essene congregation was already the sanctuary of God prior to the coming of the Davidic Messiah (cf. e.g., 1QS 8:5-9; 1QH 6:25-28); on the other, God himself would build a new temple "at the time of blessing") (11Q Temple 29:8-10; cf. 5Q13 2-6).

23. C. H. Dodd, **The Parables of the Kingdom** (London: Nisbet, 1935) see chapters two and three.

24. J. Jeremias, "Eine Neue Schau der Zukunftaussagen Jesu," *Theologische Blätter* 20 (1941) 216-22.

25. J. Jeremias, **Jesus als Weltvollender** (Gütersloh: Bertelsmann, 1930) 35-40.

26. J. Jeremias, "Die Drei-Tage-Worte der Evangelien," **Tradition und Glaube. Das frühe Christentum in seiner Umwelt** [K. G. Kuhn

Festschrift], ed. G. Jeremias, H.-W. Kuhn, H. Stegemann (Göttingen: Vanden-hoech & Ruprecht, 1971) 221-29.

   27.   See Hanns-Martin Lutz, **Jahwe, Jerusalem und die Völker: Zur Vorgeschichte von Sach 12, 1-8 und 14, 1-5** (WMANT 27; Neukirchen/Vluyn: Neukirchener Verlag, 1968) for text-critical, exegetical, and tradition-historical treatment of the texts.

   28. See K. M. Campbell, "The New Jerusalem in Matthew 5.14," *Scottish Journal of Theology* 31 (1978) 335-63.

   29.   R. G. Collingwood, **The Idea of History** (Oxford: Oxford University Press, 1946) 213-15.

   30. N. Novak, "The Christian and the Atheist," *Christianity and Crisis* 31 (1966) 51-55, p. 52.

IX

THE WORLD MISSION AND THE
EMERGENT REALIZATION
OF CHRISTIAN IDENTITY

This study deals with the relationship between the self-consciousness of early Christianity and the launching of the early Christian mission to the gentile world. From the standpoint of early Christian self-consciousness, the question is: what was it in the mind and heart of early Christianity that made the launching of the mission possible and reduced the possibility to act? From the standpoint of the history of the mission, the question is: what impact did the mission have on the self-consciousness of the early Christian Church?

Before taking up these two questions in turn (in parts two and three of this study), we shall sketch briefly the historical background and development of the launching of the mission, concentrating less on the detail of its episodes than on the conditions of its possibility.

Part one, then, is a historical sketch, which will begin with Jesus. Part two asks a set of "why?" questions. Why was there initially no mission to gentiles on the part of the community gathered around "Cephas and . . . the twelve" (1 Cor 15:5)? How explain, on the other hand, the willingness of Christian *hellēnistai* (Greek-speaking Jewish Christians) to speak the word of salvation to Samaritans (Acts 8) and gentiles (Acts 11)? What led the Antioch Christian community to sponsor a mission to the synagogues of Cyprus and south-central Asia Minor (Acts 13-14)? What explains the momentous agreement of the leaders of the Jerusalem Church with the Torah-free mission of Barnabas and Paul (Gal 2:1-10; Acts 15)? What freed Paul to launch out on his own, claiming a mandate for a worldwide mission to gentiles? Part three will raise the question: what in the end was the real impact of the mission on the self-consciousness of the first Christians?

I

Jesus understood his mission to comprehend the salvation of the world (Mark 14:24; par. Matt 26:28;[1] cf. Mark 10:45; par. Matt 20:28;[2] Matt 8:11; par. Luke 13:29;[3] Mark 4:30-32; par. Matt 13:31f.; Luke 13:18f.[4]). But how should we understand "salvation of the world"? What were the concrete, historical terms in which Jesus and his first disciples conceived of salvation for the world?

The appropriate place to begin is with Old Testament conceptions of salvation. In the consciousness of Israel, Yahweh had taken the initiative in choosing his own people out of the vast world of the peoples (Gen 11-12; Exod 19:5f.). He chose Israel and save Israel. He entered into a covenant with Israel. By that fact Israel became liable to an economy of blessings and curses, of saving interventions and condemnatory judgments, as in the oracle,

> Only you have I known
> out of all the earth's tribes;
> therefore will I punish you
> for all of your crimes (Amos 3:2).

Israel conceived good fortune and ill-fortune alike as covenantal judgments of God. But the covenant was no mere *quid pro quo* arrangement. It expressed Yahweh's elective love. Israel's transgressions of the covenantal stipulations failed to cancel out this love. If application of the covenantal dynamic to Israel meant "therefore will I punish you for all of your crimes," this same covenant grounded the hope that, though the judgment would be terrible, some would be snatched from the lion's mouth (Amos 5:15). And these few, said Amos and Isaiah and Micah and Zephaniah and the late chapters of Zechariah, were the new bearers of election and the seed of Israel to be restored.[5]

threats of punishment, but promises of restoration won out in the end.

> I know the thoughts that I think toward you, says Yahweh.
> They are thoughts of weal and not of woe,
> and they give you a future and a hope (ʾaḥărît wĕtiqwāʾ);
> then you will call upon me and come and pray to me
> and I will hear you; you will seek me
> and when you seek me with all your heart
> you will find me . . .
> and I will change the course of your destiny
>   (wĕšabtî et šĕbutekem) (Jer 29:11-14a)

The sense of the last phrase is: "I will restore your fortunes," or "I will bring about your restoration."[6] This epitomizes the hope of Israel.

Now, hope is a hoping for and a hoping in. As a hoping for, the hope of Israel was centered on the restoration of Israel. As a hoping in, it was centered on Yahweh, who was able to bring about this restoration, for he was Lord of the earth as well as Lord of Israel, and willing to bring it about, for to Israel he was father (Jer 3; 31; Isa 63; 64) and husband (Hosea), avenger and redeemer (Isa 40-55), like a suzerain committed to his liege (Exod 19-26; Deut 6; Josh 24) and like a mother bound to her children, for he had raḥămîm--a mother's compassionate tenderness--for his people (e.g., Pss 25:6; 79:8).

But Yahweh was the creator and Lord of the nations, too (Gen 1-12). In words addressed to Israel, he made promises for the nations, confirming that they had a share in blessings on Israel (Gen 12:3)[7] and, above all, in the climactic blessing of Israel's permanent restoration (cf. Isa 14:1; 56:3-7; Zech 2:15; Pss 47:10 [EVV v. 9]; 96:7-10). The reign of Yahweh, celebrated in the great Autumn festival,[8] so impinged on the classical prophet's hope of restoration as eventually to make it include not only the ingathering of Israel, but of the nations themselves. Both, perhaps, are meant in the psalm verse that says: Of Zion they shall say, 'One and all were born in her' (Ps 87:5), for everyone, no matter where he was born, would recognize in Zion his real home (Ps 87:7). Zion was the holy mountain and the navel of the earth (Ezek 5:5; 38:12).[9] It was the source of waters, hence of life, for all the world (cf. Gen 2:10-14; Ezek 47; Joel 4:18 [EVV 3:18]; Zech 14:8; Ps 46:5). Zion was the gate that divided this world from the netherworld (Ps 9:14f. [EVV vv. 13f.]). It was the site of the world sanctuary (Isa

(Ps 9:14f. [EVV vv. 13f.]). It was the site of the world sanctuary (Isa 56:7) and the goal of the world pilgrimage at the end of the days (Isa 2:2-4; 18:7; 25:6; 60:1-22; 66:18-23; Jer 3:17; Hag 2:7; Zech 8:20-23; 14:16-19; cf. Isa 14:1f.; 19:23; Ps 68:30 [EVV v. 29]). From Zion the Yahweh of Israel's future and hope would summon the whole earth "from the rising of the sun to its setting" (Ps 50:1) and the motif of Yahweh's reign conjured up the image of the princes of the peoples gathered together with the people of the God of Abraham (Ps 47:10 [EVV v.9]). The nations would bring their treasures as sacrifices to the temple court (Ps 96:8-10; cf. Ps 68:30 [EVV v. 29]).

Jesus of Nazareth presented himself to the Israel of the age of Tiberius as charged with a mission for the end of time. He announced, not a revolution, not a reform, but a fulfillment. He announced the reign of God, which the Israel of his time rightly understood to signify the divinely promised and long hoped-for restoration of Israel.[10] Moreover, by a series of stunning symbolic acts--cures and exorcisms, repeated initiatives toward notorious sinners and table fellowship with them, choice of twelve disciples (a symbol-charged number) and the sending of the twelve all over Galilee with the self-same proclamation of fulfillment, and finally a procession to the temple as the lowly and pacific "king" of Zech 9, and the many-faceted act of purging the court of the gentiles of merchants, parabolically judging the national cult and intimating its restoration--Jesus presented himself as fulfiller (cf. Zech 14:21) as well as announcer of fulfillment (cf. Isa 52:7-9).

Here, in short, was a restoration of Israel in process of realization, a restoration that confounded, dumbfounded, average expectations in Israel. It tore at the fabric of scribal authority. It violated taboos grounded in the Torah. In the cleansing of the temple, this impressive but baffling restoration lay violent hands on the untouchable. For all these things and, above all, for the claim to transcendent authority that they all implied, Jesus would pay with his life.

Unlike the Israel contemporary with him, Jesus renounced every hint of hope for vengeance on the gentiles.[11] Though he included the gentiles as beneficiaries of God's climactic and definitive saving act (of which he himself was the decisive agent),[12] he neither commanded nor commended a mission to gentiles. In accord with biblical tradition, he alluded to the salvation of the gentiles in the imagery of the post-historical pilgrimage of the peoples to restored Zion (Matt 8:11; par. Luke 13:29).[13]

Such was the inheritance of the Aramaic-speaking followers of Jesus (called *hebraioi* in Acts) who were gathered into an Easter community around Cephas and the twelve. According to Paul, in a text providing the earliest evidence of the self-understanding of this Jerusalem community, Cephas, James, and John were "pillars" (Gal 2:9)--pillars, that is, of the messianic temple of believers.[14] In its own view this eschatological sanctuary, together with the Zion on which it was established, constituted the nucleus of fulfillment of age-old hopes. This living sanctuary awaited the crowning events of history: the entry of all Israel into its appointed restoration, the return of the dispersed from all the countries to which the Lord had banished them (cf. Jer 32:37-40), the climactic hallowing of God's name, as the nations acknowledged the restoration of Israel (Ezek 36:23), and, finally, the pilgrimage of the peoples, when Zion would attain its destiny as the peak (Isa 2:2) and sanctuary (Isa 56:7) of the world. The Christian *hebraioi* of Jerusalem accordingly knew themselves as that sanctuary which Jesus was to build "in three days" (Mark 14:58; par. Matt 26:61; Mark 15:29; par. Matt 27:40; John 2:19; cf. Acts 6:14).

We thus find world salvation in the field of vision of the Aramaic-speaking Church of Jerusalem; but we do not find there the enabling conditions of a mission to the world. In the actuality of history, however, gentiles would not come into the legacy of the Jerusalem Church by a mass pilgrimage. Those who in fact came into this legacy did so thanks to an energetic missionary movement to the gentile world. According to Acts, this took place through the mediation of Greek-speaking Jewish Christians, probably converts to the first kerygma, whose distinctive horizons made a mission to non-Jews possible, and whose initiative and drive converted the possibility into action.

Acts provides seminal data on this dynamic element in earliest Christianity. They include the story of Stephen and his death by stoning (Acts 6-7); the story of Philip in Samaria (Acts 8); the story of Saul/Paul: his persecution (Acts 8), his conversion (Acts 9), and his proclamation of Jesus in Greek-speaking synagogues (Acts 9:19-21, 29); the arrival in Antioch of Greek-speaking refugees from Jerusalem, and their preaching to gentiles of Jesus as Lord (Acts 11:19f.).

These data derive, no doubt, from the *hellēnistai* themselves, via Antiochene literary sources.[15] Despite their lacunary and episodic character, the sources make it clear that the *hellēnistai* of Antioch were the initiators of a mission in gentile lands. What the sources of Acts do not tell us is how it was that a mission to the diaspora made little sense to one wing of early Christianity and made excellent sense to another. What this says about early Christian diversity is among the questions we shall entertain presently, in part two.

Paul of Tarsus looked back on his conversion experience on the road to Damascus as ordered from the start to his becoming Apostle to the gentiles (Gal 1:16). If (as is possible but not certain) Paul meant that right from the start he understood this "revelation" as a missionary mandate to win over the gentiles, perhaps he inaugurated his career immediately, in Arabia, i.e., the Nabatean kingdom (southern Transjordan, the Negev, and the Sinai peninsula) (Gal 1:17; cf. 2 Cor 11:32f.). But if so, it was an abortive experience. Paul would have learned from it that the actual fulfillment of his appointed career hinged not on personal initiative but on Church policy.

Paul may well have had something to do with the initiative of the Antioch community summarily described in the opening verses of Acts, chapter 13. In this enterprise Barnabas and Paul were partners. Their work came under attack by right-wing *hebraioi* from Jerusalem (Gal 2:4; Acts 15:1, 5), but it was affirmed by the pillars of the community: Cephas, James, and John (Gal 2:6-9; cf. Acts 15:7-19).

It may have been the so-called Antioch incident (Gal 2:11-21) and Luke's inheritance of the views of the Antioch community that together account for the distance between Acts' portrait of Paul and Paul's portrait of himself. Paul's real vocation--his independent mission to the gentiles (Gal 1:15f.; cf. 1 Thess 2:3f.; Gal 2:2, 7-9; Rom 1:5, 14; ll:13; 15:15-28)--took wing only after the dispute with Cephas and Barnabas (Gal 2:11-21), which was probably also the end of his special ties with Antioch. Thereafter he could unambiguously locate himself and his career in the missionary scenario sketched in Rom 9-11, which now accorded priority to the preaching to the gentiles. This reinterpreted, it did not sacrifice, the salvation-historical principle that went back to the policy of Antioch and, much later, found lapidary expression in Rom 1:16, "the Jew first, then the Greek." Paul now applied the principle to the divine plan as a whole. The present moment was concentrated on the salvation of the gentiles. The Apostle of the gentiles had come into his own. With the figure of Paul bent on the task of the world mission, we bring this summary sketch to a close.

II

What might account for the fact that the Greek-speaking Jewish Christians exhibited from the outset so striking an openness to Samaritans and gentiles? The charges against Stephen (Acts 6:13f.) offer a first clue. Stephen was hostile to temple and Torah, claiming "that Jesus the Nazorean will destroy this place and change the customs that Moses handed down to us" (Acts 6:14). The first part of the charge appears to reflect the word cited against Jesus in the trial before the Sanhedrin (Mark 14:58; par. Matt 26:61; cf. John 2:19). The reference of the second part of the charge is less precise, but it probably relays in garbled fashion words of Jesus such as his claim to bring the Torah to its appointed completeness (Matt 5:17), or his strictures (Mark 10:6-9; par. Matt 19:8f.; cf. Matt 5:32; Luke 16:18) on the inadequacy of the Deuteronomic legislation on divorce (Deut 24:1-4) in favor of return to what he conceived as the original ideal of marriage (Gen 2:24); or his hostility to the current halaka on the Sabbath (cf. Mark 2:27) and other topics (e.g. Mark 7:15; par. Matt 15:11). The point is that the charge against Stephen indirectly attests Stephen's appropriation of gospel traditions. Measured against the accent on the positive, the mood of confidence, the tone, the style, the bias of Cephas and the twelve as depicted in the first chapters of Acts, Stephen's interpretative retrieval and application of Jesus' words stand out as independent and distinctive. Whereas the Christian *hebraioi* were buoyed up by an optimism to which the heritage of Jesus' conflicts with his contemporaries and his harsh words on imminent judgment and ordeal, the ruin of the nation, the capital, and the temple were all very alien, the *hellēnistai* appear to have been strangely unaffected by this happy mood. Behind the charges against Stephen there probably stands an unvarnished appropriation by Christian *hellēnistai* of all Jesus' grim prophecies. The *hellēnistai* had come into possession of these traditions through the *hebraioi*, but the interpretation that they gave them was their own. If this is so, how are we to account for it?

The challenge is to account not only for a set of discrete interpretations, but for the horizon in which such moves took place. How describe and account for this horizon? A first set of indices relates to the break with the past of Jesus' historic words that the Easter event effect-

ed. In contrast to Jesus' own prophetic vision, his resurrection diverged
ex eventu from the still future and climactic coming of the reign of
God. What had not been foreseen was the single, isolated resurrection of
Jesus from the dead, an event dissociated in time from the general resurrection and the judgment. The eschatological scheme that informed the
authentic sayings of Jesus about the future[16] had posited two successive
moments: that of the ordeal (Aramaic, *nisyônāʾ*; Greek, *ho peirasmos*)
to be ushered in by his own suffering and death and to include a set of
dreadful disasters, and that of the swiftly following ("in three days")[17]
resolution of the ordeal by the revelation of "the Man" *{bar ᵉnāšāʾ*; *ho
huios tou anthrōpou)*, the pilgrimage of the nations, the judgment, the
new sanctuary in its splendor, the banquet with the patriarchs. In this
scheme the historic life of the messianic remnant or assembly *(ᵉedtāʾ hē
ekklēsia)* was coterminous with the ordeal; its *ʾabbāʾ* prayer was to be a
prayer for the ordeal;[18] its distinctive cultic meal would not only com-
memorate the death of Jesus but also invoke it in calling on the Father
to put an end to the ordeal.[19] There had been no room in this scheme for
a single resurrection to take place in the course of historical time nor,
consequently, for an interim between the resurrection of Jesus and his
public manifestation at the coming of the reign of God ("the day of the
[Son of] Man").[20] The Easter event shattered this eschatological scenario
and required that the whole be reconstituted to allow for an indeterminate segment of time between the resurrection of Jesus and his public
manifestation.

The *hebraioi* reconstituted the scenario as far as possible along
lines that had been laid down by Jesus himself. Israel had arrived at its
long hoped-for restoration in the disciples who celebrated his resurrection and now constituted the messianic community on Zion. While
awaiting the consummation of time and the ingathering of the nations,
this community would gather in its brethren by the power of the Easter
kerygma. The categories of the community's self-understanding were
grounded in the Jesus tradition: the eschatological sanctuary, the remnant of the last days, the assembly of the new covenant.[21]

But what did they make of their legacy of themes on the ordeal, such as the destruction of the temple? The opening chapters of
Acts, as we have observed, suggest a conception of the present moment
to which doom-laden prophecy was alien and irrelevant. Easter had unexpectedly inserted into the eschatological scheme of things a last moment of indeterminate (but surely brief!) duration that would accord Is-

rael a last (and surely irrestible!) appeal to enter into its heritage of messianic blessings (Acts 2:38; 5:31f.).

The Christian *hellēnistai* did not share this vision of things. Evidently, it was their understanding of the significance of the Easter event that generated the enabling conditions of their negative stand on Torah and temple and of their positive openness to Samaritans and gentiles. Contrary to the *hebraioi,* for whom Easter had reduced Jesus' prophecies of doom to provisional status, the *hellēnistai* interpreted Easter precisely as validating Jesus' woes on Israel, her capital and temple. The positive side of this view was a conception of Easter as radically transcending "this age." Its impact on those who shared in it by faith and baptism was transformative. Henceforward, life would be lived under the ascendancy of "the age to come." Temple and priesthood, Torah and halaka, were now all obsolete.

Moreover, textual indices to christology among the *hellēnistai* illuminate their missionary initiatives. The account of Stephen's trial supplies us with a reference to the Son-of-man theme (Acts 7:56), and in the story of Philip we meet a prophetic interpretation of the great Isaian passage on the suffering Servant (Acts 8:32-35). Both of these allusions to biblical sources are significant, for both sources strike the note of universalism. The salvation of the "many" (= the nations) in which the great Servant text culminates (LXX Isa 53:11; cf. 52:13) has as its only antecedent supposition the obedient suffering of the Servant. And the universal dominion of the "one like a son of man" ("all nations, tribes and languages," LXX Dan 7:14) follows immediately on his ascent to the court of the Ancient of Days (LXX Dan 7:13). The *hellēnistai* need only have identified the Easter event with the reversal of the fate of the Servant (LXX Isa 53:10b-12) and with the ascent of the "one like a son of man" (LXX Dan 7:13) to have understood this event as grounding scripturally an explicit universalism now.

Again, there are liturgical compositions produced by the *hellēnistai* and preserved by Paul that point in the same direction. A satisfactory literary critique isolates, in my opinion, a pre-Pauline distich in Rom 3:25f.[22]
This may be rendered:

> whom God displayed as the [true] propitiatory in his
> own blood/ for the remission of sins committed in
> [the time of] God's forbearance.

The primary effect of the text is to present Christ's bloody death as a divinely planned eschatological event. Its meaning had been limned in advance by the most solemn rite of the Day of Atonement, the sprinkling of blood on the propitiatory (Lev 16:14). This golden lid on the ark of the covenant had signified the presence of God, the locus of revelation, the forgiveness of sins; now these meanings were magnified by transposition to Golgotha where, for all to see, God displayed the fulfillment whose "type" had been hidden in the temple's innermost recess.

But it is a secondary aspect of the text that engages us here. The propitiatory--and, by implication, the whole economy of ritual Torah and temple--is reduced to the role of "type." The "true" propitiatory was the crucified Christ. In the perspective of this text the forgiveness of sins had awaited the climactic, definitive, unrepeatable *yôm kippur* of Golgotha. Once given this reality, temple and Torah could claim no independent significance. This sense of the text converges in approximate fashion with the accusation against Stephen.

The Philippians hymn (Phil 2:6-11) is likewise relevant to the recovery of the soteriology of the *hellēnistai*. The essential thrust of the hymn is to set the confession *kyrios Iēsous* ("Jesus is Lord!" 1 Cor 12:3; cf. Rom 10:9f.) in salvation-historical context. Resurrection, exaltation, installation as Lord were facets of the same event. The hymn gives the divine reason why (cf. v. 9, "therefore" or "this is why") of this event: it was a reward of obedience. In response to Jesus' selfless and flawless submission to God, God gave him the "name" by which he is acclaimed as divine Lord. Our present interest is in a secondary aspect of the text: the claim of the exalted *kyrios* to universal acclamation. Otfried Hofius is probably correct in understanding the full realization of the universal acknowledgement of the *kyrios* to be reserved for the end of time.[23] Still, the decisive moment, the turning point of the ages, has already taken place. In the view of the *hellēnistai* who composed this hymn[24] Easter had set the stage for the world mission.

Hebraioi and *hellēnistai* alike were convinced that the nations were rightful beneficiaries of eschatological salvation. The difference between the groups was established by a set of conceptions on the part of the *hebraioi* that the *hellēnistai* did not share: that the unexpectedly isolated vindication and glorification of Jesus created a new situation reducing his harsh prophecies of the ordeal to provisional status; that the regime of the Torah remained intact as in Jesus' day and with the radicalization that he brought to it; that (as to "when?") the entry of the gentiles into salvation would be signaled by "the day of the Man" (cf. Luke 17:22, 26, 30) in accord with Jesus' own view; that (as to "how?") this would take place by the eschatological pilgrimage depicted in the scriptures, again in accord with Jesus; that the mission of his followers was consequently limited, as in his own lifetime, to the house of Israel. Given these conceptions, the disparity between the inclusion of the gentiles in God's saving act and, on the other hand, their present isolation from messianic salvation was not felt to be enigmatic or incongruous. But in the absence of this set of conceptions and in the face of contrary convictions--that the vindication of Jesus confirmed the doom of the temple; that his expiatory death rendered the temple cult superfluous; that the glorification of Jesus already laid claim to universal acknowledgement and celebration--the world's non-entry into messianic salvation was precisely an incongruity calling for resolution.

Thus, the distinct horizons projected by the *hellēnistai* comprehended an explicit universalism, not in the mode of hellenistic humanism, but in that of realized eschatology. The Servant, now glorified, was seen to have served "many" well (LXX Isa 53:11; cf. the "many nations" of 52:15); now "all nations, tribes and languages" (LXX Dan 7:14) were called on to serve him, the Son of man installed at God's right hand (Acts 7:56; cf. Ps 110:1). The history of man's sin and God's forbearance--the ever accumulating debt and the patiently postponed settling of accounts--had come to an end on Golgotha (Rom 3:25f.). The millenary horizon evoked by the theme of Yahweh and his people now yielded to a horizon evoked by the theme of God, Christ, and the whole human race. Paul would ask, "is God God of the Jews alone? Is he not also God of the gentiles?" (Rom 3:29). God had reconciled to himself through Christ (cf. 2 Cor 5:19) not only Israel but "the many" (Mark 10:45; par. Matt 20:28; cf. Mark 14:24; par. Matt 26:28). Now "every knee" and "every tongue" (Phil 2:10f.) was to acknowledge God in acknowledging Jesus as Lord (Phil 2:11).

If the *hebraioi* were the link of the earliest community with the past of Jesus, the *hellēnistai* by their self-understanding made themselves the link with the future: not as the vanguard of Israel but as the vanguard of a purified mankind.

III

We began by sketching the beginnings of the Christian mission to the gentile world. Then, in an effort to make these beginnings historically intelligible, we offered an account of the interpretative convictions that induced Christian *hellēnistai*, first, to welcome Samaritans and gentiles into salvation and, then, to sponsor a missionary initiative in the Greek-speaking diaspora. We evoked two phases in the missionary career of Paul. Together with Barnabas, he first worked as commissioned by the Antioch community. Soon, however,--and perhaps under the impact of "the Antioch incident"--he made his work depend exclusively on an unmediated divine mandate for a worldwide mission to the gentiles.[25] The Paul of the letters is already established in this second phase of his missionary career.

We turn now to the question: what impact did the mission have on the self-consciousness of the first Christians? Obviously, a full answer would be too large, too complex, too difficult to attempt here. All the more reason, then, to focus on the heart of the matter, namely, on the resolution of policy questions that the launching of the mission made acute. This will require that we return briefly to the sequence of historical events, for to speak of "policy questions" suggests a certain conscious unity on the part of Christians as well as a conscious capacity for authoritatively settling practical issues, and the historicity of both these implications has been contested.

Both, on the other hand, find historically cogent support in Paul and in Acts. Paul, for example, affirmed the unity of the Church by his writing of letters, which was an effort to achieve *koinōnia* and a practice of realized *koinōnia*, like "the collection" for the poor among the saints in Jerusalem. Moreover, he made unity within each Church (e.g., 1 Cor 1-4; 12:4-6, 12-31; Phil 2:1-18) as well as among the Churches (e.g., Rom 16:25-27; cf. 1 Cor 16:1-4) not only a vital supposition (Gal 1:6-9; 2:2; 1 Cor 9:19-21; 10:32), but also a fully articulate theme (1 Cor 10:16f.; 12:12-31; 13:1-13). He underscored the ultimate ground of unity as one Spirit, one Lord, one God (1 Cor 12:4-6), proclaimed in one gospel (1 Cor 12:4-6; 15:1-11; Gal 1:6-9; Rom 1:16f.), re-creating mankind through baptism (1 Cor 12:13; Rom 6:3f.; cf. 2 Cor 5:16-21) and the eucharist (1 Cor 10:16f.), and eliciting from this new creation and Israel of God (Gal 6:15f.) a corporate life lived in love (1 Cor 13:1-13). If Paul made his career a career-long pursuit of ecclesial unity, this interlocks substantially and easily with inherited data in Acts and Luke's own redactional themes in Acts.

Neither in Paul nor in Acts did the concern for unity inhibit, much less paralyze, initiative. The first fifteen chapters of Acts depict a dynamic, pneumatic movement, its members venturing on one initiative after another. But the recurrent pattern was to follow up these initiatives with an effort of discernment, testing them for their coherence with the experiences, convictions, and commitments that the ecclesial community took to be normative.

Examples of this pattern of follow-up are the Jerusalem community's sending of Peter and John to Samaria in the wake of the baptizing of Samaritans by Christian *hellēnistai*; it was thus that the Samaritans "received the holy Spirit" (Acts 8:17). Again, once Peter had baptized the gentile Cornelius and his household, he was obliged by "the advocates of circumcision" (Acts 11:2) to present the rationale of this act to the Jerusalem community, which he successfully did (Acts 11:4-18). Furthermore, among the fugitives from persecution in Jerusalem there were "some men from Cyprus and Cyrene" who evangelized gentiles in Antioch. The Jerusalem community sent Barnabas to Antioch to test the legitimacy of this initiative (Acts 11:22-24). Probably in persuance of this mandate, Barnabas in turn called on Saul/Paul (Acts 11:25) to participate in the Antiochene leadership of "prophets and teachers" (Acts 13:1). Finally and climactically, the initiative of a Torah-free missionary journey (Acts 13-14) was contested by Jerusalem advocates of circumcision, but legitimized by the leaders of the Jerusalem community (Acts 15; cf. Gal 2:1-10).

The simultaneous operation in primitive Christianity of three factors--spontaneous missionary initiatives, concern for ecclesial unity, and acknowledgement of apostolic authority--generated the phenomenon of a developing Christian consciousness. The "consciousness" in question refers, not to the views of just one wing or of one faction or of one or another party within Christianity, but rather to a development on the part of Christianity as a whole between 30 A.D. and 60 A.D. In this fast-moving thirty-year period there was among the mass of Christians, be they Jews or Greeks, a far-reaching change of horizons, of self-understanding, of conscious self-shaping.[26] For, even more significant than the changing self-definition of particular groups (say, of the *hellē-*

nistai) was the inter-group impact of such change (e.g., the dialectic of
Jerusalemite and Antiochene self-definition). It is finally inescapable
that the peculiar mix of missionary initiatives, concern for unity, and
acknowledgement of authority powered and steered a general evolution
of Christian consciousness. The last and main purpose of this essay is
to establish the fact of this change and to define its character.

The conviction that ecclesial unity was a divine imperative
meant that the Jerusalem community gathered around Cephas, the
twelve, and James, "the brother of the Lord," could not regard with indifference the work--which they themselves had neither initiated nor
could in way have seen their way clear to initiate--of evangelizing Samaritans and gentiles. The same conviction of unity as divine imperative meant that when the innovations of Christian *hellēnistai* driven out
of Jerusalem to Damascus or Antioch were questioned or disallowed by
critics among the Christian *hebraioi* of Jerusalem, the innovators did
not feel free to sustain their course of action in the invulnerable conviction of being right. Rather, they sought to bring the conflict to authoritative resolution. Paul remained in this tradition. To be sure, he never
doubted the authenticity of his own vocation; but neither did he think it
meet and just that he go his own way without reference to the Torah-
observant saints of Jerusalem (Gal 2:2).[27]

How was the religious and ecclesial consciousness of these Jerusalemites affected by the successes of Antiochene Christian mission-
aries in the diaspora of the Greeks? Some scholars have been willing to
say: not at all.[28] The Jerusalemites (despite Paul's explicit testimony to
the contrary respecting the "pillars") never really approved the Torah-
free mission; "the two fronts remained" and they agreed "to differ."[29] But
one may wonder about the historical plausibility of this view. For,
while the Torah-observant life of the Jerusalemite Christians differed
from the Torah-free life of their gentile brethren in the Pauline and other
communities of the Greek-speaking diaspora, and while both wings of
the early Church agreed to differ in this sense, neither interpreted the differences as divisions rupturing ecclesial communion. Unlike the minor-
ity of dissident reactionaries among the *hebraioi*, Cephas, James, and
John could and did affirm both diversity and unity, as Paul and Barnabas
did. They did not demand that gentile converts to the common Christian
kerygma (1 Cor 15:11) be circumcised. Between Christian Jew and
Christian Greek uniformity was not imperative; hence, there was unity
amid diversity. On the side of the gentile converts in the Mediterranean

basin this is amply attested and historically certain. On the side of the Christian *hebraioi* of Jerusalem it is, though less fully attested, still solidly probable, and surely more probable than the contrary hypothesis (e.g., that the Jerusalem Church flatly refused the Pauline collection, so signifying ecclesial rupture). True, a new chapter in Christian history was opened by the events of the decade in which Cephas, Paul, and James were executed, and revolt broke out among Palestinian Jews against the empire; henceforward, the Christian center of gravity would shift from Jerusalem to Antioch and Ephesus and, eventually, to Rome. These developments, however, go beyond the limit we have set for this essay (60 A.D.).

How are we to explain the will to unity among the leaders of the *hellēnistai* and the openness to new initiatives among the leaders of the *hebraioi*? The answer proposed here is that it derived on both sides from the cardinal experience of salvation, i.e., from what the kerygma theologians of our century have named "the Easter experience of the disciples" (*das Ostererlebnis der Jünger*). This esperience was "cardinal" in the sense that on it, according to Paul, hinged the divine revelation of the gospel and the mandate to proclaim it (see, for example, 2 Cor 5:18f.).

It was on this basis, it seems to me, that Paul could mount an argumentative appeal to the *hebraioi* (represented by Cephas at a particular moment in Antioch): "we [i.e., you as much as I] . . . have come to know [i.e., by our encounter with the risen Christ] that man is made righteous not by works of the Law but through faith in Christ . . ." (Gal 2:15f.). The Easter experience, generative of the gospel and accordingly a normative index to the gospel, had totally bypassed the Torah, neither comprehending nor entailing it. Paul's appeal to Cephas had its counterpart in his appeal to the Galatians (Gal 3:2-5). They, too, had had an experience of salvation, a charismatic experience of the gifts of the Spirit of God. How had the Torah figured in this experience? In no way at all. It thus fell outside the sphere of the normative. Again, the appeal to the experience of salvation as principle of discernment was the linchpin in Peter's apologia for having baptized Cornelius and his household without requiring circumcision (Acts 11:15-17). In a word, the experience of salvation was an index to Christian identity.

"Identity" is what the core of one's allegiance makes one to be. The allegiance proper to the Christian is summed up in (to use a Pauline word) the "gospel" (*euaggelion*). They are Christians who commit themselves to the gospel, and Christian identity is what commitment to the gospel effects in those so committed. "Christian identity" and "gospel" are exact correlatives.

In the flesh-and-blood actuality of history, however, identity is realized in a cultural context. Christian *hellēnistai* differed culturally from Christian *hebraioi* already in Jerusalem of the early thirties. When identity is considered, not in abstraction from cultural context, but precisely in cultural context, I would call it self-definition. Self-definition, in other words, is identity culturally incarnated. Inasmuch as Torah piety belonged part and parcel to the horizons of the *hebraioi* of Jerusalem, they assimilated the experience of salvation in a way that left allegiance to the Torah intact. This is the point at which we must attend to the Pauline appeal differentiating between Torah piety and the heart of the Christian experience: "We [you and I] have come to know [by our encounter with the risen Christ] that man is made righteous, not by works of the Law, but through faith in Christ" (Gal 2:15f.).

We have said that "the Easter experience of the disciples" was the cardinal Christian experience, inasmuch as the gospel and its proclamation hinged on it (2 Cor 5:19; cf. 1 Cor 2:10-16; 9:1f.; 15:1-11). It was a charged experience: not only a revelation but a reconciliation--the reconciliation to God through the communion offered by his risen and glorified Son, of men who had earlier rejected the claim of this same Son (James), or abandoned him (the disciples in general), or "denied" him (Peter), or "persecuted" him (Paul).[30] Neither the prescriptions of the Torah nor its remedies for transgression had had any role in this drama of acquittal and reconciliation. It had not named and condemned the transgressions nor, much less, mediated their cancellation. The Easter experience--exclusively, integrally, normatively--had been revelation and reconciliation and mandate. It had generated the content of the gospel and the charge to proclaim it.

As foundational, the Easter experience was not merely a first experience, soon left behind. It was a lasting resource, the full sense of which could come to thematic consciousness only with time and under pressure of experience. In the last century, Carl von Weizsäcker argued that the persecution of the Jesus movement by Judaism (Acts 8:1) was the experience that "liberated the Christian faith." Persecution, that is, functioned as the means by which Christianity "came to a knowledge of itself."[31] One aspect of this observation is surely right: the matrix of the social reality that is "meaning" is, as George Herbert Mead has urged, the dialectic of gesturer and respondent.[32] The gesturer learns the meaning of his gesture by taking account of the respondent's response to it. Thus, the *hellēnistai* were only one wing of the two wings that made up the Christian community. The persecution of the *hellēnistai*[33] mediated, rather, the transition from the performative to the thematic self-definition of the *hellēnistai*.

Still, we have insisted that the inter-group dialectic of *hebraioi* and *hellēnistai*, of Jerusalem and Antioch, produced something of a common Christian consciousness. Moreover, we have already located the act that brought that dialectic to intensity. It was the launching of the Torah-free mission. This is what "liberated Christian faith." Here was the means by which it came to know itself. The mission drove the early Church to discover, laboriously, a selfhood irreducible to any and all cultural contexts. Christian identity was incarnated culturally, and that means that it was incarnated diversely. But it could not be exhausted nor swallowed up nor petrified in any of its cultural incarnations. As Paul put it, "neither circumcision nor uncircumcision is of any importance at all" (Gal 6:15; cf. 1 Cor 7:19). This inner Christian drama, set in motion by the Torah-free mission, was a drama of identity. Out of a crisis of conflicting self-definitions, Jerusalemite and Antiochene, one identity--the subjective correlative of one gospel--emerged into the light of thematic self-knowledge. A Greek adage founded on a line from Pindar bids us "Become what thou art!" Through the crisis instigated by the world mission, Christianity became what it already was: Israel restored, but far more than that, for the Israel of God was a new creation.

The figure that gave focus to this momentous self-realization was, of course, Paul of Tarsus.

> Free from all, I made myself a slave to all,
> > to win over as many as I could.
> To the Jews I became like a Jew
> > to win over Jews;
> > to those under the Law, like one under the Law
> > > (though I am not myself under the Law)
> > > to win over those under the Law;
> > > to those free of law, like one free of law
> > > > (though I am not free of God's law
> > > > but am bound to Christ's law)
> > > > to win over those free of law (1 Cor 9:19-21).

This remarkable flexibility respecting religious cultures or self-definitions is no isolated datum in Paul. When the gospel was at stake, neither circumcision nor foreskin had the slightest importance (Gal 6:15; 1 Cor 7:19). Having brought Christian identity to full consciousness, Paul could relativize all self-definitions. For example, he could put the gospel ahead of the self-definition, in itself fully legitimate, or "the strong" in Corinth and in Rome. It allowed him to differentiate between unity and uniformity. For, as we have already argued, there were two sets of opposites: unity versus division, and uniformity versus diversity. If division was incompatible with unity, and diversity with uniformity, still, there was no incompatibility of unity and diversity. Paul affirmed them both, but with this proviso: when diversity began to pose a threat to unity, he affirmed the priority of unity.[34] One gospel meant one self-identical Church, and the plurality of self-definitions, however legitimate, would not be allowed to subvert the oneness of the gospel and the correlative oneness of the Church.

From the moment of the Easter experience, the disciples became conscious of a new ecclesial, election-historical identity. But they moved from consciousness of identity to knowledge of identity only under pressure of the launching of the mission to the gentiles. The pressure was generated by theological conflicts, and the conflicts were rooted in cultural differences. The movement from mere consciousness of identity to thematic knowledge of identity concretely consisted in what Gregory Dix called "the 'de-Judaisation' . . . of Christianity."[35] The eschatological hope of Israel for definitive restoration was the chrysalis of an eschatological universalism when these hopes found fulfillment.

Publicly, Jesus proclaimed the reign of God and restoration of Israel. Privately, he taught his disciples what this meant for him: his death for the world and his glorification--to vindicate the meaning and value of that death as well as to undo its physical effects. If Jesus' death and glorification defined the gospel, the universalist thrust of that death and glorification somehow belonged to the definition. How? The world mission showed how. For, the mission brought into the light of day what had lain in the dark, a little under the surface of Israel's hopes, a little under the surface even of the Easter experience. This mission gradually but dramatically laid bare, not only to the world at large, but to Christians themselves, what the gospel was: the power of salvation for all who believe. It was news of new creation and a new mankind. The gospel was a third force, irreducible alike to Judaism and to Hellenism.[36] The identity correlative to the gospel accordingly transcended Jew and Greek, slave and freeman, male and female. This mission let Christianity know itself as mankind made new by solidarity with a new Adam lately risen from the dead (1 Cor 15:45).

NOTES

1. See Joachim Jeremias, **The Eucharistic Words of Jesus** (Philadelphia: Fortress, 1977) 179-182. Rudolf Pesch, **Das Abendmahl und Jesu Todesverständnis** (Freiburg: Herder, 1978) 90-125.

2. See Peter Stuhlmacher, "Vicariously Giving His Life for Many, Mark 10:45 (Matt. 20:28)," in **Reconciliation, Law and Righteousness** (Philadelphia: Fortress, 1986) 16-29.

3. See Joachim Jeremias, **Jesus' Promise to the Nations** (London: SCM, 1958) 55f. Jacques Dupont, " 'Beaucoup viendront du levant et du couchant . . .' (Matthieu 8, 11-12; Luc 13, 28-29)," *Sciences Ecclésiastiques* 9 (1967) 153-167. Of the attempts to break down the historical ascertainment yielded by this word of Jesus, namely, that he envisaged the eschatological pilgrimage of the nations at the consummation of time, none, so far as I can judge, has succeeded. An example is Dieter Zeller, "Das Logion Mt 8,11f/Lk 13,18f und das Motiv der 'Völkerwallfahrt,' " *Biblische Zeitschrift* 15 (S1971) 227-237; 16 (1972) 18-95.

4. See B. F. Meyer, **The Aims of Jesus** (London: SCM, 1979) 163f., 214f.

5. Ibid. 224-235, especially 225-229.

6. See Ernst Ludwig Dietrich **SWB SBWT. Die endzeitliche Wiederherstellung bei den Propheten** (Giessen: Töpelmann, 1925). On the eschatology summed up in the words "the restoration of Israel," see E. P. Sanders, **Jesus and Judaism** (London: SCM, 1985) 77-119.

7. See the sagacious treatment of this text in Gerhard von Rad, **Genesis. A Commentary** (Philadelphia: Westminster, 1972) 159-161.

8. See John Gray, **The Biblical Doctrine of the Reign of God** (Edinburgh: Clark, 1979).

9. Shemaryahu Talmon, "har gibh^c^ah," **Theological Dictionary of the Old Testament**, (Grand Rapids: Eerdmans, 1974-), III, 427-447, see 437f., has urged that the navel motif is absent from the Hebrew Bible. If this should prove to be so, the thematic complex "navel of the earth" will have en-

tered the tradition of Israel in the intertestamental period (see, e.g., LXX Ezek 38:12), complementing the already age-old complex of Zion themes. In the New Testament the entire thematic complex is attested by Matt 16:17-19; see Meyer, **Aims**, 185-197.

10. See Meyer, **Aims**, 133-135, 171-173, 220-222. For direct evidence of how the Israel of Jesus' time related "reign" and "restoration," see the relevant parts of the *Qaddiš* and *Tephilla;* **Aims**, 138; 289 note 34.

11. Jeremias, **Jesus' Promise to the Nations**, 40-46.

12. See Meyer, **Aims**, 164, 167f, 171, 184, 247, 298 note 130.

13. See above, note 3.

14. See Ulrich Wilkens, "*stylos*," **Theological Dictionary of the New Testament**, (Grand Rapids: Eerdmans, 1964-1974) VII, 732-736, see 734f.; also, C. K. Barrett, "Paul and the 'Pillar' Apostles," in **Studa Paulina** [J. de Zwann Festschrift] eds. J. N. Sevenster and W. C. van Unnik (Haarlem: Bohm, 1953) 1-19, see 12-16.

15. See Adolf von Harnack, **Die Apostelgeschichte** (Leipzig: Henrichs, 1908) 169-173; Joachim Jeremias, "Untersuchungen zum Quellenproblem der Apostelgeschichte," *Zeitschrift für die neutestamentliche Wissenschaft* 36 (1937) 205-221, repr. in **Abba** (Göttingen: Vandenhoeck & Ruprecht, 1966) 238-255; with qualifications, Martin Hengel, "Between Jesus and Paul," in **Between Jesus and Paul** (London: SCM, 1983) 1-29; see p. 4.

16. See Joachim Jeremias, "Eine neue Schau der Zukunftsaussagen Jesu," *Theologische Blätter* 20 (1941) 216-222; the substance of this not easily accessible article is given in Meyer, **Aims**, 202-209.

17. On the sense of the "three days" in Mark 14:58; par. Matt 26:61, see the whole essay of Joachim Jeremias, "Die Drei-Tage-Worte der Evangelien," in **Tradition and Glaube** [K. G. Kuhn Festschrift] eds. G. Jeremias, H.-W. Kuhn, H. Stegemann (Göttingen: Vandenhoeck & Ruprecht, 1971) 221-229.

18. See Meyer, **Aims**, 208. For greater detail both on the prayer and on the ordeal as its context, see Joachim Jeremias, "The Lord's Prayer in the Light of Recent Research," in **The Prayers of Jesus** (London: SCM, 1967) 82-107.

19. Otfried Hofius, " 'Bis dass er kommt': I Kor xi. 26," *New Testament Studies* 14 (1968) 439-441, has shown that the temporal clause *achri hou elthę* in 1 Cor 11:26 carries the nuance of a purpose clause. This attests eucharistic celebration as a cry for the parousia and the reign of God, in thematic parallel with the Our Father.

20. In addition to the references in note 16 above, see C. H. Dodd, **The Parables of the Kingdom** (London: Nisbet, 1935; repr. London-Glasgow: Collins [Fontana] 1961) 63.

21. See B. F. Meyer, **The Church in Three Tenses** (Garden

City: Doubleday, 1971) 4-12.

22. See B. F. Meyer, "The pre-Pauline Formula in Rom. 3.25-26a," *New Testament Studies* 29 (1983) 198-208.

23. See Otfried Hofius, **Der Christushymnus Philipper 2,6-11** (Tübingen: Mohr, 1976) 41-55.

24. See the treatment of Reinhard Deichgräber, **Gotteshymnus und Christushymnus in der frühen Christenheit** (Göttingen: Vandenhoeck & Ruprecht, 1967) 128-131.

25. Gregory Dix, **Jew and Greek** (Westminster: Dacre, 1953) 31-32, 48-50, had the merit of attempting to reconstruct the way in which Paul's call as Apostle of the gentiles concretely impinged on the history of missionary policy. Whether Paul early initiated a missionary career among gentiles is unclear. If he did, he learned in time, as the letter to the Galatians indicates, to make it cohere with ecclesial policies and commitments.

26. These are the three moments that together constitute "self-definition" in my use of the term; see B. F. Meyer, **Self-Definition in Early Christianity**, ed. Irene Lawrence (Berkeley: Center for Hermeneutic Studies in Hellenistic and Modern Culture, 1980) especially 6-9.

27. This is explicit in Paul (e.g., Gal 2:2); it is also among the vital suppositions without which the data from both Paul and Acts for the reconstruction of what actually happened would lose their intelligibility. The identification of such indispensable suppositions was a basic and signally successful technique in Dix's account of the passage of Christianity into the gentile world. See **Jew and Greek**, 29-51.

28. E.g., Rudolf Meyer, *"peritemno,"* **Theological Dictionary of the New Testament**, VI, 72-84, see 83: "Gl. 2:7 shows us, of course, that fundamentally freedom from *Ioudaismos* was simply noted in Jerusalem . . ." This follows Eduard Meyer, Hans Lietzmann, and others.

29. Rudolf Meyer, *"peritemno,* 83.

30. See Peter Stuhlmacher, "Jesus' Resurrection and the View of Righteousness in the Pre-Pauline Mission Congregations," in **Reconciliation, Law and Righteousness** (see above, note 2) 54.

31. Carl von Weizsäcker, **The Apostolic Age of the Christian Church**, 2 vols. (New York: Putnam, 1897) vol. 1, p. 75.

32. On Mead's paradigm, see Gibson Winter, **Elements for a Social Ethic** (New York: Macmillan, 1966) 17-29, 88-104.

33. On this topic and on the synagogues in question, see Martin Hengel, "Between Jesus and Paul, " 17-25, with the notes on 148-154.

34. Bengt Holmberg, **Paul and Power** (Lund: Gleerup, 1978) 25, cites with seeming approval a view of Traugott Holtz to the effect that the supreme value for Paul was not the unity of the Church but the truth of the gospel. The question, however, is whether Paul dissociated the two. "The strong"

in Rome might be said to have had the better of their argument with "the weak," so far as the truth of the gospel was concerned; but Paul, invoking the reign of God, urged them to put up with the weak for the sake of "perfect harmony" with one another, "one heart and voice" in glorifying God (Rom 14:13-15:6).

35. Dix, **Jew and Greek**, 109.

36. Dix makes a final point: the process by which Christianity ceased to be Jewish did not thereby make it Greek. "It became itself--Christianity." Or, "if we are to be positive, then [not the 'Hellenising of Christianity' but] the 'Catholicising of Christianity' must serve," **Jew and Greek**, 109. As the writer of Ephesians saw (Eph 3:1-21), Paul, by the divine gift of insight into "the secret" of salvation in Christ, became the mediator of this process.

X

CRITICAL REALISM
AND BIBLICAL THEOLOGY

Socrates discovered the difference between making sense of things and making sense of the ways people make sense of things.

They made sense of things first of all by the meanings and values that grounded, shaped, and animated their way of life. Socrates seized on these lived meanings and values under such names as excellence, justice, beauty, piety, courage, self-control, happiness. But the story of the Socratic effort to define them made it clear that there were two levels of meaning: a primary, spontaneous level on which men used everyday language, and a secondary, reflexive level on which they might try to say exactly what they meant by it. Altogether at home on the first level, the Athenians were surprised to find themselves so swiftly bewildered and baffled on the second. Moreover, they saw no clear need of operating well on this second level and, as we know from the hemlock at the end of the story, they came to resent the curious mix of modesty and presumption with which Socrates insisted on it.

But how right Socrates was! In the practical affairs of life primitive men, whether of antiquity or in the modern era, are as intelligent and reasonable as any others. Yet it remains, as Bernard Lonergan has observed, that all their activites and all their living are "penetrated, surrounded, dominated by myth and magic."[1] Furthermore, what holds for primitives holds also for the ancient high civilizations. Myth and magic penetrated and dominated "both the routine activities of daily life and the secret aspirations of the human heart."[2] Both myth and magic had meaning, but it was meaning gone astray. Hence, the importance of the Socratic enterprise. "The [critical] mediation of meaning is not idle talk but a technique that puts an end to idle talk."[3] At a deeper level than all its political and economic arrangements and all the wars and revolutions that have set them up or swept them away, the story of Western civilization is a record of the inheriting and abandoning, the adopting and rejecting, of meanings and values, and of the role played in this drama by the critical effort to make sense of them and gain some control over them. Like the dream before the therapist has decoded it, spontaneously lived meanings and values generate uncanny primitive power. In pre-critical culture this power is moderated only by common sense, the resources of which, limited as they are to everyday practicalities, are unequal to the task of taming the superabundant energies of imagination and image, passion and affect. But once the Socratic mediation of meaning--the critique that makes sense of how men make sense of their lives--takes hold, pre-critical life is remembered as a shadow-world seen against the wall of a cave.

Biblical theology is a critical mediation of meaning. As such, it is a break with the unexamined life and specifically with the un-self-suspecting appropriation of the proverbs, songs, and stories that J. H. Plumb referred to as "the past" in the phrase "the death of the past": a popular tradition in the service of interests of party, class, church, or nation.[4]

It is an abiding temptation of the retrieval that purges popular conceptions of the past to bypass the hard task of finding the truths amid the illusions. Far more compelling is the joy of attack and the unmasking of old men's lies. Critique can be heady; it can degenerate into a demonic honesty that insists on victims. Let justice be done, though heaven fall and the world perish. Moreover, the critique that revels in laying illusion bare easily meshes with the critique powered by alienation and self-defined as liberation.

This is anything but new to biblical research. In the wake of Richard Simon (1638-1712) and Benedict Spinoza (1632-1677), modern biblical studies took shape as twin streams, one of continuity, the other of discontinuity, with biblical religion. Simon and Spinoza respectively might be named their patrons. On technical matters (lexicography, textual criticism, environmental research, and so on) the two streams have run parallel, but in spirit and purpose they have diverged, orthodox and pietists being pitted against neologists and rationalists in the eighteenth century, conservatives against liberals in the nineteenth century, conservative Protestants and mainstream Catholics against demythologizers and ideologically secular historians of biblical religion in the twentieth century.

Both streams or wings of biblical scholarship have made tangible contributions to technical progress. The differences between them have always been hermeneutical. The strong point of the tradition of discontinuity (dogma-free scholarship) has been its resolutely critical stance. Its weakness has lain in the sometimes latent, sometimes patent, alienation pervading its critical distance from the biblical text. Conversely, the strong point of the stream of continuity (religious and theological conservatism) has been its connaturality with the text; its weakness, a propensity to harmonize divergences and to underestimate the discontinuities between past and present. The interpretative ideal is somehow to comprehend these extremes and occupy the space between them, to temper the warmth of connaturality with the coolness of critical distance.

Biblical theology is a historical project, but it is also more than a historical project. As a reconstruction of religious institutions and allegiances in ancient Israel and early Christianity, it belongs to the history of religions. It would accordingly build on the achievements of the history-of-religions school (1890-1920), i.e., on the recovery of the contexts conditioning ancient Israel, early Judaism, and Christianity at its birth in Judaism and during its early development in the Levant, Egypt, and on the north shore of the Mediterranean basin. But a biblical theology worthy of the name will stand apart from the history-of-religions school and from the school's contemporary successors insofar as they have enlisted the historical enterprise in the cause of emancipation from classical or historical or dogmatic Christianity. The school's hermeneutical dilemma--its spontaneous and cultivated recoil from just those phenomena that it had set out to understand--is of a piece with this basic orientation. Genuine biblical theology belongs rather to the Simon stream of continuity with biblical tradition. Unlike the history-of-religions school, it conceives of primitive Christianity not as a liberating alternative to classical Christianity but as its radically homogeneous foundation.

Again, it conceives of the critical spirit not as closing off religious allegiances in favor of the objectivity of positivism but as serving them in accord with the objectivity of critical realism. Here the adjective "critical" (from *krisis*, "judgment") implies a thoroughgoing valorization of the scholastic adage, *ens per verum innotescit* ("being becomes known through the true"). Reality, that is, comes to light not through acts like looking at a tree or kicking a stone but through the act of true judgment, by which reflective intelligence climaxes the discursive and often laborious process of trying to find out what is true. The noun "realism" signifies that, as the strict correlative of truth, reality is the goal of the drive to know. A great epistemological tradition thus finds new affirmation, but in contradistinction to the naive affirmation of common sense (Samuel Johnson's kicking of a stone in refutation of Berkeley), critical affirmation is founded on a leisurely examination of cognitional data.

As Lonergan undertook it, the examination had a seemingly modest purpose: to settle matters of fact.[5] Cognitional fact emerged from attentiveness to cognitional data, the effort to understand these data, and to secure such understanding as correct. But the ascertainment of cognitional fact had momentous negative and positive consequences. Negatively, it broke the spell of "cognitional myth"[6] or "picture-thinking"[7] or "the notions of knowledge and reality . . . formed in childhood,"[8] namely, that knowing is like seeing and that reality is what is there to be seen. These were the notions that down through the centuries had provided "the unshakable foundations of materialism, empiricism, positivism, sensism, phenomenalism, behaviorism, pragmatism . . . ."[9] Positively, the ascertainment of cognitional fact led to an acknowledgment of the idealist critique of these primitive notions (they overlooked the essential role of acts of intelligence) but, equally as important, it led to the transcending of idealism, too. Whereas Kant had posited an immediate relation of subject to object exclusively through sense perception,[10] Lonergan argued (from the utter unrestrictedness of human intentionality, which in particular cases terminated in true judgments) that human cognitional activities had as their object, being; that the activity immediately related to this object was questioning; that all other cognitional activities, including sense knowledge as well as understanding and judgment, were mediately related to the object, being-- mediately, because they were the means of arrival at the answers in and through which the goal intended by questioning was attained.[11]

Having broken both with the stubborn illusion that sense knowledge yielded reality and with the equally illusory idealist correction to the effect that it yielded appearance,[12] Lonergan could reconstitute the world that existed prior to questions and answers, the merely given, not yet wondered about, questioned, or construed "world of immediacy," made present by acts of sensing; from it he could differentiate the "world mediated by meaning," made present in the first instance by attending to, catching on to, adopting the words and phrases, customs and convictions, preferences and values of one's human environment.

Object and objectivity differed in accord with the differences between these two worlds. In the world mediated by meaning, "object" was what was intended by questions and known when the questions were satisfactorily answered. In the world of immediacy, "object" was merely the term of extraverted consciousness, whatever was seen, heard, touched, tasted, smelled. Corresponding to these two meanings of object, there were two meanings of objectivity. In the world of immediacy the condition of objectivity was "to be a successfully functioning animal."[13] But in the world mediated by meaning, objectivity had several components. Experiential objectivity lay in the giveness of data. Normative objectivity arose when the exigences of intelligence (namely, for insight in response to questions) and of reasonableness (namely, for the logic relating insight to the conditions of its truth) were met. Terminal or absolute objectivity resulted from the combining of normative and experiential objectivity, just as the conclusion of the syllogism "if X, then Y; but X; therefore Y" resulted from the combining of the major and the minor propositions.[14]

This exigently precise gnoseology opened onto a metaphysics entirely free of obscurantism, to an ethics of freedom and responsibility, and to a positive account of general transcendent knowledge (the rational affirmation of God) and of special transcendent knowledge (the anticipation of religion that emerges from the antithesis of God and evil).[15]

To biblical scholarship a philosophic base of this kind would render the inestimable service of "removing what prohibits" (*removens prohibens*), e.g., freeing the exegete, historian, and theologian from inhibitions and prohibitions such as those associated with the so-called "scientific world view," itself grounded in obsolete notions of science (unalterable law) and nature (a mechanistic determinism) and in an account of science as not only a model of all knowledge, but a negative norm of answers to non-scientific questions.

The lack of a solid and liberating philosophic base is evident throughout the history of modern biblical studies. Besides other factors, a philosophic inadequacy respecting human history lay behind the strong current of Marcionitism, already emergent in the Reformation, that clouded prospects of a satisfactory biblical theology from the days of Hegel (Israel's religion was inferior to Greek and Roman cults) and Schleiermacher (there was no special divine revelation in the legalistic religion of the Old Testament) through the era of Friedrich Delitzsch (the Old Testament in content and history was unconnected with the New; Jesus was not a Jew) and Harnack (there is no longer any excuse for keeping the Old Testament as part of the canon) to that of Hirsch (the Old Testament is alien and theologically superfluous) and Bultmann (the function of the Old Testament in the canon is to dramatize the failure of its way to God).[16] The philosophic options actually operative among biblical scholars, so far from functioning to neutralize the intrusive prohibitions of bias, added their own obstacles to the appropriation especially of the Old Testament scriptures (Spinoza provides a dramatic early example). First rationalism, then cosmopolitan idealism, and, in Germany, the harsher forms of the law-and-gospel dialectic that might appear in any era, all contributed to theological antipathy toward the Old Testament down to the present day.

What philosophic options have in fact controlled modern biblical scholarship? In the Enlightenment, rationalism reigned. This yielded in the first half of the nineteenth century to Hegelian schemes of development (Vatke in the Old Testament, Baur and the early Strauss in the New). In the latter nineteenth century these in turn gave way to the positivism and Neo-Kantianism that in various modulations have held sway ever since. A positivist conception of objectivity in particular has passed without notice into biblical criticism, except where explicitly philosophic reflection has commended a more sophisticated, Neo-Kantian, hermeneutic (e.g., Bultmann, Hans Jonas) or an allied "reflective philosophy" (e.g., Paul Ricoeur).[17] Add to this a potent strain of fideism--the meeting ground of Karl Barth and his followers with numberless non-Barthians--and one has the names of the few sets of ideas that have exercised remote control over biblical exegesis, history, and theology for the past two hundred years.

There is no doubt, however, that the authority of all these traditions has collapsed or waned, "seeping out of them," in Eric Voegelin's phrase.[18] True, an unthematic positivism has hung on, tough as crab-grass, protected by the simplicity with which its adherents disclaim any interest in theory. Bultmannianism, on the other hand, lost its ascendancy with awesome suddenness and has been succeeded, especially in North America, by the turn of structuralism, literary theory, and the application of sociology and anthropology to the Bible. Some of these developments have already had an impact on the whole field of biblical studies. Rather than review them for their possible contributions, however, I would like to offer a single example, particularly relevant to present purposes, of how literary criticism, itself provisioned by biblical conceptions, can contribute in turn to biblical theology.

Frank Kermode set his lectures on "the sense of an ending" under the specific rubric of making sense of the ways we try to make sense of our lives.[19] History makes sense on condition that it is going somewhere, that it has a point, goal, end. Our drive to make sense of our lives says why we thrive on epochs, each defined by a beginning and an end. For, we are born and we die *in mediis rebus*, our birth not coterminous with any beginning nor our death with any ending but our own. To make sense of our lives, however, we need the "fictions" of beginning and end. We need to be somehow inserted not into an empty duration of *chronos* (time) but into a time-span charged with *kairoi* (seasons) by the prospect and hope of a meaningful end. Hence our insatiable interest in the future: it is time-redeeming.[20]

What Suzanne Langer called the "virtual" time of books is a fictive model of world time.[21] The plot of novel or drama allows action to escape mere chronicity. All plotting requires that an end bestow meaning on the whole sequence. Such is the time of the novelist; its correlation with our existence in time--the correlation between fiction and reality--gives Kermode's observations on fictive beginnings and ends and fictive correspondences between them their peculiar interest. The devices of fiction become pointers to our efforts to make sense of our lives and help us to fix attention on how the resources work that allow us to do so.

This line of reflection, splendidly illustrated by fiction, nevertheless raises a problem for the reader, anticipated by Kermode. The problem bears on the fictive as fictive, i.e., as "consciously false." Genuinely critical intelligence will not be taken in by the Nietzschean view that the falsity of an opinion is no objection against it, the only relevant question being how far it is life-furthering. The danger of such rakish abstractions has been far too garishly illustrated by the agreement of the Nazis on the irrelevance of true and false and their conviction that death on a large scale was supremely life-furthering. The appalling results would seem to force the issue of whether "true and false" remains a matter of indifference precisely with respect to what is supposedly "life-furthering." Kermode's solution, however, is not so direct. It addresses the issue of truth only tangentially, by distinguishing between fictions and myths. Fictions can degenerate into myths whenever they are not consciously held to be fictive. Myths differ from fictions by presupposing total and adequate explanations of things and calling for absolute assent. Fictions, on the other hand, are for finding things out. They are pragmatic: not hypotheses but models, not subject to disproof but only to obsoleteness through neglect.[22]

Is this satisfactory? The most important of the fictions in question do not in fact function exclusively or primarily as devices for finding things out. For Kermode our imposition of a plot on world time (crucial to the positing of a meaning for history) is a fiction. But while this meaning may serve as a tool or resource in the service of further inquiry, before it is such a tool it is already far more than a tool. The sources of intelligibility in the face of otherwise meaningless time are not reducible to the category of heuristic device.

Again, the need that called this "fiction" into being: is it a need for real or for fictional meaning? Kermode himself succumed to the dangerous charm of Wallace Stevens's bleak pragmatism. A fiction, by definition "consciously false," is the object of "the act of finding/What will suffice."[23] But this offers irony, not plausibility. Just as for Plato the work of the artist was at two removes from reality, so for critical realism a fictional meaning of history is at two removes from sufficing. First, myth, since by definition it is *not* "consciously false," will surely serve better on a pragmatic level than fiction. For more than half a millennium Stoic myth nerved countless ancients to order their lives and especially to confront tribulation and death with courage. Had the Stoics thought that their world view was a fiction, could this massive, six-hundred-year fact have obtained? Hardly. The consciously false--that is, fiction--would not have sufficed. Second, the unconsciously false--that is, myth--will not suffice, either. For there is sufficiency and sufficiency. We are surely right in finding something insufficient in the paranoid schizophrenic's elaborate and cunning construal of seemingly innocent data as evidence of conspiracy and persecution. The account satisfies him but not us.We refuse to think that just because he is satisfied with it his account is as good as any other; that his satisfaction is self-sufficient, all that counts; that he has managed to place "the act of finding/ What will suffice." On this deeper than pragmatic level Stoicism, too, in the measure in which it was moored in a myth-ridden monism, failed to suffice even while it flourished. True, it sufficed pragmatically: in a limited sense it worked. But it did not achieve its goal of access to and harmony with the real. Its realism was flawed and fragmentary. The human need, however, is not only for meaning but for valid meaning. Neither noble myth nor exquisitely contrived fiction can adequately meet this need.

This observation, to be sure, does not settle the matter of fictions nor deny the utility of the category. The "concordances" to which Kermode alludes and which play so important a part in both Testaments (e.g., through the schemes of prophecy and fulfillment or of type and antitype) are often undeniably artificial, i.e., fictions. But are they "consciously false"? It seems that the theory of fictions borrowed by Stevens and Kermode from Hans Vaihinger, the founder of "as if" philosophy, stands in need of revisions and refinements. When Paul allegorized the story of Sarah and Hagar and their sons (Gal 4:22-31), he was operating as a trained and resourceful exegete, no doubt fully conscious of having himself brought their freight of meaning into existence for the first time. It is a figure; it has a fictional dimension. It hardly follows that Paul conceived of it as consciously false, or that by failing to regard it in this light he unintentionally slipped into myth.

Like the categorical revision that differentiates between a real and a merely fictional meaning for history, a more differentiated account of interpretative fictions is clearly in order. In neither case can we allow ourselves to pay the price for even so conscious and erudite an immersion in the contemporary as Kermode's. It is unsatisfactory that any meaning or value falling outside the purview of a cultivated contemporary sensibility should somehow without argument slip the pull of reality and float off into the weightlessness of fiction. If changing sensibility had the power to reduce to fiction whatever it no longer reverenced or believed, the imposition of a plot on time would, for much of the contemporary world, be no more than a fiction. But changing sensibility--though it changes much, very much--has no such power. To assure our contemporaries that, when we say we can no longer believe this or that, we mean that some of our old fictions are now obsolete and that we accordingly need new fictions with which to replace them, is to offer them a serpent in place of fish and a stone in place of bread. Two things are missing here: a criterion for distinguishing between the fictional and the real and the will to insist on the distinction.

Once the distinction is again respected, however, Kermode's

exploration of the conditions of intelligibility in fiction can be made to throw a powerful light on structures of human meaning. The sense of an ending in fiction has intense clarity as a heuristic resource for capturing the sense of an ending in history as this stamped and pervaded biblical tradition and came to undergird the civilization of the West until our century, in which by no coincidence an art, a theatre, a literature, and a philosophy of the absurd have prospered. The effective mediation of biblical meaning is conditioned precisely by a recovery of the magnetism of the end. Historically, this magnetism appeared first as (pre-Exilic) hope for *a new year* within history, then as (Exilic and post-Exilic) hope for a final sabbath and eighth day of the universe under new heavens on a new earth. Can we make real sense of this way of making sense of human life? What in it, untransposable, belongs simply to its own period? And if anything in it belongs by right of truth and inheritance to us, how can we appropriate it?

In the sphere of the human spirit inheriting is an act of faith, choice, and retrieval. "Faith" here has a weaker than biblical sense. It is merely an initial openness and provisional readiness to agree, an attitude that a reader normally brings to a book. "Choice" has a strong sense. It is a free and discriminating decision. "Retrieval" is an act of appropriation. It integrates into a present context something chosen from a past context. From their first days Christians have inherited in this way. Intent on the scriptures, they discovered their inheritance there. They chose it and retrieved it, correlating the present--the fulfillment that was Easter--with the past: the promise to Abraham (Gen 12:2f.) and the "types" of Isaac preserved (Gen 22:12), the servant glorified (Isa 53:10-12), the "one like a man" made king (Dan 7:13f.). . . .

Biblical theology brings critique to acts of appropriation. It is not merely a survey of biblical literature with a view to presenting its theological content. William Wrede[24] rightly discerned that biblical theology conceived in this way was unwittingly on its way to becoming a history of religion and religious literature, a genre to which theological conceptions were irrelevant except as objects of critique. Wrede proposed that this process be pushed to its logical conclusion. He was mistaken, however, in expecting that biblical theology would thereby drop out of existence. What has actually happened in the wake of Wrede's clarification is that biblical theology has been helped to find its vocation.

What Wrede saw he saw clearly, and what he did not see clearly he did not see at all. Some of his successsors, having recognized as he did the futility of a theology that mistook itself for the merely recognitive and reconstructive activities of exegesis and history, concluded (as the religiously and theologically tone-deaf Wrede could not) that the specific difference of biblical theology lay precisely at the point where the meaning of the biblical text was released from its original matrix. The past as past is dead, but it is the recurrent miracle of historical intentionality, be it pre-critical or critical, that it quickens the past by bringing it to life in present knowledge and quickens the present by bringing to it hot coals from the ashes, new possibilities from the riches, of the past.

History is first of all reconstruction, but successful reconstruction maximizes a new possibility: to transpose meanings and values from the contexts of the past to the context of the present. It is this vital act of transposing that makes the vast effort of exegesis and history finally worthwhile. In this respect interpretation and history are on a par. At the conclusion of his theology of the New Testament Rudolf Bultmann observed that, though interpretation and history were reciprocally determining, one might ask which was finally in the service of the other. His own answer gave the primacy to interpretation, on the supposition "that [the New Testament writings] have something to say to the present."[25] This is a sound supposition. It does not, however, rule out the possibility that history, too, has something to say to the present and that it has things to say that were not said by any New Testament authors.

To Christians this should be obvious on a moment's reflection, for besides the linguistic meaning by which Jesus and the evangelists who interpret him announce the news of salvation, there is the incarnate meaning that charges Jesus' life, death, and resurrection, incising his words and the words of the evangelists, as nothing else could, in the human memory and heart. This incarnate meaning shines out of his symbolic acts (the call and sending of the twelve, the exorcisms and cures, the non-fasting, the dining with notorious "sinners," the cleansing of the temple), his almost wordless passion, his death, his resurrection from the dead. If two millennia of Christian exegesis have still not plumbed the depths of the gospels' linguistic meaning, two millennia of Christian contemplation have similarly failed to exhaust the incarnate meaning of this lived history. Both continue to have "something to say to the present."

The so-called myth of transparency[26] accordingly is itself illusory; biblical texts evoke and attest extratextual realities without reference to which the texts themselves lose their force. As Luther succinctly put it, "whoever does not understand the things cannot draw the sense from the words" *(qui non intelligit res non potest ex verbis sensum elicere).*[27] The conclusion that history as well as interpretation belongs to a living biblical theology thus finds at least oblique reinforcement.

The principal questions preliminary to biblical theology (conceived as bearing on the whole Christian Bible) are two: first, what binds the Old Testament to the New as the field of this inquiry? Second, is there any criterion of authenticity for biblical theology?

There is no single answer to the first question, but there is a single foundation for all the relevant answers. The Old Testament is bound to the New through the election-historical mission of Jesus, vindicated by his resurrection from the dead. The mission of Jesus supposed, continued, and climaxed the election history of biblical Israel; and the God of Israel, sweeping aside the judgments of Jew (Mark 14:64; par. Matt 26:66; John 19:7) and gentile (Mark 15:15; par. Matt 27:26; Luke 23:25; John 19:16) and undoing their lethal effects, vidicated the authenticity of the claim of his Son by raising him from the dead. According to the claim of Jesus, response to his proclamation decided the destiny of individuals (Mark 8:38; par. Matt 10:33; Luke 12:8f.; 9:26), towns (Mark 6:11; par. Matt 10:14; Luke 9:5; 10:11; Matt 11:21-24; par. Luke 10:12-15), the capital (Matt 23:37f.; par. Luke 13:34f.) and nation of Israel (Mark 9:50; par. Luke 14:34f.; Matt 24:37-39; par. Luke 17:26-30; Luke 12:39f.; 13:6-9; 21:34f.). The resurrection of Jesus, far from leaving such questions behind, gave them final definition. Henceforward, the messianic restoration of Israel was realized in the community of Jesus' followers, and in time even gentiles would share in constituting "the Israel of God" (Gal 6:16). Thus, the permanent bond with the history and scriptures of Israel was forged from the first moment of the life of Christianity and held as Christianity developed through time.

The New Testament writers, partly reflecting Jesus himself, could and did conceive of this bond, first, as the fulfillment of promise (Gal 3:8; 4:28f.; Rom 4:13-25; Acts 2:16-21), prophecy (Luke 24:26f., 46f.; Acts 2:23, 34f.), and type (1 Cor 10:6; Rom 8:32); second, as the completion of the incomplete, in accord with the divinely foreordained eschatological measures of time (Mark 1:15), revelation (Matt 5:17), sin (Matt 23:32; 1 Thess 2:16; Rom 1:29), suffering (Col 1:24), and the whole drama of history (Eph 1:9f.); third, as the contrary dynamisms of the promise and the Law (Gal 3:6-29; Rom 4:1-5:21). Contemporary discussion has brought variously motivated critique to bear on all these conceptions[28] and has added new themes to the discussion: the continuities between the Old Testament and the New in history, conceptuality, and language.[29] (This discussion too, belongs to the task.)

Is there any criterion of authenticity for biblical theology? There are many, no doubt; but let it suffice here to name just one factor, necessary though not sufficient for biblical theology. It is the affirmation of God as Lord of nature and Lord of human events, Lord of his people, and Lord of all mankind. A biblical theology that limits the Lordship of God whether to the sphere of the natural order (eighteenth-century rationalism) or to that of moral conversion (nineteenth-century liberalism) or to that of the religious conversion of the solitary individual (twentieth-century existentialism) retrieves too little of the biblical legacy to make good the claim to authenticity.

But can we today affirm the Lordship of God in harmony with the attestation and celebration of his Lordship in biblical tradition? Can we so affirm it as to prolong and share in the way that ancient Israel and Apostolic Christianity made sense of things? Can we not only make sense of this way of making sense, but adopt it as our own? Is this, in fact, the condition of our own escape from mere chronicity, the condition of our having a time-redeeming future of our own? So it seems, and so it has seemed to many in our century who have pondered these questions and made an affirmative answer the center of their thought: e.g., among biblical scholars, Gerhard von Rad[30] and Oscar Cullmann;[31] among theologians, Pierre Teilhard de Chardin[32] and Wolfhart Pannenberg;[33] among philosophers, Karl Löwith[34]] and Josef Pieper.[35] No doubt, the category of salvation history and the role played therein both by the history of biblical traditions and by modern conceptions of history have been rightly subjected to critique and refinement, but in ever more refined form it remains the heart of the matter.

Biblical theology is not a fixed Platonic essence, but in large measure is what the biblical theologian makes it. In conclusion, then, let me summarize the specifications for a biblical theology worthy of engaging the best efforts of our generation. It is not divided into Old Testament theology and New Testament theology, but embraces both (as well as exploiting non-canonical literature, where it is relevant) in one "biblical" theology. It is not interpretation only but interpretation and history. It is not purely descriptive, but intent on the transposition of meaning to the present. The past accordingly is not thought of as irremediably discontinuous with the present but as open to critical retrieval; the meanings to be retrieved are not fictional but real; the effort to retrieve them centers both on first-level "meaning," which makes sense of things, and on the second-level "meaning of meaning," which makes sense of the way the men and women of the biblical tradition made sense of things. The task, then, is necessarily approached not under positivist or Neo-Kantian constraints but in the manner of critical realism; not from a dogma-free platform but from within commitment to historical Christianity.

These are specifications for a biblical theology that counts. They break cleanly with both the familiar simplicities in which conservative biblical scholarship has bogged down and with the pathological modes of sophistication that have lately pioneered new ways of trivializing the New Testament. The ultimate goal includes a recovery of personal and social foundations, first among Christians, then all through the formerly Christian West--a materially rich world increasingly starved for basic, valid, and coherent meaning.

The kind of biblical theology specified here is not easily achieved. Obviously, it supposes a powerful collaborative effort of scholarship. Less obviously but more crucially, it supposes a community of scholars made up of authentic men and women--and the cost of discipleship is higher than the cost of scholarship. Sheer realism led Lonergan to make this issue of human and Christian authenticity the touchstone of effective theological collaboration.[36] But realism takes as much account of the forces that favor as of the forces that frustrate great projects, and in respect of the great project briefly outlined in these pages, a powerful favoring force is the fact that authenticity is the deepest need, the highest gift, and the most prized achievement of the human being.[37]

NOTES

1. Bernard Lonergan, "Dimensions of Meaning," in **Collection. Papers by Bernard Lonergan**, ed. F. E. Crowe (New York: Herder & Herder, 1967) 252-267, p. 257.

2. "Dimensions," 257.

3. Ibid.

4. J. H. Plumb, **The Death of the Past** (London: Macmillan, 1969), especially "The Sanction of the Past," 19-61.

5. Bernard Lonergan, **Insight. A Study of Human Understanding** (London and New York: Longmans, 1957, repr. London: Darton, Longman & Todd, 1983) 3-374.

6. Lonergan, **Method in Theology** (New York: Herder & Herder, 1972) 239f.

7. "The Subject" in **A Second Collection. Papers by Bernard Lonergan**, ed. W. F. J. Ryan and B. J. Tyrnell (London: Darton, Longman & Todd, 1974) 76-78.

8. **Method in Theology**, 213.

9. Ibid, 214.

10. **Kritik der reinen Vernunft**, A. 19, B. 33.

11. "The Subject," 78f. See also **Method in Theology**, 262f.: answers refer to objects mediately, namely, insofar as they connect with the objects only through the questions that intend those objects.

12. Sense knowledge alone yields not reality, not appearance, but data. See **Insight**, 252f. on the duality of "elementary" and "fully human" knowing.

13. **Method in Theology**, 263.

14. "**Insight** Revisited," in **A Second Collection**, 275.

15. See **Insight**, 385-549 on metaphysics; 595-633 on ethics; 634-686 on general transcendent knowledge; 687-730 on special transcendent knowledge.

16. See A. H. J. Gunneweg, **Understanding the Old Testament** (London: SCM, 1978) 116-118 on Luther and Agricola; 152 on Hegel; 119, 152f. on Schleiermacher; 153-156 on Delitzsch; 39, 119 on Harnack; 155-157 on Hirsch; 158f., 224f. on Bultmann.

17. On the common ground among the cognitional theories of Jonas, Bultmann, and Ricoeur, see Frederick Lawrence, "Method and Theology as Hermeneutical," in **Creativity and Method. Essays in Honor of Bernard Lonergan**, edited by M. L. Lamb (Milwaukee: Marquette University Press, 1981) 86-89.

18. Eric Voegelin, **Order and History. I: Israel and Revelation** (Baton Rouge: Louisiana State University Press, 1956) xiii.

19. Frank Kermode, **The Sense of an Ending. Studies in the Theory of Fiction** (Oxford: Oxford University Press, 1966; repr. 1981) 3.

20. Ibid., 47-52.

21. Suzanne K. Langer, **Feeling and Form. A Theory of Art** (New York: Scribner's Sons, 1953) 109-119. Langer's view is cited in **The Sense of an Ending**, 52.

22. **The Sense of an Ending**, 39.

23. Ibid., 42.

24. William Wrede, "The Tasks and Methods of 'New Testament Theology'," in Robert Morgan, ed. **The Nature of New Testament Theology. The Contribution of William Wrede and Adolf Schlatter** (London: SCM, 1973) 68-116, esp. 84-95.

25. Rudolf Bultmann, **Theology of the New Testament**, 2 vols. (New York: Scribner's, 1951-55) vol. 2, 251.

26. Frank Kermode, **The Genesis of Secrecy: On the Interpretation of Narrative** (Cambridge: Harvard University Press, 1979) 118f.

27. Cited by Hans-Georg Gadamer, **Truth and Method** (New York: Seabury, 1975) 151. Valentine Cunningham, "Renoving That Bible: The Absolute Text of Post-Modernism," in **The Theory of Reading**, ed. Frank Gloversmith (New Jersey: Barnes & Noble, 1984) 1-51, offers a brilliant exposition of the impossibility of maintaining textual meaning while dispensing with reference to extratextual reality.

28. For a brief discussion of salvation history, the history of promise, the argument from prophecy, and typology, see Gunneweg, **Understanding the Old Testament**, 179-212. On the slow transition in Old Testament scholarship from the category of "prophecy and fulfillment" to that of "historical development," see Ronald E. Clements, "Messianic Prophecy or Messianic History?" *Horizons in Biblical Theology* 1 (1979) 87-104.

29. On the theme of the continuity of revelation and of literary traditions as theological justification for the historic fact of the Christian canon, see Hartmut Gese, "Erwagungen zur Einheit biblischer Theologie" in **Vom Sinai zum Zion. Alttestamentliche Beitrage zur biblischen Theologie** (Munich: Kaiser, 1974) 11-30. On continuity of doctrine, conceptuality, and language, see Gunneweg, **Understanding the Old Testament**, 223-236.

30. Gerhard von Rad, **Old Testament Theology, Vol. 1: The Theology of Israel's Historical Traditions** (New York: Harper & Row, 1962) 50-56, 105-115, 127f., 316-318.

31. Oscar Cullmann, **Salvation in History** (London: SCM and New York: Harper & Row, 1967) esp. 48-64.

32. Pierre Teilhard de Chardin, **The Future of Man** (London:

Collins [Fontana] 1964.

33. Wolfhart Pannenberg, "The Revelation in God of Jesus of Nazareth," in **Theology as History,** ed. J. M. Robinson and J. B. Cobb (New York: Harper & Row, 1967) 101-123; "Die Auferstehung Jesu und die Zukunft des Menschen," *Kerygma and Dogma* 24 (1978) 104-117.

34. Karl Löwith, **Meaning in History** (Chicago: University of Chicago Press, 1949); **Nature, History and Existentialism and Other Essays in the Philosophy of History** (Evanston: Northwestern University Press, 1966).

35. Josef Pieper, **The End of Time. A Meditation on the Philosophy of History** (London: Faber and Faber, 1954); also **Hope and History** (New York: Herder and Herder, 1969) 29-44.

36. **Method in Theology,** 235-293.

37. Ibid. 254.

INDEX OF
BIBLICAL PASSAGES

OLD TESTAMENT

Genesis
1:12   175
2:10-14   175
2:24   179
11-12   174
12:2f   204
12:3   175
22:12   20

Exodus
19-26   175
19:5f   175
2:8   169

Leviticus
16:14   182

Deuteronomy   42
6   175
24:1-4   179

Joshua
24   175

2 Samuel
7:13   164
7:13f   163, 165

1 Chronicles
17:12f   163, 165

Job xiii   42

Psalms   42
2:7   165
9:14 [13]   175
25:6   175
46:5   175
47:16 [19]   175, 176
50:1   176
68:30 [29]   176
79:8   175
87:5   175
87:7   175
89:27   165
96:7-10   176
96:8-10   176
110:1   183
110:3   165

Qoheleth   42

Wisdom   42

Isaiah	xiii	Ezekiel	
2:2	177	5:5	175
2:2-4	176	36:23	177
7:9	166	38:12	175, 192
8:9f	166	38:14-16	166
14:1	175	47	175
14:1f	176		
14:26f	166	Daniel	42
14:32	166	7:13	181
17:12-14	166	7:13f	204
18:7	176	7:14	181, 183
19:23	176	8:10	111
25:6	176	12:2f	111
26:19	111		
28:16	166	Hosea	42
29:2f	166		
29:18f	30	Joel	
35:5-7	30	2:1-20	166
40:55	175	4:18 [3:18]	175
43:3f	169		
52:7-9	176	Amos	
52:13	181	3:2	174
52:15	183	5:15	174
53:10	169		
53:11	183	Zephaniah	
53:10-12	181, 204	3:8	166
53:11	181		
56:3-7	175	Haggai	
56:4	176-177	1:1f	164, 165
60:1-22	176	2:7	176
61:1f	30	2:20-23	164, 165
63	175		
64	175	Zechariah	42
66:18-23	175	2:15	175
		6:12f	163-5
Jeremiah		8:20-23	176
3	175	9	176
3:17	176	12:2-4	166
29:11-14	175	14:2	166
31	175	14:8	175
31:31-34	169	14:16-19	176
32:37-40	177	14:21	176

Non-Cannonical Texts
4QFlor 1-13   164
4QFlor 11   165
1QS 8:5-9   171
1QH 6:25-28   171
1QH 11:10-14   111
Pss Sol 3:16   111
2Bar 49-51   111
2Bar 50:1-3   111, 113
2Bar 61-63   111

NEW TESTAMENT

Matthew
5:3f   30
5:17   29, 30, 179, 207
5:21f   30
5:32   179
5:33f   30
5:38f   30
5:43f   30
8:11   174, 176
8:11f   191
8:20   161
9:6   161
9:9   167
9:10f   167
9:11   167
9:12   168
9:13   168
10:14   206
10:23   30, 126
10:33   206
11:5   30
11:9   167
11:21-24   206
11:25-27   121
12:7   168
12:8   161
13:3ff   174
13:11   121
15:11   179

16:13   159
16:13-20   168
16:15   159
16:16-19   164
16:17   121
16:17-19   192
16:18   166, 170
16:28   126
18:14   168
19:8f   179
20:14f   168
20:28   169, 174, 183
21:42   154
22:29f   111
23:10   161
23:32   30, 207
23:37f   206
24:37-39   206
26:1   170
26:28   169, 174, 183
26:60-64   169
26:61   163, 166, 177, 179
26:64   159
26:66   206
27:14   159
27:26   206
27:40   170, 177

Mark
1:15   30, 207
2:10   161
2:14   167
2:15f   167
2:16   167
2:17   168
2:27   179
2:28   161
4:11   121
4:30-32   174
6:11   206

Mark cont'd

7:15	179
8:27	159
8:27-30	169
8:29	159
8:38	206
9:1	126
9:31	30
9:41	161
9:50	206
10:6-9	179
10:45	30, 169, 174, 183
12:10	153
12:24f	111
14:24	30, 169, 174, 183
14:58	162, 163, 166
14:57-62	169
14:58	170, 177, 179
14:58-62	164
14:62	159
14:64	206
15:2	159
15:15	206
15:29	170, 177
16:12	111

Luke

5:2	167
5:24	161
5:27	167
5:29f	167
5:30	167
5:31	168
5:32	168
6:5	161
7:34	167
7:36-50	167
7:37f	167
8:10	121
9:5	206
9:18	159
9:18-21	169

9:20	159
9:26	206
9:27	126
9:58	161
10:11	206
10:12-15	206
10:21f	121
12:8f	206
12:39f	206
13:6-9	206
13:16	168
13:18f	174
13:28f	191
13:29	174-176
13:34f	206
14:16f	168
14:22-24	30
14:34f	206
15:1f	167
15:7	168
15:10	168
15:11-32	168
16:18	179
17:22	183
17:22-30	160
17:24-30	30
17:26	183
17:26-30	206
17:30	164, 183
19:5	167
19:9f	168
19:10	168
20:17	154
20:34-36	111
21:34f	206
22:20	169
23:3	159
23:25	206
24:26f	29, 206
24:31	111
24:36-53	111
24:46f	29, 206

John

1:14	61, 63
1:41f	159, 168
1:42	166
2:19	170, 177, 179
2:19-21	165
6:44	121
6:51	169
6:68f	159, 169
15:5	121
18:37	159
19:7	206
19:16	206
20:19-23	111

Acts

2:16-21	29, 206
2:23	29, 206
2:33	29
2:34f	29, 206
2:38	181
3:18	29
3:22	29
5:31f	181
6-7	177
6:13f	179
6:14	163, 170, 177, 179
7:56	181, 183
8	173, 177
8:1	188
8:17	185
8:32-35	181
9	177
9:19-21	177
9:29	177
11	173
11:2	185
11:4-18	185
11:15-17	187
11:19f	177
11:22-24	185
11:25	185

13	178
13-14	173, 185
13:1	185
15	185
15:1	178
15:5	178
15:17-19	178
26:23	111

Romans

1:3f	43
1:5	178
1:14	178
1:16	178
1:16f	184
1:29	30, 207
3:25f	43, 181, 183
3:29	183
4:1-5:21	207
4:13	25, 61
4:13-25	29, 206
4:25	43, 61, 111
6:3f	184
8:18-27	114
8:21	126
8:22f	114, 116
8:23	105, 114
8:26f	114
8:29	154
8:29f	111
8:32	29, 206
8:34	43, 111
9-11	42, 178
10:9f	43, 182
11:13	178
12:6	30
15:8	29
15:15-28	178
16:25f	45
16:25-27	184

1 Corinthians	55
1-4	184
2:1	45
2:7	45
2:10-16	188
2:11	121
7:19	189, 190
9:1f	188
9:16f	30
9:19-21	184, 189
10:6	29, 206
10:16f	184
10:17	61
10:32	184
12:3	182
12:4-6	184
12:12-31	184
12:13	184
13:1-13	184, 185
15	47, 100, 103-5, 109-11, 120
15:1-11	111, 184, 188
15:3-5	111
15:3-8	63
15:5	173
15:11	186
15:12-34	111, 118
15:19	120
15:20	111, 118
15:21	118
15:21-28	63
15:23	45, 113
15:24	45
15:35	112
15:35-49	114, 125
15:42-49	113
15:45	111, 191
15:49	118
15:50	108, 110, 112, 116
15:50f	45
15:50ff	103, 105
15:50-55	114
15:50-57	63, 112-114, 116
15:51	105, 110, 112, 115, 125
15:51f	116, 125
15:52	105
15:53f	113-15
16:1-4	184
16:7	120

2 Corinthians	103, 108
1:9	104
1:20	30
2:17	30
4-5	105
4:14	104
5	107, 110
5:1f	107
5:1ff	103
5:1-4	115, 116
5:1-10	102-3, 108-9
5:2	105
5:2-4	110, 114-16
5:2-5	115
5:2-8	105
5:4	105, 114-15
5:5	114
5:6-9	105, 110, 115-16
5:10	107
5:16-21	184
5:18f	187
5:19	183, 188
5:19f	30
11:32f	178

Galatians	
1:6-9	184
1:15f	178
1:16	178
1:17	178
2:1-10	185

2:2	178, 184, 186
2:4	178
2:6-9	178
2:7	193
2:7-9	178
2:9	177
2:11-21	178
2:15f	187-188
3:2-5	187
3:6-29	207
3:8	29, 206
4:5	25
4:22-31	203
4:28f	29, 206
6:15	189-90
6:15f	185
6:16	30, 206

Ephesians

1:3-10	45
1:9f	30, 207
2:20f	154
3:1-13	45
3:1-21	194

Philippians 103

1	100
1:21ff	102, 103
1:21-23	110
1:23	102, 105, 110, 116
2:1-18	184
2:6-11	157, 182
2:9	182
2:10f	183
2:11	183
3:8f	102
3:11	104

Colossians

1:18	154
1:24	30, 207

1 Thessalonians 102

2:3f	178
2:13	30
2:16	30, 207
4	100, 103, 108-11, 116
4:13-17	103
4:13-18	125

Hebrews

2:10-18	154

1 Peter

2:6f	154

Revelations

1:5	154

Non-Canonical Thomas

32	166

INDEX OF NAMES

Abelard, Peter 60
Agricola, Johannes 209
Akenside, Mark 39
Aquinas, Thomas ix, xiii, 5, 9, 10, 158
Aristotle 5, 44, 82, 151
Arnold, Matthew 66
Athenasius 54
Augustine 52, 91, 96
Aune, David E. 144
Auden, Wystan Hugh 53
Austin, J. L. 50

Baker, Russell 83, 95
Balthasar, Hans Urs von 31, 52
Barbour, R. S. 143
Barr, James 65
Barrett, C. K. 192
Barrett, William xv
Barth, Karl xiv, 14, 58, 71, 109, 200
Barthes, Roland 16
Bauer, Bruno 91, 122
Baur, Ferdinand Christian 94, 99, 100, 101, 105, 122, 200
Beardsley, Monroe C. 20, 37-40, 49, 52
Berkeley, George 84, 198
Betz, Otto 163, 171
Billerbeck, Paul 42, 53
Bloch, Ernst 127
Bornkamm, Günther 57, 73, 126, 148
Boswell, James 84, 95
Brown, Raymond E. 13, 53
Buber, Martin 22, 50

Bultmann, Rudolf xiv, 14, 43-47, 50, 54, 55, 57-63, 71, 73, 74, 89, 94, 109, 125, 127, 139, 148, 149, 150, 155, 163, 171, 200, 205, 209, 210
Burkert, Walter 95

Caesar, Julius 153
Calvert, D. G. A. 143
Campbell, K. M. 172
Carnap, Adolf 50
Cassirer, Ernst 12, 15
Chadwick, Owen 122
Charles, R. H. 96, 104, 110, 123
Chrysostom, John 91, 96
Clements, Ronald E. 46, 54, 210
Clement of Alexandria 54, 91, 96
Collingwood, R. G. ix, 44, 53, 62, 75, 94, 132, 144, 148, 150, 152, 154, 166, 172
Collins, John J. 54, 73
Conzelmann, Hans 73
Cooper, Thomas 73
Coreth, Emerich 126, 127
Crane, Hart 38
Croce, Benedetto ix
Cross, F. M. 13
Cullmann, Oscar 207, 210
Cunningham, Valentine 16, 210
Cyril of Alexandria 54

Dahl, Nils Alstrup 159, 160, 170
Dalman, Gustaf 42, 53, 151, 153, 163, 165, 170, 171
Daly, Robert 79, 80, 94

Dante, Alighieri ix, 22
Davies, W. D. 107, 110, 114, 124
Deichgräber, Reinhard 193
Delitzsch, Friedrich 91, 200, 208
de Lubac, Henri 51
Derrida, Jacques 16
de Saussure, Ferdinand 20, 49
Descartes, René 26, 28, 32, 57, 60
Dietrich, Ernst Ludwig 191
Diodore of Tarsus 54
Dix, Gregory 157, 170, 190, 193, 194
Dodd, C. H. 55, 96, 106, 110, 119,
    123, 124, 164, 165, 171, 192
Donoghue, Denis xii, xv
Doran, Robert 51
Drews, Arthur 91
Driver, S. R. 53
Dungan, David xiv
Dupont, Jacques 108, 125, 126, 191

Ebeling, Gerhard 22, 50, 58, 59, 73,
    149, 155
Einstein, Albert 44, 79
Eisler, Robert 91
Ellis, E. Earle 138, 143, 144
Engnell, Ivan 163, 171
Euclid xi

Farrer, Austin 170
Fish, Stanley 52
Fitzmyer, Joseph A. 13
Frege, Gottlob 20, 50
Freud, Sigmund 13, 14, 24, 26, 28, 94
Frye, Northrop ix, 12, 14, 15
Fuchs, Ernst 58, 59, 73, 74, 148

Gadamer, Hans-Georg 14, 20, 22, 23,
    26, 49, 50, 51, 59, 65, 68, 69, 75,
    92, 96, 117, 127, 210
Gager, John G. 72
Galileo Galilei 151
Gerhardsson, Birger 144

Gese, Hartmut 210
Glick, Nathan 94
Gnilke, Joachim 108, 109, 124
Gogarten, Friedrich 25
Goguel, Maurice 163, 171
Goodspeed, Edgar J. 113
Goppelt, Leonhard 61, 74
Goulder, Michael 152, 155
Grant, Robert M. 72
Gray, John 191
Gunneweg, A. H. J. 209, 210

Habermas, Jürgen 14
Hanson, J. S. 13
Harnack, Adolf von 74, 91, 192, 200,
    209
Harner, Philip B. 53
Harrington, Daniel J. 73
Harvey, Van 152, 153, 154, 155
Hegel, G. W. F. 4, 10, 11, 26, 28, 60,
    61, 91, 99, 122, 200, 209
Hegermann, Harold 53
Heidegger, Martin 78
Heisenberg, Werner 79
Hengel, Martin 61, 74, 75, 192, 193
Heracleitus 22, 23
Hirsch, E. D. 20, 36, 37, 39, 40, 49,
    50, 52
Hirsch, Emmanuel 200, 209
Hill, David 144
Hofius, Otfried 192, 193
Hoffmann, Paul 109, 125
Hoffmann, J. G. H. 163, 171
Holmberg, Bengt 193
Holtz, Traugott 193
Hook, Sidney 78
Hooker, Morna D. 136, 138, 143, 144,
    170
Hopkins, Gerard Manley xii
Horsley, Richard A. 13
Hume, David 69

Irenaeus 31

Jakobson, Roman 12
James, William 167
Jaspers, Karl 78
Jeremias, Joachim ix, xiii, 42, 43, 52,
  53, 55, 94, 108, 110, 113, 124, 125,
  134, 144, 151, 153, 155, 156, 164,
  165, 171, 172, 191, 192
Jerome 91, 96
Johann, Robert O. 127
Johnson, Samuel xi, 84, 198
Jonas, Hans 55, 89, 200, 209

Kabisch, Richard 99, 100, 103, 122
Kant, Immanuel 9, 10, 28, 32, 198
Käsemann, Ernst 57, 58, 59, 73, 130,
  143, 148, 149, 150, 155
Keats, John xii
Kee, Howard Clark 72
Kennedy, H. A. A. 104, 114, 123
Kermode, Frank 21, 49, 50, 201, 202,
  203, 210
Kertelge, Karl 73
Kierkegaard, Soren ix, 13, 78
Knox, Wilfred L. 96, 106, 107, 110,
  119, 123, 124
Kuhn, Karl Georg 43, 53

Lang, Friedrich 109, 125
Langer, Suzanne 201, 210
Lash, Nicholas 66, 75
Lawrence, Frederick 95, 209
Leibniz, Gotfried Wilhelm 18
Lewis, C. S. 53, 127
Lichtenberg, G. C. 41
Lidzbarski, M. 171
Lietzmann, Hans 193
Lodge, David 16, 52
Lonergan, Bernard J. F. ix-xv, 4-15,
  23, 34, 44, 50, 51, 52, 53, 69, 71,
  75, 78, 86, 94, 95, 96, 127, 128,
  142, 145, 150, 151, 152, 154, 155,
  158, 159, 170, 195, 198, 208, 209
Löwith, Karl 207, 211

Lüdemann, Hermann 101, 105, 122
Luedemann, Gerd 108, 110, 124, 125
Lührmann, Dieter 143
Luther, Martin 21, 51, 62, 68, 117,
  206, 209
Lutz, Hanns-Martin 172

MacArthur, Harvey K. 143
Malherbe, Abraham J. 72
Malina, Bruce J. 73
Marcel, Gabriel 78, 127
Maritain, Jacques 78
Marx, Karl 26, 28
Marxsen, Willi 135, 144
McCarthy, Dennis J. 51
Mead, George Herbert 188, 193
Meyer, B. F. 54, 55, 74, 96, 124, 144,
  154, 170, 191, 192, 193
Meyer, Eduard 193
Meyer, Rudolf 193
Mill, John Stuart 50
Miller, Hillis 16
Minkowski, Hermann 44
Moltmann, Jürgen 127
Morissette, Rodolphe 109, 125
Moule, C. F. D. 143
Muddiman, J. B. 138-39, 144-45
Müller, Christian 73
Mure, G. R. G. 3-4, 10, 14
Mussner, Franz 161, 170

Navone, John 73
Nero Claudius Caesar 132
Nestorius 54
Neugebauer, A. 53
Newman, John Henry ix, 22, 45, 50,
  52, 66, 74, 75, 78, 92, 99, 122
Nietzsche, Friedrich 26, 78, 87, 90, 91,
  201
Nineham, Dennis 152, 155
Novak, Michael 167, 172

Origen 54

Pannenberg, Wolfhart 61, 74, 207, 211
Parson, Talcott 14
Pattison, Mark 99
Perry, Ralph Barton xii
Pesch, Rudolf 13, 79, 80, 191
Pfleiderer, Otto 91, 96, 101, 103, 104, 105, 106, 110, 119, 121, 122, 123
Philip the Chancellor 45
Pieper, Josef 90, 96, 117, 119, 120, 126, 127, 128, 207, 211
Pilate, Pontius 166
Plato 9, 96, 202
Plevnik, Joseph 125
Plügge, Herbert 120, 127
Plumb, J. H. 196, 209
Plummer, Alfred 113, 126
Pound, Ezra ix
Pythagoras 96

Quinton, Anthony 50

Rahner, Karl 52
Ranke, Leopold von 14, 155
Reimarus, Hermann Samuel 94
Reitzenstein, Richard 163, 171
Ricoeur, Paul 14, 15, 24, 26, 50, 51, 200, 209
Rilke, Rainer Maria ix, 22, 23, 79
Ritschl, Albrecht 88
Robertson, Archibald 113, 126
Robertson, John C. Jr. 3
Robinson, James M. 53, 54, 58, 63, 73, 74, 75, 95, 127
Roloff, Jürgen 61, 74
Russell, Bertrand 79

Sabatier, Auguste 105, 123
Sanders, E. P. 13, 191
Scheler, Max 14
Schlatter, Adolf 108, 113, 126, 210
Schlegel, Friedrich 28

Schleiermacher, Friedrich 91, 200, 209
Schlier, Heinrich 120, 127
Schmid, Hans Heinrich 73
Schnabel, Franz 122
Schniewind, Julius 109
Schopenhauer, Arthur 78
Schürmann, Heinz 48, 49, 55, 59, 61, 74, 143
Schweitzer, Albert 99, 100, 102, 105, 106, 122, 123, 154
Scroggs, Robin 72
Sevenster, J. N. 115, 126
Shakespeare, William xi, 83
Shiner, Larry 51
Shostakovich, Dmitry 79
Simmel, Georg 14
Simon, Richard 32, 93, 196, 197
Smith, Jonathan Z. 72
Snell, Bruno 12, 15
Socrates 153, 195, 196
Solzhenitsyn, Alexander ix, 31, 52
Spencer, Herbert 44
Spengler, Oswald 78, 94
Spinoza, Benedict 32, 43, 93, 119, 196, 200
Stein, Robert H. 143
Stevens, Wallace 202
Strauss, David Friedrich 43, 60, 61, 74, 94, 122, 135, 144, 200
Stravinsky, Igor 79
Stuhlmacher, Peter xiv, 13, 15, 22, 50, 57, 59, 61, 62, 64, 65, 66, 67, 71, 72, 73, 74, 75, 93, 96, 127, 191, 193
Suetonius, Gaius 132, 133

Tacitus, Cornelius 132
Talmon, Shemaryahu 191
Teichmann, Ernst 96, 103, 104, 106, 108, 109, 110, 119, 122, 124
Teilhard de Chardin, Pierre 14, 137, 207, 210
Theissen, Gerd 72, 155

Theodore of Mopsuestia 54
Toynbee, Arnold 13
Trautmann, Maria 143
Troeltsch, Ernst 5, 32, 43, 61, 62, 74,
   149, 155
Tylor, Edward Burnett 44

Vaihinger, Hans 203
Valéry, Paul ix, 79
Vatke, W. 200
Vico, Giovanni Battista 26, 28
Voegelin, Eric 14, 200, 210
Vögtle, Anton 144
von Rad, Gerhard ix, 94, 191, 207, 210

Waugh, Evelyn ix
Weber, Max 40
Weiffenbach, Wilhelm 124
Weiss, Johannes 99, 122, 126
Weizsäcker, Carl von 188, 193
Wernle, Paul 105
Whitehead, Alfred North 18, 49, 79
Wilkens, Ulrich 192
Wimsatt, William K. Jr. 20, 40, 49, 52
Winter, Gibson 193
Wrede, William 204, 205, 210

Yeats, William Butler ix

Zeller, Dieter 191
Zimmerli, Walther 42, 53